Ugo Balzani

Italy

Ugo Balzani

Italy

ISBN/EAN: 9783337229948

Printed in Europe, USA, Canada, Australia, Japan

Cover: Foto ©Andreas Hilbeck / pixelio.de

More available books at **www.hansebooks.com**

EARLY CHRONICLERS OF EUROPE.

ITALY.

BY

UGO BALZANI.

PUBLISHED UNDER THE DIRECTION OF THE COMMITTEE
OF GENERAL LITERATURE AND EDUCATION APPOINTED BY THE
SOCIETY FOR PROMOTING CHRISTIAN KNOWLEDGE.

LONDON:
SOCIETY FOR PROMOTING CHRISTIAN KNOWLEDGE;
NORTHUMBERLAND AVENUE, CHARING CROSS;
43, QUEEN VICTORIA STREET; 26, ST. GEORGE'S PLACE, HYDE PARK CORNER;
AND 135, NORTH STREET, BRIGHTON.
NEW YORK: E. & J. B. YOUNG AND CO.
1883.

PREFACE.

IN attempting to give a popular account of the Italian chroniclers of the Middle Ages, I have tried to avoid all unnecessary display of erudition, and to present the book in as simple a form and as free from quotations and notes as possible. If I have not been able to keep myself rigorously to this rule, it has been because I desired as far as I could to make the book not wholly without value to more special students, since, if I am not mistaken, this is the first work which professes expressly to narrate the history of medieval Italian chronography. Hence I have made a diligent study in the best editions of the text of all the authors mentioned in this book, and before passing judgment upon them have tried to see all that others had thought and written on the same points.

As for the general structure of the book, if I have been sometimes rather diffuse in treating of the various historic periods which it traverses, I trust that I may be forgiven for this, considering that it is not easy, nor would it be a good plan, to speak of historical writers, without taking into account the times in which they lived and of which they wrote. Thus I have often been led to enlarge on the lives of the writers whose works I was examining, and this I have done because it seemed to me that in no other way could I give so clear an idea of the times described by them, and of the reasons why they wrote. In Italy more than elsewhere the history of the Middle Ages was related by men who took an active part in the events which they recorded, from the earliest to the latest times, from Cassiodorus and Gregory the Great to Albertinus Mussatus, Dino Compagni and Giovanni Villani. Also, in order to make the reader better acquainted with the disposition, nature, and style of the various chronicles, I have introduced long and numerous extracts from them, translated from the Latin, Greek, or Italian originals. These passages have been translated by my wife, who has also given its English garb to the rest of the book, sharing with me the labour and the interest of compilation. In rendering these fragments the translator has striven to be true to the letter of the originals, but where some, from their obscure and confused Latin, made a literal translation impossible, she has done her best to adhere closely to the intention of the authors. The number of books which I had to consult is too great for me to mention them all, but I have tried to acknowledge those which have rendered me more special service, both from gratitude, and in order that any reader wishing to push his inquiries further may know where to turn for information. The first chapters were printed (through involuntary delay on my part) many months before the last. For this I am sorry, as it has prevented me from making use of two recent publications—the edition of the *Acts of the Neapolitan Bishops*, made by Signor Capasso of Naples, and the edition of Jordanes, by Theodor Mommsen; yet neither would have changed substantially what I had already written. What those first chapters, however, do recall is a memory bringing with it a sense of regret. Before they were sent to be printed, they had been read by the late

Canon Robertson, of Canterbury, and honoured with his suggestions and approval. I hoped to have been able to express to him in this place my gratitude, whereas I can only place it on record, as a poor tribute to one for whom I feel deep reverence. Assuredly he is missed by many in England, as he is by me, for the generous and gentle qualities of his heart, while he is regretted by all, whether in England or Italy, who have studied his works and admired that calm and keen serenity of judgment which is one of the highest attributes of a faithful historian.

UGO BALZANI.

ROME,
December, 1882.

CONTENTS.

CHAPTER I.

DECLINE OF HISTORY WITH THE DECLINE OF ROME—ITS REVIVAL IN THE TIME OF THE GOTHS—CASSIODORUS—HIS HONOURS AND THE POLITICAL TENDENCY OF HIS WORKS—HIS LOST HISTORY OF THE GOTHS AND THE "LIBRI EPISTOLARUM VARIARUM"—COMPENDIUM BY THE GOTH JORDANES OF THE HISTORY OF CASSIODORUS—THE DIVISIONS BETWEEN ROMANS AND GOTHS FOMENTED AT CONSTANTINOPLE—GOTHIC WAR NARRATED BY PROCOPIUS OF CÆSAREA—MERITS AND IMPORTANCE OF THIS AUTHOR—MINOR WRITERS ... 1

CHAPTER II.

SAD CONDITION OF ITALY IN THE EARLY PERIOD OF THE LOMBARD INVASION—GREGORY THE GREAT—COLLECTION OF HIS LETTERS—THEIR GREAT IMPORTANCE FOR THE HISTORY OF ITALY—THE BOOK OF DIALOGUES—THE EDICT OF ROTHARI—THE "ORIGO LANGOBARDORUM"—AND MINOR WRITINGS UP TO PAULUS DIACONUS—HIS LIFE—HIS WORKS AND ESPECIALLY HIS HISTORY OF THE LOMBARDS 40

CHAPTER III.

DECAY OF ITALIAN CHRONOGRAPHY—THE "LIBER PONTIFICALIS"—THE ACTS OF THE NEAPOLITAN BISHOPS—AGNELLUS OF RAVENNA—POLEMICAL WRITINGS OF AUXILIUS AND VULGARIUS—THE MONASTERIES AND THE SARACEN INVASIONS—FARFA: THE "CONSTRUCTIO"—LIVES OF THE SAINTS OF ST. VINCENT ON THE VOLTURNO — THE "DESTRUCTIO"— MONTECASSINO: CHRONICLE OF ST. BENEDICT—CATALOGUES—TRANSLATIONS OF RELICS—"HISTORIA" OF ERCHEMPERT—CHRONICLE OF SALERNO—ANDREW OF BERGAMO—PANEGYRIC OF BERENGARIUS—STATE OF LAY EDUCATION IN ITALY—POLITICAL CONDITIONS—LIUTPRAND—IMPERIALIST WRITINGS—BENEDICT OF SORACTE—VENETIAN CHRONICLE OF JOHANNES DIACONUS ... 91

CHAPTER IV.

INTELLECTUAL MOVEMENT IN THE ELEVENTH AND TWELFTH CENTURIES—REFORMS IN THE CHURCH AND THE CONTESTS REGARDING THE INVESTITURES—REVIVAL OF ECCLESIASTICAL CULTURE AND OF HISTORICAL RESEARCH IN THE MONASTERIES—MONASTIC REGISTERS AND CHRONICLES—THE MONASTERY OF FARFA AND THE WORKS OF GREGORY OF CATINO—THE "CHRONICON VULTURNENSE"—RENAISSANCE OF ARTS AND LETTERS AT MONTECASSINO PROMOTED BY THE ABBOT DESIDERIUS—THE MONK AMATUS AND HIS HISTORY OF THE NORMANS—LEO OSTIENSIS AND PETRUS DIACONUS, HISTORIANS OF MONTECASSINO—HISTORICAL WRITINGS OF SOUTHERN ITALY—LEGENDARY CHRONICLE OF THE MONASTERY OF THE NOVALESA 146

CHAPTER V.

THE LATER CONTRIBUTIONS TO THE "PONTIFICAL BOOK" —BRUNO OF SEGNI—WIBERT OF TOUL—PAUL OF BERNRIED—"ANNALES ROMANI"—PETRUS PISANUS — PANDULPH — BOSO— POLEMICAL WRITINGS — ST. PETER DAMIANI—BONIZO'S "LIBER AD AMICUM"— THE LIFE OF ANSELM OF LUCCA—DOMNIZO'S LIFE OF THE COUNTESS MATILDA—THE LETTERS OF GREGORY VII. 186

CHAPTER VI.

NEW PHASES OF ITALIAN THOUGHT FROM THE TWELFTH TO THE FOURTEENTH CENTURIES — SOUTHERN WRITERS OF THE NORMAN AND SUABIAN TIMES— SABA MALASPINA — HISTORIANS OF THE SICILIAN VESPERS—LIVES OF THE POPES—LIFE OF COLA DI RIENZO—LOMBARD MUNICIPAL WRITERS OF THE FIRST PERIOD—OTHO OF FREISING—GENERAL HISTORIES— MUNICIPAL WRITERS OF THE SECOND PERIOD—FRA SALIMBENE OF PARMA — CHRONICLERS OF VARIOUS CITIES OF CENTRAL AND NORTHERN ITALY—CHRONICLERS OF LOMBARDY AND OF THE MARCA TRIVIGIANA —ALBERTINUS MUSSATUS 226

CHAPTER VII.

THE CHRONICLERS OF THE MARITIME REPUBLICS : VENETIAN CHRONICLES — MARTIN DA CANALE — ANDREA DANDOLO—THE GENOESE ANNALISTS FROM CAFFARO TO JAMES D'ORIA—PISA : PETRUS PISANUS—BERNARD MARANGO—THE CHRONICLERS OF THE REST OF TUSCANY AND PRINCIPALLY THE FLORENTINES — DINO COMPAGNI—THE VILLANI 292

INDEX 338

EARLY CHRONICLERS OF EUROPE.

ITALY.

CHAPTER I.

DECLINE OF HISTORY WITH THE DECLINE OF ROME — ITS REVIVAL IN THE TIME OF THE GOTHS — CASSIODORUS — HIS HONOURS AND THE POLITICAL TENDENCY OF HIS WORKS — HIS LOST HISTORY OF THE GOTHS AND THE "LIBRI EPISTOLARUM VARIARUM" — COMPENDIUM BY THE GOTH JORDANIS OF THE HISTORY OF CASSIODORUS — THE DIVISIONS BETWEEN ROMANS AND GOTHS FOMENTED AT CONSTANTINOPLE — GOTHIC WAR NARRATED BY PROCOPIUS OF CÆSAREA — MERITS AND IMPORTANCE OF THIS AUTHOR — MINOR WRITERS.

IN the decline of Rome, and the slow dissolution of Latin unity, not only was all national feeling and life destroyed, but also the art—almost the will—

of writing history was lost. The old world was dying in the West, and with it were fading away the last gleams of the old civilization. The grand inspiration of Livy, and the powerful utterances of Tacitus, had ceased ages before, and gradually every spring was drying up, so that in the fifth century the story of that dark and uncertain period must be laboriously sought for among the few writers with whom we still meet, and who, with the exception of Ammianus Marcellinus, were not generally historians even in name. Prudentius, Claudianus, Rutilius Numatianus, St. Jerome and the principal fathers of the Church—such are the insufficient sources to which the historical student of this age must turn; and the reason for this is not far to seek. Where public life languished, it was natural that the records of the life itself should languish also. And while history was dying out among the natives of Italy, it could not spring all at once into life among the first invaders. To them the art was wanting, nor could the wish to turn the living traditions of their songs into history come to them naturally, unless they first learnt this art in Italy, or at least found some one among the vanquished disposed to write the narrative of their deeds. But for this end, it was necessary first that vanquished and victors should commingle and learn to feel in common, so that while one brought new blood and energy to the enervated country, the other infused into these new elements what remained of former learning. Such a commingling was not to be expected in the case of the first invaders who swept down from the Alps rather for rapine than for conquest, but appeared for a moment to be possible with the Goths ; and it is indeed in their time that the devotion to past memories temporarily revives, and that, so to speak, the narratives and historical documents of the Middle Ages begin.

Certainly of all the German nationalities the Goths were the most open to civilizing influences, and most capable of assimilating Latin culture and of identifying themselves with the old races among whom they had come down, while bringing into them new and salutary elements of vitality. Even to-day the German language has to refer for its origin to the Gothic translation of the Bible left by Ulphilas, and to the fragments of a harmony of the Gospels. A strong people of distinct originality, they could not, after their long contact with the Latin and Greek nations, neglect such rich intellectual traditions, nor treat with contempt the exquisite creations of classic art and the legislative wisdom which in the Justinian code presented a synthesis of the work of many ages. And if the Goths were capable of appreciating the traditions of antiquity, these traditions, on the other hand, had still life enough in them to command the respect and admiration of their vigorous foes. If a strong nation could ever have been formed out of the two elements, the Roman and the barbarian, it could only have happened with the Goths, and at that time. The majesty of the Empire still survived, and still the Latin element was so strong as to offer the barbarians more hope of union than of conquest. Later, after many struggles, after long and disastrous wars, impoverished, exhausted, and depopulated, while her Grecian rulers thought less of defending her than of satisfying their greed, Italy had grown powerless, and the new invaders regarded with contempt what remained of the old authority and the old civilization of Rome. But it was different during the Gothic period, and the reign of Theodoric (A.D. 493–526) shows a continual desire to unite the German and Roman elements, and to join the two people in a common brotherhood of feeling and of thought. Cassiodorus, who held the highest offices of the State during a very long part of the Gothic dominion—from the reign of Theodoric to that of Vitiges—directed all his efforts towards this object, and did all that lay in his power to root firmly in the soil this new kingdom. "What we aim at, with God's help, is that our subjects should lament the not having come sooner under our rule." These words which Cassiodorus puts into the mouth of Theodoric, seem to express a fixed purpose, and to explain whither his actions tended.

And while he was at the head of public affairs, his literary labours were conceived in the same spirit, and assisted him in this object. He may well be said to have represented his age in letters as well as in politics. The court of Theodoric had become a centre round which the survivors of the ancient civilization clustered, and there many works originated which carried on the memory of this culture into the Middle Ages. And in truth the school of the grammarians—Donatus, Macrobius, Marcianus Capella—finds its descendants about this time in Priscianus and Cassiodorus, whose confused style and obscure and inflated Latin was to win the admiration of a later age. The Aristotelian philosophy owed much of its influence on mediæval thought to the greatest scholar then living, Severinus Boetius, a man of noble character, made famous by his misfortunes and by the book which he wrote under their inspiration. The old pagan learning was never destroyed, notwithstanding the complete victory of Christianity; and these men, by christianizing it to a certain extent, made it more acceptable to later generations. Nor were the Goths altogether strangers to this intellectual movement, for some of them in the court of Ravenna allied themselves to the learned Romans, and followed their studious example. The existence of the Gothic philosophers, Athanarid, Hildebald, and Marcomir, has not been established with certainty, although they are mentioned in an ancient document; but there is no doubt that Theodatus, a relation of Theodoric and later himself king of the Goths, was much given to philosophical studies, and styled himself a follower of Plato. The high-minded and unfortunate Queen Amalasuntha had an amount of culture rare for her time and in her sex, and we shall presently have occasion to speak of the Goth Jordanes, who fortunately made a compendium of the history of the Goths by Cassiodorus, the history itself being lost.

Magnus Aurelius Cassiodorus, born in Samnium, of a noble family, and early initiated into public life, sided with those of the Roman patricians who thought it advisable that their country should cast in its lot with the barbarians, and thence form a kingdom, to which the twofold element might insure unity and strength. During the reign of Odoacer (A.D. 476-493) he held various public offices, and Theodoric not only confirmed him in them, but raised him to the highest dignities and entrusted to his care the most important State questions. We have already said how the writings of Cassiodorus, which have a direct or indirect historical aim, are in accord with his public life, and are all calculated to draw closer the bonds of brotherhood between Romans and Goths. Indeed, he wrote a short chronicle with the special object of glorifying Theodoric; but this work, full of inflated praises, is a very poor thing, and consists only of a chronological sketch badly put together and full of errors, which have been pointed out and severely commented upon by Theodor Mommsen. On the other hand his history of the Gothic people, divided into twelve books, appears to have been a work of much greater value, and to have been more in harmony with the learned and scholastic tendencies of that day. But this work was soon lost, and we can only judge of it, and that but imperfectly, from the compendium of Jordanes. The spirit of this history is sufficiently indicated by the words with which the King Athalaric announced to the Roman Senate the appointment of Cassiodorus as Prefect of the Prætorium. "Not only," he says, "has Cassiodorus magnified his present lords, but going backwards he has extended his inquiries into the ancient cradle of our race, discovering from his researches in documents what was hardly any longer remembered, even by the hoary traditions of our old men. He brought forth the kings of the Goths from the oblivion wherein they lay in the remote hiding-places of antiquity. He established the illustrious lineage of the Amali, proving clearly that our race has been royal for seventeen generations. He made the origin of the Goths part of Roman history, collecting as it were into one garland the hardy plants which he found dispersed throughout the fields of literature. Consider how much affection he showed you in praising us, by teaching that your prince's family had been distinguished from remote ages, and that as you were always held to be noble, so you should be ruled over only by an ancient race of kings." Here we see clearly the political aim of the book. To the Roman whose pride in his country's history increased as its power diminished, it was desirable to show that these barbarians who had come down from the North to divide the land with him were also of noble extraction and could boast of a glorious history. For this end, says Wattenbach, did Cassiodorus employ all his learning. "It had long been easy to believe that the Goths and Gætæ were all one people, but no one had yet tried to demonstrate the relationship. This was done by Cassiodorus. He wove together the special historical recollections of the Goths, and the contents of their ballads, with what he found about the Gæti in Greek and Roman records; and because the Greeks constantly called both Goths and Gæti Scythians, he brought in the whole of the primitive history of the Scythians and did not hesitate to call the Amazons also Goths. In the same way the Amali" (this was the name of Theodoric's family), "whose greatness was celebrated in the Gothic Sagas, were represented as being the immediate descendants of Zamolxis and Sitalkes, and the Romans were left to find some consolation in this for the bitterness of a foreign yoke."[1]

We have quoted above some words addressed to Cassiodorus by the Kings Theodoric and Athalaric. These words written by Cassiodorus himself are contained in a collection of letters which, during

---

[1] Wattenbach, *Deutschland's Geschichtsquellen im Mittelalter*, i. 59. Berlin. 1877–78.

his public life, he was called upon to write in the names of the sovereigns whom he served. This collection is divided into twelve books, and the letters being addressed principally to important personages or to great institutions of the State, may be said to contain in order all the acts of government by which the Gothic kings and their ministers regulated public affairs in Italy until the beginning of the reign of Vitiges. Their importance for Italian history is incalculable. The lost history of the Goths could not itself have given such clear evidence as to the moral and political conditions of the Italians, or as to the relations existing between them and their invaders, nor could it have given so much information with regard to the life of that day and the state of men and things. Such documents speak to posterity with an eloquence which mere contemporary history can never reach. Thus when Theodoric announces to the Roman Senate the elevation of Cassiodorus to the dignity of Patrician, and praises his merits and those of his ancestors, we may from his words infer the respect still felt for the name of Rome, and the Roman point of view from which the Gothic king regarded the invasions of Attila :

"But what we most especially desire is that the light of dignity should shine upon your assembly. . . . For the father of this candidate [Cassiodorus] was associated with the Patrician Ætius for the assistance of the Commonwealth. . . . He was sent, and not in vain, to Attila as ambassador. He regarded him without alarm whom the Empire feared, and heeded not, being shielded by the truth, those terrible and threatening faces, nor hesitated to reply to the arguments of him who, seized by I know not what fury, seemed to seek the dominion of the world. He found the king severe, he left him pacified. . . . He sustained by his courage those who were timid, nor were those imagined to be unwarlike who were represented by such ambassadors. He brought back a peace which had been despaired of."

And these other words very clearly establish what were the judicial conditions of the two nations united under Theodoric's sceptre, as well as giving a true though sad picture of the degenerated manners of the Roman nobility. In one of those tumults which a bad habit introduced from Constantinople rendered frequent in the party strifes of the amphitheatre, a patrician of the name of Theodoric and the consul Importunus had acted unjustly to some of the populace who belonged to the party opposed to them in the games, and caused one of them to be killed. Cassiodorus, speaking in the person of the king, wrote about it to the magistrate in the following severe and resolute manner:—

"If we moderate the manners of foreign nations who are under our law, if all that is associated with Italy must submit to Roman law, how much more should the capital of the State show greater reverence for the laws, since the grace of dignity should shine as an example of moderation? For where can a modest spirit be found, if violent acts disgrace the nobles? . . . But lest the gossip of the populace should offend distinguished men, some account must be kept of this presumption. If any one impudently use injurious language against a most reverend senator when he is passing, let it be held a crime to have preferred speaking evil to speaking well. But who can insist on serious manners at a spectacle? Those who go to the circus are not Catos. Whatever is said there by the people in their gaiety should not be regarded as abusive language. It is the place which excuses a certain excess. And if their garrulity is patiently borne, it will be found to be an honour to the princes."

Temperate and generous words which are in harmony with these others, addressed to the Senator Sunivadus, sent by King Theodoric into Samnium to settle some disputes between the Romans and Goths:

"Enter therefore the province of Samnium. If any dispute has arisen between any Roman and the Goths, or between any Goth and the Romans, thou shalt decide upon it with due consideration of the laws, nor can we permit that those shall live under an unequal law whom we wish to protect with a single judge. Thou shalt therefore decide on both sides what is just, for he who merely thinks of equity must not respect persons."

It was, therefore, with good reason that Theodoric praised Cassiodorus for having made his reign famous by introducing integrity of conscience into the court; and profound tranquility among the people.[1] Here, at the entrance of the Middle Ages, we feel still in the letters of this last of Roman statesmen, that the ancient order of things is not yet extinct, and that there is still some life and vigour left in Roman civilization. And in truth no civilizing element is neglected in them. As in the maintenance of the Roman laws, so also we see a constant watchfulness for the preservation of the monuments and works of art scattered throughout Italy. In these letters we find him at one time intent on recovering for the public enjoyment a bronze statue stolen at Como; at another, on restoring the baths of Spoleto, or on rebuilding dilapidated aqueducts, or on sending to Ravenna the columns and marbles lying unused in Rome which might serve to adorn new monuments there, since the degenerate condition of art was unfavourable to new ornamental work. In one letter

---

[1] "Nostra fecisti eximia tempora prædicari. Ornasti de con scientiæ integritate palatia, dedisti populis altam quietem" (*Variarum*, iii. 28). A fine example of antique tolerance may also be found in the following words of a letter to the Roman Senate, written in consequence of the burning of a synagogue during a tumult against the Jews: "Quia nolumus aliquid detestabile fieri unde romana gravitas debeat accusari. . . . Hoc enim nobis vehementer displicuisse cognoscite ut intentiones vanissimæ populorum usque ad eversiones pervenerint fabricarum, ubi totum pulchre volumus esse compositum" (*Variarum*, iv. 43).

to Boetius there is honourable mention made of music, while in another addressed to the same there is interesting evidence of the condition of mechanical studies at that time, and from this latter are made the following extracts :—

"So the lord of the Burgundians has earnestly begged of us to send him a clock worked by water flowing under the wheel, and which is also marked by the whole light of the great sun, as well as the workmen for putting it up. So that what we are daily accustomed to, may, if they can obtain this thing of delight which they ask for, seem to them a miracle. . . . The mechanician is, if we may say so, almost an associate of nature, disclosing what is hidden, altering what is manifest, playing with miracles, imitating so well that the imitation is not suspected but is supposed to be genuine. Thou wilt prepare for us, therefore, this aforesaid clock as soon as possible, because we know that thou art specially expert in these matters, in order that thou mayest become known in that part of the world whither otherwise thou couldst not reach. So may foreign nations recognize through thee that we have such distinguished men of science as are read of. How often they will not be able to believe what they see! how often they will think that the truth is but a deceptive dream! And when they have recovered from their astonishment, they will not dare to think themselves our equals, when they know that we have wise men who invent such wonders."

It is painful, however, to find Theodoric staining the glory of his reign in his last years by cruelly putting to death this very Boetius so glorified in this letter, as well as his illustrious father-in-law, Symmachus. Perhaps this unjust sentence is a sign that the Roman patriciate was beginning to separate itself from the Goths, and that the agreement between the two nationalities was less easy than had been hoped at first. Unfortunately the official letters of Cassiodorus can throw no light upon this, and the absence of positive historical data obliges us to content ourselves with hypotheses. At any rate, whatever turn events may have taken, and whatever may have been the spirit of the Roman nobles, Cassiodorus was faithful to his ideas of reconciliation, and at the death of Theodoric he remained in his post near Amalasuntha, who reigned for some years in the name of her son Athalaric, then a child. During this regency the divisions between the Goths and Romans grow more evident, especially touching the education of the young king, which the principal Goths wished should be free from any literary tendency, and entirely devoted to bodily exercise and warlike arts. In the mean while the imperial Government at Constantinople added to the flame, and by encouraging these discords between the two races, as also those of the Goths among themselves, hoped to be able to take advantage of them in order to recover the Italian provinces. After the death of the young

Athalaric, his mother, Amalasuntha, reigned for some time by herself; but neither her great intelligence, nor the fact of her being Theodoric's daughter, could save her from the suspicions of the Goths, so that at one moment finding herself in danger she entered into treaty with the Emperor Justinian with the object of escaping from Italy and seeking an asylum at Constantinople. Afterwards, however, flattering herself that she might thus retain her hold upon the throne, she gave her hand in marriage to Theodatus, a cousin of her own and a descendant of the Amali, who had formerly been her enemy, but whom she hoped to conciliate by associating him in the kingdom. Theodatus, a mean and cowardly man, as soon as he had ascended the throne, confined Amalasuntha in an island of the lake of Bolsena (*Vulsinium*), and there afterwards had her murdered. He reigned alone for some time, but finding his position a precarious one, and desirous above all of leading a quiet life, he offered to give up the kingdom to Justinian, asking in exchange riches and peaceful honours on the Bosphorus. But when the Goths perceived that their cowardly king had betrayed them, they deposed him, and overtaking him as he was escaping to Ravenna, stabbed him to death. Then lifting Vitiges, one of their valiant warriors, on their shields, they proclaimed him king; and Cassiodorus, who during all these events had remained in office, wrote in the name of the new king the following letter, which we quote at length because it seems to us like a trumpet-call, ushering in the fateful and adventurous war which was at hand.

"Vitiges the king to all the Goths. Although every good fortune is to be considered as a gift from the Deity, nor is there any good thing but we know that it comes direct from Him, yet more especially we should refer the source of royal dignity to superior judgments, which have ordained whom He would that His people should obey. Hence, rendering gratefully most humble thanks to Christ, the Author of all things, we announce that the Goths' own kinsmen, amidst drawn swords, and according to the manner of our ancestors raising us on their shields, have conferred on us with God's approval the kingly dignity, that arms might bestow that honour to which war had already given a claim. For behold I was elected not in secret chambers, but in the midst of the open camp; I was sought not with delicate discourse of flatterers, but with clashing trumpets, that the Gothic people, roused by such sounds to the desire of native valour, might find a martial king to reign over them. And indeed how long could men of valour, brought up amidst raging wars, endure a prince whose fame was insecure, however much he might presume on his prowess? It follows necessarily that the reputation which a nation enjoys depends on the leader whom it has deserved to have. For, as you may have heard, I came, called forth by the danger of my kinsmen, to share with them all a common fortune; but they would not allow me to be merely their general, seeing as they did that an experienced king was wanted. So that you are responding to the intentions first of Divine grace, and then of the Goths, inasmuch as you have made me king by your unanimous votes. Lay aside, therefore, all fear of injury, all suspicion of loss; fear no harshness from us. We who are experienced in war have learnt to love valiant men. Add to this, that I have been a witness to the exploits of each of you. For it is not necessary that I should be told of your deeds by any one, since I, the companion of your labours, know them all. The arms of the Goths are not to be broken by any change in my promises. All that we do shall be for the national good: we shall have no private predilections, and we promise to pursue all that may do honour to the royal name. Finally, we promise that in everything our government shall be such as it should be for the Goths after the illustrious Theodoric, a man so singularly and successfully adapted for the cares of a kingdom that each prince may justly be considered illustrious according as he is seen to follow his counsels. Hence he should be credited as a relation of his who is able to imitate his deeds. And therefore, while you continue diligent for the advantage of our kingdom, be reassured as to its internal administration, by the help of God."

This letter, and one addressed by Vitiges to

Justinian announcing his election, and exhorting him to peace while showing no fear of war, are the two last important letters to be found in this collection by Cassiodorus; and it appears to us an instructive sign of the times to find none addressed to the Roman Senate. It is not quite certain at what time Cassiodorus gave up public life, but it is commonly supposed to have been on the fall of the kingdom of Vitiges, and after the first great defeat of the Goths. Taking, however, into account both the abrupt cessation of his letters and the finding no mention of him in the histories of Procopius, as well as the new political tendency, we think it probable that he retired even earlier, disheartened, and having lost all confidence in a good understanding between the Goths and Romans, which would nevertheless have been necessary at that time for the preservation of the Gothic kingdom. At any rate, he had about the year 540 given up the world, and withdrawing to the Abruzzi, near Squillaci, he founded there a monastery (*Monasterium Vivariense*), where he passed the rest of his life in peaceful solitude and literary occupations. There, in addition to the works he had already composed, he had a history of the Church compiled and translated;[1] and in the ninety-

---

[1] This, which is known by the name of *Historia Tripartita*, as having been compiled from the Greek writers Socrates, Sozomen, and Theodoret, became for ages the popular authority on the subject in the Western Church.

third year of his age, he himself wrote a treatise on orthography for the use of his monks, on whom he had laid the obligation of copying books. We have no record of the year in which he died, but he may have lingered on to see the new invasion of Italy by the Lombards, and his life may have closed amid calamities from which he had vainly tried to preserve his country, by encouraging the foundation of a Gothic-Roman kingdom.

If such was the aim of Cassiodorus, the same may be said of the Goth Jordanes, who seems also to have held that the safety of the Goths lay in their union with the Romans under the rule of the Amali—Theodoric's descendants. Jordanes[1] belonged to a noble Gothic family, connected by relationship with the Amali. His grandfather had been notary and chancellor to the king of the Alani, Candac in Mesia, and he also was a notary before embracing an ecclesiastical career. Like Cassiodorus, and perhaps in imitation of him, he is often as a writer elaborate and sententious, but like him also, he was under the influence of the same ideal, and Stahlberg has clearly shown that he saw no other hope but that for the future of his nation. On that account he not only took no part in the struggle which followed between the

---

[1] It is a vexed question whether the name of this writer is Jordanes or Jornandes. We adopt, however, with Wattenbach and Mommsen, the form Jordanes, which is that found in the best manuscripts of the Gothic historian's works.

Goths and the Empire, but seems rather to have sympathized with the Greeks than with his own countrymen. His very relationship with the Amali and the traditions left by Theodoric, who, while maintaining his independence, showed himself respectful towards the Empire and a friend of the Romans, naturally led Jordanes to side with a party which looked with little favour on the ideas prevailing in his day among the Goths. For it is certain that about that time there was a party among the Goths, which regarded as a misfortune the fall of the Amali dynasty, and the separation from the Romans. To this party Jordanes belonged. In various parts of his compendium, he mentions the child Germanus, who, according to him, should have ruled the destinies of the two nationalities united in one. And this explains why in his work he hardly mentions Totila, whom he of course regarded as a usurper. It also appears certain that he wrote his book, not in Italy but at Constantinople, where he was one of those who accompanied Pope Vigilius in his exile from the year 547 until 554. This also explains why he was not able to have the history of Cassiodorus before him while he was making his compendium of it, and was obliged to trust entirely to his memory. He tells this himself in the preface, and it appears that he compiled it for the convenience of the Pope and his followers, and on this account he narrates at more length the ancient history of the

Goths; and his value as a source of Italian history is diminished by his alluding but briefly to contemporary events. Jordanes is also the author of a book entitled *De regnorum successione*, or *De breviatione chronicorum*, which is worth little and compiled principally from Florus. Wattenbach has already observed that what gives most value to Jordanes is his historical point of view, according to which the Roman Empire, linked through successive ages with the generations of the Old Testament, is destined to endure throughout all time till the end of the world. Besides this conception of the universality of Rome, we find in him a special importance as the representative of that Gothic party which desired to throw in their lot with the Romans, and endeavoured to create a mixed nationality.[1]

---

[1] To give an idea of the style of Jordanes we add here, in a note, a fragment which may prove interesting to the reader; it is a portrait of Attila. "A man born into the world for the devastation of nations, and for the terror of all countries, feared everywhere from the formidable reputation in which, I know not by what chance, he was generally held. For he was haughty in his gait, casting his eyes round him in all directions, so that his power might be apparent even from the boastful motions of his person; a lover indeed of war but moderate in action, strong in counsel, gracious to suppliants and benevolent to those once taken into his confidence; short of stature, broad shouldered, with a large head, small eyes and thin beard; his hair was sprinkled with white, his nose was flat, his complexion dark,—all indications of his origin. And although it was his character to be confident in great undertakings, still his assurance was increased by the discovery of the sword of Mars, always held sacred by the Scythian kings, and the finding of which on the following

But this party had fallen for ever with the dynasty of the Amali, and henceforth every tie between the two races was severed. The Emperor Justinian, seeing that all his negotiations were in vain for regaining Italy peacefully, prepared to reconquer it with the sword. Belisarius, already famous for his victories over the Vandals in Africa, was sent into Italy, and while Theodatus was still reigning (535, 536) became master of Sicily and Naples. When Vitiges was raised to the throne, he retired to Ravenna, not feeling himself perhaps strong enough to withstand the first shock of the Greek army, and Belisarius took advantage of this to seize immediately upon Rome. Here begins in truth the heroic period of this war, one of the most memorable ever fought. Vitiges collected all the Gothic forces, and with an army of about a hundred and fifty thousand men, marched from Ravenna to Rome, which he besieged. But through his perseverance and military talents, Belisarius was able to make a successful resistance, and, after an obstinate struggle and indescribable sufferings from famine and pestilence, Rome was

---

occasion is thus related by the historian Priscus : Once a certain shepherd, he says, saw one of his herd limping, and not understanding the cause of its injury, he followed carefully the traces of blood, and came upon a sword which the heifer had accidentally stepped upon while grazing, and digging it up he immediately carried it to Attila, who was greatly rejoiced by this present, for in his ambition he considered that it conferred on him the kingdom of the world, and that success in war was assured to him by the sword of Mars."

relieved from this the first siege of the war, and the strength of the Gothic army was greatly exhausted. But the war continued throughout Italy. Everywhere there were battles and sieges, cities taken and retaken. From Milan to the neighbourhood of Rome the country was devastated, the harvests destroyed, and hence over a large track of Italy a distressing famine decimated the people (A.D. 537, 538). The war was continuing with all its evils, when a Frank army of about a hundred thousand men came down unexpectedly from the Alps like a cloud of locusts, and scattering round them devastation, fire, and rapine, overran a great part of Italy, and returned by Liguria laden with spoils. Shortly afterwards Ravenna, besieged by the Greeks, was obliged to surrender, and Belisarius, taking Vitiges with him as a prisoner, returned to Constantinople, after having refused the offer of the Italian kingdom from the Goths (A.D. 540). These then chose for their king, first Ildibald, then Eraric, who were both assassinated after reigning but a few months. Their successor was a hero, Totila, who, having collected and disciplined what forces remained, succeeded quickly in regaining almost the whole of Italy, except Ravenna and Rome, by taking advantage of the discords among the Greek captains left behind by Belisarius. This great general, being then sent back to Italy, began the struggle afresh, but, being short of soldiers and besieged at Ravenna, he could not as he wished go immediately to the assistance of Rome, which was closely surrounded by the Goths, and when he later made great efforts to do so they were fruitless. Rome in the mean time resisted for long, in spite of famine and every kind of suffering, but at length fell into the hands of Totila. When the Gothic king had made himself master of the city, and had probably recognized that he could not defend himself successfully within its vast circumference, he dismantled the walls, and having driven out all the citizens, he left it completely deserted and marched southwards. Belisarius lost no time in reoccupying the city, and notwithstanding its ruined condition was able to defend it against repeated assaults, while a desultory war continued throughout Italy (547). In consequence of palace intrigues, Belisarius was recalled to Constantinople, and again Grecian influence waned in Italy. Totila again took possession of Rome, and advancing on Sicily succeeded in occupying it also; while the Franks, taking advantage of the weakness of both Greeks and Goths, made another descent to spread havoc through Venetia and Liguria (548–552). Narses, then chosen general-in-chief for the war in Italy, improved the prospects of the Greeks, who, after a successful naval battle with the Goths in the Adriatic, were able to raise the siege of Ancona. Then reinstating themselves in Corsica, Sardinia, and Sicily, they continued to wander fighting over the whole of Italy, until, the two armies arraying all their forces against each other at Tagina in Umbria, the Goths were totally routed after a hard fight, and Totila was killed (552). The Goths replaced their fallen hero by another, and elected King Teias at Pavia, while the Greeks accomplished other undertakings in the south, took Rome, and laid siege to Cuma, where the Goths kept their treasure under the guard of Aligern, the brother of Totila. The new king, Teias, then gathering together what still survived of the Gothic army, and marching from Pavia through almost the whole of Italy, arrived at Nocera, at the foot of Vesuvius; and there was fought the last decisive battle, in which the Goths were completely and finally subdued, and Teias found a death which deserved to be held in remembrance.

We should have no contemporary account of this heroic war unless Procopius, who took part in all the wars conducted by Belisarius, had fortunately left us a narrative of it. On that account we have recalled this war to our readers' minds, and given this brief statement of the events treated by the Greek historian before entering on a more special mention of him and his work.

From Cæsarea in Palestine, where he was born, Procopius came to Byzantium in the time of the Emperor Anastasius, and soon attracted the attention of the Government by his remarkable talent and learning. Justin the Elder, in a moment of great difficulty for the Empire, when the Persians were carrying on the war against the Greeks with success, appointed Procopius as counsellor to Belisarius. Later Justinian wished him to remain in that capacity during the wars in Africa and Italy, in which he rendered excellent service to the State in various missions, and was of much use to the great captain of the Empire. When Belisarius was recalled after the subjugation of Africa, Procopius remained behind with Solomon, who had succeeded Belisarius in the command of the army, and was commissioned to establish firmly the authority of the Empire there, which, owing to the rapidity of the conquest, was not thoroughly secured. He has himself given us an account of his doings in Persia, Africa, and various parts of Italy; nor can he be accused of boastfulness in speaking of himself. His useful services, though of secondary importance, were well rewarded; and after being inscribed among the senators, he rose, in the thirty-fifth year of Justinian's reign, to the high dignity of *Præfectus Urbis*. About that time he had already written his histories, and published all except the last book, which he called *Anecdota*, but which is better known by the name of *Historia Arcana*. In this book, which was not published till after the death of Justinian, many palace intrigues are revealed which place the imperial court in an unfavourable light; and Justinian the emperor and his wife Theodora, who before ascending the throne was, as is well known, an actress in the circus, more especially suffer in this *Historia Arcana*, which, disclosing vices unmentioned in the previous books, has caused doubts to be entertained of the truthfulness of Procopius. Justinian's reign, however, was no less remarkable for its vices than for its virtues, and so offered a wide field for descriptions which, while differing, might nevertheless be truthful; moreover this is not the place for examining these accusations, nor the defence made for Procopius. Putting aside the *Historia Arcana*, which has no direct reference to Italy, as well as the accounts of the wars carried on by Belisarius in Africa and Persia, we need only examine that part of his history which refers specially to the Gothic war. What he says on this subject is doubly valuable, both because, at the side of the great commander, he took a personal part in it all, and also on account of the great impartiality he shows in treating of the Goths, for whom he often expresses a sincere admiration which does him credit. As an eyewitness he describes with telling effect, not only that disastrous war which lasted eighteen years, but also the train of evils which it involved, and he indicates clearly the condition of utter exhaustion and weakness in which Italy was left at the end of that struggle. A Greek writer in a period of decadence, it is very apparent that his book was written at Constantinople and not at Athens; and his style as well as his language suffered from the poverty of the age, and is very far from the simple purity of the ancients. Nevertheless it is wanting neither in vigour nor in colouring, and his book, very superior to contemporary Latin literature, is a model of good taste when compared to the writings of Cassiodorus. When he describes the famine which desolated the whole of Italy, and the maladies which ensued and destroyed so many more of its inhabitants, he finds colours in which to depict it that are dark and terrible in their distinctness, and such as were needed to tell the story of the famished wretches who wandered about in search of corpses wherewith to satisfy their hunger. The very brevity with which he narrates the death by famine of fifty thousand peasants in Picenum alone (the Marche), and of many more who died in the parts beyond the Ionic Gulf, is very forcible, and gives a clear idea of the low ebb to which the resources of Italy must have fallen during that war, and of how exhausted the country was at the end of it. If space had permitted, we should willingly have given this passage, but we must content ourselves with the following short description of another famine which devastated Rome during one of the many sieges which occurred at that period:

"In the meantime the famine enduring and increasing grew into a great evil, and suggested strange sorts of food repugnant to nature. First of all Bessas and Conon, who were the chiefs of the garrison in Rome (and who happened to have a large quantity of corn stored up within the walls of the city), having kept back what was wanted for the soldiers, sold the rest for large sums to the wealthy Romans; for the price of a medimnus (a measure of about twelve gallons) was seven gold pieces. But those whose means did not allow of their spending so much on food, paid a quarter of this price for a medimnus of bran and ate it, while necessity made it taste to them most sweet and dainty. And an ox which the soldiers of Bessas took in a sally, was sold to the Romans for fifty gold pieces. But any Roman who had a dead horse or anything else of the kind, was accounted very fortunate, inasmuch as he could luxuriate upon the flesh of the dead animal. But all the rest of the people lived only on the nettles which grew in great quantities everywhere on the walls and ruins of the city. And that the pungency of the plant might not sting their lips and throat, they boiled them well first before eating them. While therefore the Romans had gold coins they bargained with them, as has been said, for wheat and bran; but when these came to an end, they carried their household goods to the market, and exchanged them for each day's food. But at last, when neither the emperor's soldiers had any more corn to sell to the Romans, there remaining only a little for Bessas himself, nor the Romans had anything left to offer in exchange, they all had recourse to the nettles. But as this food did not suffice for them, and they had not even of it as much as they could eat, their bodies gradually wasted away. And their colour having soon become livid made them look exactly like spectres. And many while walking and still chewing the nettles between their teeth, suddenly fell to the ground dead. And many others, impelled by starvation, destroyed themselves, when they could no longer find either dogs or rats or other living things to feed upon. And there was one Roman, the father of five children, who surrounded him, dragging at his garments and imploring him for food. But he, neither lamenting aloud nor letting his confusion be seen, but hiding away his misery with great strength of mind, desired his children to follow him as if he would give them food. And when he reached the bridge over the Tiber, having put his cloak to his face and covered his eyes with it, flung himself into the river in the sight of his children and of all the Romans who were present. Afterwards the imperial governors, having extorted more money, gave as many Romans as wished for it permission to escape whither they would. So only a few remaining behind, all the rest rushed off in haste wherever they could. And most of them died on their journey either by sea or land, their strength being already quite exhausted by famine. And many were taken by the enemy and killed. For to this condition had fortune brought the Senate and people of Rome."

The avarice of the Greek captains, Bessas and Conon, who meanly took advantage of the scarcity of provisions in order to enrich themselves, is not passed over in silence here by the Greek writer, and further on he reproaches them with it in severe terms. On the other hand, in sharp contrast with this baseness of the Greeks, we find the conduct of Pope Pelagius, who interceded in dignified language with the conqueror Totila for the lives of the Romans, against whom the Goths on entering the city began to act with great cruelty. To this Totila agreed, taking possession, however, for himself and his Goths, of the ill-gotten treasures of Bessas; and at the same time all the patrician houses were pillaged:

"And thus it happened to the other Romans and Senators, and more especially to Rusticiana, the wife of Boetius and daughter of Symmachus, who had always given all her substance to the needy, that they had now to beg bread and the other necessaries of life from their enemies, clothed in the garb of slaves or peasants. For they went round knocking at the doors of the houses, asking for food, nor was it regarded by them as a disgrace. And the Goths insisted that Rusticiana should be put to death, accusing her of having bribed the Roman officers to destroy the statues of Theodoric, in order to avenge the murders of her father

Symmachus and of her husband Boetius. But Totila would not allow any injury to be done her, and saved from outrage both her and all the other women, for which moderation he received great praise."

We see from this touching incident, in which Procopius does honour both to Totila and to the last remains of the Roman nobility, what serenity of judgment he possessed, as well as the quality, so precious in an historian, of being able to seize on facts in their true proportions, and to place them before the reader in such a manner that they give a fair general idea of the conditions of the period described. We think, however, that his good and bad qualities as a writer are all represented in the following account of the decisive battles fought at the foot of Vesuvius, with which Procopius concluded his history of the Gothic war:

"At the foot of Mount Vesuvius there are springs of good water, and a river called Draco flows from them, which passes very near to the town of Nocera; and the two armies were encamped on the opposite sides of this river. But the Draco, though it contains but a small quantity of water, is not fordable either by horsemen or foot soldiers, for it contracts its bed into a narrow space, and breaks away the ground on either side to a considerable depth, so that its banks are very steep. Whether this results from the nature of the ground or of the water I do not know. And the Goths, having seized on

the bridge and encamped close to it, placed wooden towers on it, and various machines, including what they called *ballistra* (βαλλίστρα), in order that they might from the top of them wound and harass the enemy. For, as I have said, it was impossible to come to hand-to-hand combat on account of the river which was between, so that both for the most part attacked each other with missiles, approaching as near as they could on their respective banks. A few single combats did take place, when some Goth occasionally crossed the bridge to challenge fight. And so the two armies spent the space of two months. But thence the Goths were masters of the sea, near which they were encamped, and could hold out as long as their ships brought them the necessary provisions. Afterwards the Romans took the enemies' ships by the treason of the Goth who was in command of the whole fleet, and also innumerable ships from Sicily and the rest of the Empire came to their assistance. At the same time Narses, placing wooden towers on the bank of the river, succeeded in entirely subduing the spirit of his antagonists. But the Goths, having lost heart and being pressed for want of food, escaped to a mountain near, called by the Romans in Latin the *Mons Lactis*. Thither the Romans could not pursue them on account of the badness of the ground. But soon the barbarians began to repent having gone up there, for provisions were still scarcer, so that they could by no means feed
IT.

either themselves or their horses. Therefore they, thinking it more desirable to die in battle array than by slow starvation, came down when the enemy were least expecting it, and made a sudden attack upon them. The Romans withstood them as they were, not ordering themselves according to their captains, or companies, or places, nor arranged in any sort of order among themselves, but defending themselves against the enemy with all their might, each man where he happened to be. Then the Goths, having left their horses, formed into a deep phalanx with their faces all turned to the enemy, and the Romans seeing this also left their horses, and all drew up together in the same array.

"And here I shall describe a battle very remarkable, both in itself, and in the courage displayed so clearly by Teias, who proved himself second to none of those whom we call heroes. And the desperate condition in which they found themselves, urged on the Goths to valour; while the Romans, although they saw that they were desperate, opposed them with all their might, being ashamed to give way to those whom they had already beaten: so that both attacked with great impetuosity those nearest to them, these seeking death, the others glory. And the battle beginning early in the morning, Teias, defended by his shield and brandishing his spear, stood with a few others in a conspicuous position before the phalanx. When the Romans saw him, they thought that if he fell the whole line of battle would be more easily broken up, so that all who claimed to be courageous, and they were many, banded together against him, some thrusting their spears at him, some hurling them against him. But he, hidden behind his shield, received all the spears on it, and then suddenly falling upon them destroyed many. And when he saw that the shield was full of the spears sticking in it, he handed it to one of his shield-bearers, and took another. Thus he continued to fight for a third part of the day, and then his shield being transfixed with twelve spears, he was powerless either to move it at will, or to beat off his attackers. But he merely called in haste to one of his shield-bearers, without quitting his post or stepping back as much as an inch, or allowing the enemy to advance, and without turning round or covering his back with his shield, or standing sideways; but he stood with his shield as if fastened to the ground, dealing death blows with his right hand, with his left keeping all at a distance, and calling by name on his shield-bearer. And when the latter brought him a shield, he immediately changed for it the one he held which was heavy with spears. In the mean time it happened that his breast was uncovered for a short moment, and a javelin chanced to hit him then, and killed him instantly. And some of the Romans fastened his head to a pike and carried it about, showing it to both armies—to the Romans that they might be encouraged, to the Goths that, losing all hope, they might cease from the war. Yet not on this account did the Goths give up fighting, although they knew for certain that their king was dead. But when it grew dark, both separating passed the night in their armour, and rising early the next morning drew out again in the same order, and fought until nightfall, neither giving way to the other, nor turning nor losing hold for a moment, although many were killed on both sides, but they stuck to their work, being infuriated against each other. For the Goths well knew that they were fighting their last battle, while the Romans thought it beneath them to be beaten. At last the barbarians, sending some of their chief men to Narses, told him that they were persuaded that they were contending against God, for that they felt His power set against them; so that, comparing this truth with what had happened, they wished now to change their minds, and desist from the struggle, not, however, so as to obey the emperor, but to live independently together with some of the other barbarians. And they asked that the Romans should let them retreat in peace, and not grudge them reasonable treatment, but should give them, as maintenance for their journey, all the money which they each had stored in their castles in Italy. And when Narses was deliberating on this, John, the son of Vitalianus, advised that this request should be granted; and that they should not continue to fight with men prepared to die, nor put further to the proof a valour which resulted from despair of life, and which was equally disastrous to those who showed it and to those who encountered it. 'For it should suffice,' he said, 'to wise men to be victorious; wanting too much is likely to turn out prejudicial to both parties.' This counsel pleased Narses, and they agreed that those who were left of the barbarians, after collecting their own possessions, should immediately clear out of the whole of Italy, and should on no account fight any more against the Romans. In the mean time about a thousand of the Goths, leaving the camp, proceeded to the city of Pavia and the countries beyond the Po; and Indulph, whom we have already mentioned, was among those who led them. But all the rest confirmed by oath what had been agreed upon. Thus the Romans took Cumæ, and all the other places, and this was the end of the eighteenth year of the war with the Goths, which was written by Procopius."

The whole history of this age is contained in Cassiodorus and Procopius, but there are some other writers who also deserve to be mentioned. Agathias continued, also in Greek, the history of Procopius, with a narrative of the later exploits of Narses, and may be consulted with advantage touching the last events of the Gothic war after the death of Teias. Marcellinus Comes has left us a dry Latin chronicle, which, beginning in the time of Theodosius, extends to that of Justinian (A.D.

379-558); but, notwithstanding its dryness, it has a value especially for the chronology of certain facts, with regard to which something also may be extracted from the chronicle of Marius Aventicensis. Far superior to these, both for interest and importance, is Magnus Felix Ennodius, bishop of Pavia. Of a noble and doubtlessly Gallo-Roman stock, he seems to have been born at Milan, and certainly lived there as a child. He was bound by ties of blood or friendship to all the first men of his time—to all those most distinguished either by learning or birth. He was married and had one child, but later he and his wife left the world for the religious life. After becoming deacon, Ennodius remained in that rank for a long time, till he was raised to the dignity of bishop of Pavia, where he died about the year 521. He had a great reputation in his day as a rhetorician, and wrote, both in his own name and in that of others, an immense number of orations, letters, and epitaphs for which he was very famous. But his principal fame originated from a panegyric in honour of Theodoric, and a book in defence of Pope Symmachus. The panegyric, written as far as we can judge about 507 or 508, was probably recited either at Ravenna or Milan. It is a writing in the worst possible taste, containing all the defects of the style of Cassiodorus, without his redeeming qualities. Its historical value is owing to the absence of other documentary evidence rather than to any intrinsic importance of its own, and is inferior to his letters or to his life of St. Epiphanius, bishop of Pavia. The letters written chiefly to the great men of his time contain much valuable information for the students of that epoch. The life of St. Epiphanius is the portrait of a wonderful character — of a man entirely dedicated to works of charity, and especially to the ransom of those whom the barbarians, in their incursions, carried off with them as slaves far away from their country. Besides this interesting portrait, it gives us a vivid picture of the troubled and disastrous age immediately preceding the Gothic times, to which, bad as they were, still worse were to succeed.

CHAPTER II.

SAD CONDITION OF ITALY IN THE EARLY PERIOD OF THE LOMBARD INVASION—GREGORY THE GREAT—COLLECTION OF HIS LETTERS—THEIR GREAT IMPORTANCE FOR THE HISTORY OF ITALY—THE BOOK OF DIALOGUES—THE EDICT OF ROTHARI—THE "ORIGO LANGOBARDORUM" AND MINOR WRITINGS UP TO PAULUS DIACONUS—HIS LIFE—HIS WORKS AND ESPECIALLY HIS HISTORY OF THE LOMBARDS.

ITALY was not freed by the fall of the Gothic kingdom. Belisarius and Narses had been able to break the power of the Goths, but could not create a sufficient barrier against fresh attacks. The Empire of the West was indeed falling to pieces, and the tie which bound it to the Eastern Empire only served to increase its difficulties. The Byzantine court, enfeebled by corruption, could not stand alone, and wasted the strength of Italy by a dominion which was neither national nor altogether foreign. Hence the ruin of Italy. As we have already said, had it been possible to carry out the idea of Cassiodorus, and fuse the Goths in the Latin race, perhaps a real Italian kingdom might have resulted, capable of struggling, on the one hand against the new barbaric invasions, and on the other against the sordid pretensions of the Byzantines. With something like an Italian nationality secured, as far as the age would allow, perhaps Roman civilization would not have died out for so long a series of centuries, and the times of the renaissance might have been matured earlier and with less effort. But human vicissitudes are subject to historical laws, as deep and inscrutable as all other decrees of Providence; and perhaps, on the contrary, humanity along this painful path has made quicker progress than it could otherwise have done. Yet who can help feeling some regret when he looks back now over the long array of evils which, after so many misfortunes, were still reserved for the *Alma mater* of modern nations?

The first invasion and establishment of the Lombards in Italy marks the most ill-starred period of Italian history. Arriving from Pannonia under the leadership of a fierce and valiant king, Albuin, the Lombards descended into Italy but few years after the last defeat of the Goths. They met with little resistance. The Exarch Longinus, an insignificant man, had succeeded Narses, and the cities, left to themselves, made what defence they could. In a few years the dominion of the Lombards, begun in Friuli, extended over a great part of Italy. They lived rudely, and treated with ferocity the vanquished, from whom they differed in religion, being in part Arians, in part still idolaters. Rapine and slaughter spread misery and desolation around, and justified the lamentations of Pope Pelagius II. when writing to the Bishop Aunacarius of Auxerre: "And how shall we not mourn when we see so much innocent blood shed before our eyes, the altars desecrated, and the Catholic Faith insulted by these idolaters?" The juridical condition of the Italians under their new conquerors was a grievous one during the whole time of their dominion, which lasted two centuries until it was struck down by the power of Charlemagne. The ancient civilization already tottering received a last blow, and it was with difficulty that it still retained some lingering spark of life, and the tradition of the great Roman name.

And it was indeed in Rome that the seed of a future revival was sown. In those hours of trial Rome was undergoing a great transformation, and the ancient empress of the world, fallen from her early grandeur and with the barbarians at her gates, was preparing for a new and not less vast domination, to which we only refer here on account of its immediate importance to Italian history, and without touching on the great ecclesiastical problems which grew out of it, or on the good and the evil which resulted from it. While Italy was being wasted by Byzantine bad government at Ravenna and by Lombard devastations, a man of genius, Gregory the Great, rose from the chair of Peter to defend Italy, and, as it would seem unconsciously inspired by Roman traditions, sowed the seeds of the universal supremacy of the Church. Certainly no one could have been more adapted than he was to carry out this great transformation, which was destined to be so lasting and so fruitful in its consequences. "In the case of few other men," writes an historian recently, "have both nature and fortune shown more gracious concord; but few also have shown themselves more anxious to spend aright their gifts, to turn them to best account, and to regard them only as the patrimony of others. Descendant of an illustrious patrician stock (believed to have been the Anician family: his father was the Senator Gordianus, and among his ancestors he counted a pope, Felix IV.), he had inherited, together with the considerable rent-roll of his forefathers, their robust nature and their good judgment. The dignity of the Roman and the ardour of the Christian were combined in Gregory, as in no other pontiff either before or after him."[1]

Such a man could not but find himself of necessity in the midst of all the events of his time,

---

[1] B. Malfatti, *Imperatori e Papi*, Milano, Hoepli, 1876.

and reflect in all his writings the age in which he lived; hence his works, written with quite a different aim, have in later times acquired the greatest importance for history, in consequence of the almost complete absence of contemporary historical records. Born about the year 540, while Belisarius was contesting the dominion of Italy with the Goths, he studied at Rome grammar, rhetoric, philosophy, and law. Entering upon public life, he was raised while still very young to the dignity of prætor or prefect of the city, but notwithstanding these political cares he, a man of thought as well as action, could not be prevailed upon to alter his habits of piety and contemplation. With that untiring activity which never failed him, and under the inspiration of St. Ambrose and St. Augustine, whom he calls clear and deep wellsprings of learning, he devoted himself to the study of theology, while he made use of his great riches to found six monasteries in Sicily, and a seventh in Rome on the Celian, *ad Clivum Scauri*, where there is still a church called by his name. He retired into this monastery somewhat later, in order to live in austere seclusion far away from public affairs, but for a short time only, as he was not allowed for long to escape from them. His illustrious lineage, the power of his intellect, the celebrity he had already acquired, were such as to make it impossible for him to pass unnoticed. Pope Benedict I. ordained him deacon in order to entrust to him one of the seven *regiones* of Rome; and his successor, Pelagius II., sent him as *Apocrisarius* to treat about the affairs of the Church at Constantinople. There, during the time of his embassy, he gained the favour of the emperor; and so greatly did his reputation increase that, after his return to Rome, on the death of Pelagius in the year 590, the Romans unanimously declared him pope. His resistance, and even flight from Rome, could not save him from the burthen of that great dignity. The wish of the people and clergy of Rome was ratified at Constantinople by the emperor, and he had to resign himself to accept an office which inspired him with the greater awe, inasmuch as his heart and intellect alike led him to take a more comprehensive view of the great responsibilities it imposed. Those calamitous times required fresh efforts daily from his lofty ministry, and suggested fresh thoughts; but his mind, with its yearnings towards heaven, returned constantly to the recollection of his lost peace, and regretted with infinite tenderness the solitude of his monastery: "The grief which I constantly suffer is old indeed now from habit, and yet it is ever fresh. My chafed soul remembers what she once was in the monastery, how she used to rise above fleeting things, and only thinking of heavenly matters, passed out of the boundary of the flesh, by virtue of contemplation, and death became dear to her as the beginning of life and the reward of her works." With such lamentations he one day confided his griefs to a friend who had surprised him sitting in a solitary place and meditating on his sorrow in silence. But neither his ascetic tendencies, nor the infirmities from which he suffered, sufficed to deter him from the duties of his office. A Roman heart beat in his breast, and he dedicated himself to his sacred calling with a firmness worthy of the olden times. His mind, not less than his zeal, extended afar the beneficent action which made him a centre to different nations, and a guide to the new civilization which, as yet unsuspected, owed its new-born life to his impulse. From all these continuous cares, animated by a charity both intense and comprehensive, there originated among other works a volume of most remarkable letters, which form the highest testimony to his noble life, and at the same time the most important historical monument of his age. These letters, divided into fourteen books according to the fourteen years of his pontificate, and written to every class of persons, describe admirably the conditions of the times, and give a faithful picture of what life was then like, while confirming or maintaining the record of facts either little or not at all known. In its simplicity and freedom from all ornament each one indicates the circumstances which called it forth; and regarding them as a whole, we gather from them what were the habitual reflections and aspirations of the pontiff.

The style of the prophets, of which we distinctly feel the influence in his other works, has not such hold upon him when he sets forth his thoughts and wishes fervently and spontaneously, without literary aims, and almost always hurried by the urgency of the matter. Hence his letters, free from mystical bombast, flow along easily and remind us sometimes of the simple and dignified Latin of an earlier period. The subjects of them are exceedingly varied, and treat of every matter from the highest ecclesiastical and political questions to the minute administration of the Church's possessions, and from the anxious care of individual souls to the pathetic narrative of his own long and almost continual sufferings, moral and physical. But the production here of some of these letters may serve better than anything else to give an idea both of their importance and of the miserable condition in which Italy then was. Thus the following letter addressed to the Empress Constantina, in order to obtain from the emperor some alleviation of the hardships undergone by the islands of Corsica and Sardinia, shows what the Greek government was like, and how Italy was torn in pieces by the double tyranny of her new and of her old oppressors:

"Since I know how much our most gracious lady considers the heavenly kingdom and the life of her own soul, I think that I should be committing a great fault if I were silent with regard to those things which are suggested to me by the fear of Almighty God. Having heard that there are many Gentiles in the island of Sardinia, and that, according to their depraved custom, they still sacrifice to idols, and that the priests of the island have become lax in preaching our Redeemer, I sent one of the Italian bishops there, who with the help of God converted many of these Gentiles to the faith. But he has informed me of a sacrilegious matter, namely that those who sacrifice to idols pay a tax to the judge that it may be permitted to them; of whom some now, being baptized, have given up sacrificing to idols, yet still this tax which they had been accustomed to pay for that purpose is exacted from them by the same judge, even after baptism. And when he was found fault with by the bishop for this, he answered that he had promised to pay so much for his post, which he could not do unless by these means. But the island of Corsica is oppressed by such extortions on the part of the tax-gatherers, and by such burthen of taxation, that the inhabitants can hardly satisfy these demands even by selling their own children. Whence it happens that these islanders are obliged to desert their holy Republic, and to escape to the most accursed nation of the Lombards. And indeed what could they suffer from the barbarians more oppressive or cruel, than that they should be driven to sell their children? And in the island of Sicily a certain *carthularius* on the sea-coast is said to cause so much injury and oppression by invading the possessions of individuals, and without any lawsuit affixing orders of eviction on houses and farms, that if I tried to relate all the things told me of him, I should take up more than a large volume. All which things, therefore, may our most gracious lady attend to, and comfort the groans of the oppressed. For I am quite sure that they have never reached your pious ears, for if they had they would not have lasted until now. Make them known, on fitting occasion, to your devout lord, that he may remove such a heavy load of sin from his own soul, from the Empire, and from his children. And I know well that he will perhaps say that he sends to us, for the expenses of Italy, all that is collected from the abovementioned islands; but I answer—let him give less for the expenses of Italy, and let him remove from his Empire the tears of the oppressed. And perhaps on that account so much outlay expended on this country avails so little, because it is provided for partly by sin. Let therefore your most gracious lordships command that nothing henceforth be collected sinfully, for I am persuaded that even if less is contributed to the necessities of the commonwealth, it will still be more advantaged. And should it even happen that it receives less advantage from these smaller contributions, it is nevertheless better that our temporal life should suffer than that any hindrance should be placed in the way of your eternal life. Consider with what thoughts, with what feelings must these parents tear themselves away from their children, in order not to be further racked. And whoever has children of their own should know well how to feel for the children of others. Let it therefore be enough for me to have suggested these things, in order that your piety might not be ignorant of what is happening in those parts, and I might not be arraigned by the severe Judge for my silence."

Witnessing the continual devastation of Italian territory, and being conscious that the Imperial Government hindered more than it helped, Gregory tried as often as he could to conclude temporary truces with the Lombards, in order that Rome at least, and the provinces still belonging to the Empire, might find some rest from the horrors of continuous warfare. But Romanus, the exarch of Ravenna, actuated by a narrow and jealous policy, threw obstacles in his way, and among other things broke up an agreement upon which he was entering with Ariulph, the Lombard duke of Spoleto. There resulted from this an incursion of Lombards round Rome, with slaughters and ravages up to the very walls. The pontiff, overcome by grief, fell ill, and only recovered in order to meet with fresh vexations. Agilulph, the king of the Lombards, wishing to regain possession of some cities taken from him through treason by the Greeks, moved rapidly from Pavia towards Tuscany, regained

Perugia, and did not stop till he reached the walls of Rome, whence he spread havoc on all sides. The pontiff, who at that time was expounding Ezekiel to the Romans in a course of homilies, was so overwhelmed by these calamities that he could not continue his exposition. "Everywhere," he exclaimed, "we see mourning, everywhere we hear groans; cities are destroyed, castles are sacked, the fields are devastated, the whole land has become a desert. Some we have seen carried into captivity, some mutilated, others put to death." And further on, excusing himself to his flock for not continuing, he adds: "Let no man blame me if I shall cease after this discourse, for as you all see, our tribulations have increased. Everywhere we are surrounded by the sword, everywhere we are in instant peril of death. Some have returned to us with their hands cut off, others are announced to us as captives or dead. I am now obliged to refrain from further exposition."

But while he was doing all that he could to alleviate the misfortunes of his country, and grieved over them both as a Christian and a citizen, the imperial dignitaries were trying to undermine his authority at the court of Constantinople, and accused him of having allowed himself to be deceived by the Duke of Spoleto, and hence to have deceived the emperor. Gregory indignantly defended himself, and wrote to the emperor with great frankness and resolution:

"If the slavery of my land were not increasing daily, I would say nothing of the contempt and derision in which I am held. But what pains me is this, that while I am not believed, Italy is dragged more and more under the yoke of the Lombards. I say to my devout lord: let him think every evil of me; but with regard to the weal of the commonwealth, and the liberation of Italy, let him give heed to no one, but believe facts more than words. And let not our lord in his earthly power be so readily indignant with the priests, but in consideration of Him, whose servants they are, lay his commands upon them in such way as to show them proper reverence. I will now briefly relate what I have had to suffer. First of all, the peace which, without loss to the commonwealth, I had made with the Lombards of Tuscany, was disturbed; and when it had been disturbed, the soldiers were taken away from Rome, some killed by the enemy, the rest placed at Narni or Perugia, and, in order to hold Perugia, Rome was abandoned. And when Agilulph came, things were worse; then I had with my own eyes to see Romans, like dogs, with a rope round their necks going to be sold in France. We indeed, thanks be to God, escaped from their hands, being shut up in the city; but then an effort was made to inculpate us because there was not corn enough in the city, where, however, as I explained another time, it cannot be kept for long. Nor do I grieve for myself; for having a quiet conscience, I confess that as long as my soul is in safety I hold myself prepared for everything. But I do grieve for those heroic men, the Prefect Gregory, and Castorius *magister militum*, who did everything that could be done, underwent during the siege immense fatigues of day and night watches, and nevertheless incurred afterwards the severe displeasure of the sovereigns. Whence I plainly see that it was not their actions but my person that injured them, and that after having gone through these fatigues with me, with me now they are suffering tribulations. And as to what is hinted to me of the terrible judgment of Almighty God, I pray by the same Almighty God that the piety of my sovereigns may repeat this no more. Since we cannot know what this judgment will be, and Paul the estimable preacher says, 'Judge nothing before the time, until the Lord come, who both will bring to light the hidden things of darkness, and will make manifest the counsels of the hearts.' This I say briefly, because I, unworthy sinner, trust more in the mercy of Jesus than in the justice of your piety. And may God guide here with his hand my devout lord, and in that terrible judgment find him free from every crime; and may He make me pleasing, if it is needful, to men, but in such a way that I may not transgress His eternal grace."

These calumnies, however, and obstacles did not prevent him from negotiating fresh truces with the

Lombards, and thus trying to save Italy, especially the country districts, from those wars which involved so much misery. There was then reigning over the Lombards, Agilulph, formerly duke of Turin, a prince of great valour, but of a tolerably conciliatory character, who had been called to the throne by Queen Theodolinda when she was left a widow on the death of King Authari, and was invited by the nobles to decide the destinies of the kingdom by selecting a second husband among the Lombard dukes as successor to the king who had died. This princess, a lady of noble qualities, Bavarian by birth, and in faith a Catholic, exercised a great and salutary influence in the affairs of the kingdom, and in the counsels of her husband, and was often a peacemaker. From the letters of Gregory we can also discern in what high esteem he held her, and how he hoped by her means to draw to the Catholic faith the Lombards who, as we have already said, were followers partly of the Arian heresy, and partly still of rude and superstitious idolatry. And indeed he lived to see his desire at least partially fulfilled; and it is supposed that Theodolinda's persuasions induced Agilulph to abandon Arianism, as in England those of Bertha secured the conversion of Ethelbert. Certainly after Agilulph the Lombards began gradually to hold the same faith as the Italian people, and this fact was of great political significance, since it helped to lessen the division between the two nations, and, as far as was

possible, to bring about that fusion between them
to which, however, the existence of the Eastern
Empire always offered a serious obstacle. About
that time the Cathedral of Monza was founded by
Theodolinda, and to it she presented the so-called
iron crown which was used at the coronation of
all the kings of Italy from that time; and after
having crowned Charlemagne and Napoleon is still
preserved there, and lately bore its part on a solemn
occasion behind the bier of Victor Emmanuel, the
reviver of the Italian kingdom. Agilulph having
had a son (A.D. 603), he had him baptized according
to the Catholic ritual, and Gregory, delighted at this
event of which he well saw the full importance,
sent his praises and congratulations to Theodolinda
in a letter which we give here :

"The writing which you lately sent us from the
Genoese countries made us sharers in your joy, both
on account of the son given to you by the grace of
Almighty God, and because we know, what is very
praiseworthy in your excellency, that he is made a
member of the Catholic faith. Nor could we have
believed otherwise of your Christianity than that
you should endeavour to protect, by the assistance
of the Catholic righteousness, him whom you received by Divine favour, both that your Redeemer
might recognize you as His devoted handmaiden,
and that the new king of the Lombard nation
might be nourished in His fear. Whence we pray
Almighty God that He should both keep you in the

way of His commandments, and should make this your most excellent son Adolowald proficient in His love. So that as here he is already great among men, he may also become glorious by good deeds before the eyes of our God. But that which your excellency wrote that we should answer our most beloved son Secundinus, the abbot, with respect to those things which he wrote to us with great acumen, who would delay attending to his petition or your wishes which are for the profit of many, unless hindered by illness? But we are held by such an infirmity of gout, that not only we cannot dictate, but cannot even bear the fatigue of speaking, as also your ambassadors the bearers of this letter have known, for they both found us ill on their arrival, and they are leaving us now at their departure in extreme danger, and in a struggle for life. But if Almighty God wills it so, I shall recover, and shall answer all those things which he hath written with so much acumen. And I have sent you also by the bearers of this the acts of that synod called together by Justinian of pious memory, that this aforesaid son of mine may study them, and know that all that he has heard against the Apostolic Chair, and the Catholic Church, is false. For God forbid that we should accept the meaning of any heretic, or should deviate from the ways of our predecessor Leo of holy memory. But we receive whatever is laid down in the four holy synods, and we condemn whatever is disapproved.

And we also have directed that these relics should be given to our most excellent son Adolowald, the king; that is, a cross with the wood of the holy cross of our Lord, and the volume of the holy Gospel enclosed in a Persian case; also to my daughter, his sister, I have sent three rings—two with purple and one with a milk-white stone; which things I beg may be given to them by you, in order that our love for them may be graced by your excellency. We also pray with paternal affection, while mindful of all courteous greeting, that you should thank our most excellent son the king your consort, in our name, for the peace made; and should incite him in all ways for the future to peace, as you are accustomed to do, so that you may find, in the presence of God, among your many good works, the mercy shown to an innocent people who might otherwise have perished in a great ruin."

The letters which we have chosen, not without hesitation among so many, may serve to give an idea of the sort of light they throw on the history of Italy at that time. But the vastness of Gregory's intellect, as well as the inspirations he drew from his high office, and the width of his Christian charity, did not allow of his restricting the sphere of his action to Italy alone, and hence his volume of letters become a source of universal history. And indeed we are much assisted in judging of the state of Europe during his lifetime by the letters to France, especially those directed to the famous

Queen Brunichild,[1] and those sent to Spain where his principal correspondent was that Leander, bishop of Seville, who induced King Recaredus and his Visigoths to abandon the Arian heresy. In the same way the letters directed to Constantinople, Alexandria, and to other places in the East and in Africa, describe the state of the most distant countries and their intercourse with Rome. Gregory's relations with England, and the part he took in the conversion of this country, are famous. The venerable Bede in his collection of English traditions has left a well-known narrative of them, which was repeated through all the Middle Ages, and quoted again lately in another volume of this series.[2] In this narrative it is related how Gregory,

---

[1] This correspondence of Gregory's with the profligate queen of the Franks has been blamed by some historians. According to them Gregory should not have been on such courteous terms with a woman whose name has come down to us covered with infamy. We cannot think the reproach is altogether justified. At that time the Church in France suffered great injury from the simony which prevailed in the elections of the bishops. Gregory was fighting with all his might against this scandal, and he constantly appealed to Brunichild to put a stop to it. His position with regard to this singular woman was, therefore, a far from easy one; and it seems to us that this should be taken into account in judging the conduct of a man whose virtues and the purity of whose intentions are so generally admitted. More serious would appear to us the other reproach made against him for the letter in which he recognized the authority of the tyrant Phocas, the bloody usurper of the throne of Constantinople. But here, also, we must take into account the responsibility which Gregory felt with regard to the destinies of so many nationalities who looked to him as to their only protector.

[2] *Early Chroniclers of Europe: England*, by James Gairdner, p. 10 et seq.

not yet pope, having seen in Rome some English slaves, being struck by their beauty, and hearing that they were idolaters, conceived the idea of converting, or rather reconverting, England to the faith; and having obtained permission, set out as a missionary to this land. But hardly had he begun his journey before the Roman people rose to demand his immediate return, and obliged the pope to recall him. This story, which is not confirmed by anything in Gregory's writings, shows nevertheless both the veneration which was felt for him in England some centuries after his death, and his affectionate solicitude for that mission to which his letters continually bear witness. We hope that we shall not be exceeding the limits of this work, specially dedicated to the history of Italy, if we quote a few passages from Gregory's letters, in which he speaks of this undertaking which originated with him, rejoices over its success, and directs it with his instructions. He writes thus to Eulogius bishop of Alexandria :—

"But since I know that you rejoice in all the good done both by yourself and others, I give you in return the same pleasure, and announce not dissimilar things. For whereas the English nation, in a distant corner of the world, had hitherto remained superstitiously worshipping stocks and stones, I was induced by your prayers on my behalf to send, with the grace of God, a monk of our monastery to preach to it; who, being made a bishop by the

German bishops with my permission, and encouraged by them, journeyed to this aforesaid people at the end of the world, and already has written to us of his welfare and of his work. For he and those who were sent with him shine with so many miracles among this people, that it is clear that they imitate the remarkable apostolic virtues which they teach. And on the occasion of the Christmas festival of this first indiction, we hear of more than ten thousand English having been baptized by this our brother and fellow-bishop. And I tell you of all this, that you may know what you can do in Alexandria by your speech, and in the ends of the world by your prayers. For your prayers prevail where you are not present, while your holy labours are made evident in the place where you are."

Later in this letter—remarkable for its tone of natural satisfaction as well as for its humble faith—he alludes to a great contention which he had in the East with John the Faster, patriarch of Constantinople, with regard to the title of universal bishop, which Gregory declined for himself and would not recognize in others. But this question, which gave rise to many of Gregory's letters, and to some of the most important for the history of the Church, is outside the limits of our inquiry, and we must not enter into it. We shall rather conclude these quotations with some passages of a letter written to Augustine himself with regard to his apostolate in England:

"Glory to God in the highest; peace on earth, goodwill towards men. As the dead grain of corn, falling into the ground, bore much fruit that it might not reign alone in heaven, so by His death we live, by His infirmity we are strengthened, by His suffering we are saved, by His love we inquire for our brethren in Britain whom we know not, by His grace we found those for whom we ignorantly inquired. But who could adequately here describe how much joy had sprung up in the hearts of all the faithful, that the English nation, by the operating grace of Almighty God, and by the labours of thy fraternity, has been suffused with the light of the holy faith, after the darkness of error was expelled; that it now with virtuous resolution tramples upon the idols to which it submitted before in abject terror; that it worships Almighty God with a pure heart; that it is protected by the rules of holy teaching from lapsing into unrighteous dealing; that it submits to the Divine precepts, and is intellectually raised; that it humiliates itself to earth in prayer lest it should be abased to earth in spirit? Whose work is this but His who said, 'My Father works until now, and I work'? . . . Thou shouldst rejoice that the souls of the English are drawn by outward miracles to inward grace, but thou shouldst tremble lest, amid these wonders which occur, the weak spirit should be elated by presumption, and while raised to honour without, should fall within by vain glory. . . . For the disciples of truth should rejoice in nothing but in that good which they have in common with all, and thence there will be no end to their rejoicing. It remains, therefore, dearest brother, that while thou art doing these things outwardly through God's co-operation, thou shouldst always inwardly judge thyself with discrimination, and with discrimination understand both what thou art in thyself, and what grace there is in that people for whose conversion it is that thou didst receive the gift of performing these miracles. And if thou remember to have ever offended against our Creator either in word or deed, recall this always to thy mind, that the memory of thy guilt may keep down the rising pride of thy heart; and whatever power thou mayst receive, or hast already received, to do miracles, consider that this is a gift not to thee, but to them for whose salvation it is conferred upon thee. . . . But I say these things because I desire to humble the soul of him who hears me; yet let also thy humility have perfect trust. For I, a sinner, hold a sure hope that thy sins are already forgiven by the grace of our Almighty Creator, and of our Redeemer, God, and Lord, Jesus Christ; and that on that account thou art chosen that the sins of others may be forgiven through thee. Nor wilt thou hereafter be grieved by any guilt, who strivest to cause joy in heaven over the conversion of many. For thus our Founder and Redeemer says, when speaking of the repentance of man, 'Verily I say unto you, there shall be more joy in heaven over one sinner that repenteth, than over ninty and nine just persons which need no repentance.' And if there is so great joy in heaven over one that repenteth, what must the joy be over a whole nation converted from their errors, who, embracing the faith, condemn with penitence the evils which they before committed? In this joy therefore of heaven and the angels, we repeat the very words of the angels with which we began. Let us say therefore, let all of us say, ' Glory to God in the highest; and on earth peace, goodwill towards men.' "

In the year 604, on the 14th of March, Gregory the Great ended a life which had been so virtuously and usefully spent. With the cessation of his correspondence the history of Italy loses its surest guide in that age. Some others also of Gregory's works have a certain historical importance on account of their allusions to contemporary or recent events, and especially valuable among them are the Dialogues. This strange book is one of those which most fascinated the imagination of the Middle Ages, and in it Gregory related the life and miracles of St. Benedict, and of various other Italians, who had a reputation for holiness in his day, and most of whom were either known to him or to persons with whom he was acquainted. It is a collection of quaint, fantastic legends, and it is certainly characteristic of the age to find so much childish credulity in a man of such remarkable intellect.

Still these legends are of great value, both because they are mixed up with real events, and on account of their allusions to places and monuments then existing, and to the usages and principal personages of the day.

After the death of Gregory, almost all direct and contemporary testimony to historical facts in Italy ceases during the Lombard period. The most important document is the Edict of King Rothari (A.D. 643), which, with the additions made by succeeding kings, constitutes the Lombard code of laws. Rothari prefixed to the Edict a prologue, which in the absence of other documents is of importance, as it gives a carefully compiled list of the Lombard kings with the names of their families, and an exact genealogy for ten generations of the family of the Arodi, to which Rothari himself belonged.

Until Rothari collected them, the Lombard laws had never been written, but were handed down orally from generation to generation. And the same thing happened with regard to their enterprises generally. Like every other primitive Germanic race, they committed to song the ancient legends which narrated both the deeds of their ancestors, and, what they prized greatly, the genealogies of their families. About the year 670 a Lombard tried to gather rudely from these songs some hints regarding the descent of his people, and this work of his, called *Origo Langobardorum*, was also added to the prologue of the Edict of Rothari. Before these efforts there existed a history of the Lombards compiled by Secundus, bishop of Trent (d. 612) : of this history, which seems to have been valuable but is now entirely lost, there only remains mention in the writings of Paulus Diaconus, which we are now about to examine. The follower of Prosper of Acquitaine who carried his continuation as far as the year 671, and a *Magister Stefanus* who about 698 composed a very rude poem in praise of King Cunipert, are the only contemporary sources which we have besides the *Origo* and the Edict, and they are all the work of writers of Latin origin. The Lombards, more than any other German people, were slow in acquiring Latin culture, and began to acquire it only when their rule was near its setting. However, as Wattenbach observes,[1] the grammarians who, notwithstanding the unfavourable nature of the times, had always continued their labours, began gradually to find disciples among the Lombards, and when the rule of these approached its end, they had educated for this foreign nation the historian who, like Jordanes, should after their fall at least preserve the memory of their mastery. This historian was Paulus Diaconus, and we now proceed to treat of him at some length, as being the most distinguished writer of this early part of the Middle Ages in Italy.

---

[1] Wattenbach, *Deutschland's Geschichtsquellen im Mittelalter*, vol. I. ch. ii. § 6.

Paulus Diaconus has left us some records of himself here and there in his writings, and hence we can follow the traces of his life, which was certainly a remarkable one. His lineage was ancient, and according to the favourite custom of the Lombards, he does not omit to give us its history, into which is woven a great deal that is legendary. Leupchis, whom he mentions as the founder of the family, had descended into Friuli with Albuin on the occasion of the first Lombard invasion of Italy, and died there, leaving five sons of tender age, who soon afterwards were taken prisoners in an incursion of the Avari and carried far away from their country. After a long captivity one of them, Lopichis, having reached man's estate, succeeded in escaping by flight. His journey was an adventurous one, full of hardships and dangers amidst the Alps. He first met with a wolf which guided him on his unknown road, and then, when the wolf mysteriously disappeared, the path was shown to him in a dream, and following it he finally reached Friuli. There he found the deserted house where he was born, and was able by the help of his relations, who recognized him, to restore it and to found his family. From Lopichis descended Arechis, from Arechis Warnefrit, who married a certain Theodolinda, and had about the year 720 a son, who was Paulus Warnefridus, or as he is more generally called, Paulus Diaconus.

The grammarian Flavianus—nephew of another

grammarian, Felix—was Paul's master in literature. While still a child he studied the Greek language, profitably as we believe, notwithstanding his modest assertion to the contrary in after days. It is not certain where he studied under Flavianus, whose name, as well as his uncle's, indicates his Italian origin, but it seems probable that it was at Pavia in the very court of the king, according to the ancient German custom. Certainly Paul was at court in the time of King Ratchis (A.D. 744-749), for he relates having himself seen that king, after a banquet, show the famous goblet which Albuin had made of the skull of Cunimund, king of the Gepidi. As is known, Albuin, having killed King Cunimund in battle and afterwards married his daughter Rosamund, used on solemn occasions to drink out of his skull, from which a cup had been formed. One day he commanded that the goblet should be handed to the queen, calling upon her to drink gaily with her father. This horrible outrage, which later was cruelly avenged by Rosamund, appeared so great to Paul that he exclaims, while relating it to us, " Lest this should seem incredible to any, behold I speak the truth in Christ; for indeed I saw on a certain feast-day King Ratchis holding this cup in his hand and showing it to his guests."

This anecdote, which we have introduced here as an instance of the rude ferocity of the first Lombards, helps us to follow the private history of Paul's life, nor is this the only episode in which we find him in intimate relations with the princes of his time. The earliest writing of Paul's which remains (A.D. 763) is a poem on the six ages of the world, the verses of which form an acrostic on the name of *Adelperga Pia*, the daughter of the Lombard King Desiderius and wife of Arechis, duke and later prince of Benevento. This princess, who had been a pupil of Paul's, always remained his friend, and invited him later to enlarge and continue the Roman history of Eutropius. It also appears that he composed the epitaph in verse for Queen Ansa, the mother of Adelperga, whose body was brought back to her native country from France, whither she had followed her husband Desiderius when the Lombard kingdom was overthrown by the power of Charlemagne. The lines of the inscription, the style of which seems certainly that of Paul, breathe a profound melancholy, and bear witness to the affection of the author for his Lombard lineage. It is not known with certainty when he received holy orders, nor whether he had received them before entering the cloister, but it does not seem improbable that he went as monk to Montecassino at the time that Ratchis, hurled from his throne, found a refuge there. And there the solemn peace of the cloister gained such empire over Paul, that perhaps he would never have been persuaded to leave it unless the force of circumstances had called him forth. After the fall of the Lombard kingdom there broke out in 776 a revolt against the Franks, especially in the Duchy of Friuli; and even if Paul was a stranger to this revolt, certainly his brother Arechis took part in it, and was for this reason taken prisoner to France, while all his possessions were confiscated. This circumstance must have been the origin of a legend regarding Paul, which arose about the tenth century and was widely diffused for a long time afterwards. According to this story, Charlemagne sent Paul into exile, suspecting his complicity in a conspiracy, and confined him in the small island of Tremiti on the Adriatic coast, whence he succeeded after some time in escaping by miracle, and taking refuge first at Benevento, afterwards at Montecassino. In all this there is not a shadow of truth; on the contrary, six years after the exile of his brother Arechis, when Charlemagne had already come to Rome and shown much moderation and clemency in State affairs, and also a desire to encourage letters, we find Paul addressing the victorious monarch in verse, imploring that his brother may be restored to his family, whose miserable condition he describes in vivid colours and with great pathos. To insure the success of his appeal Paul left his monastery and crossed the Alps, in order to betake himself to the court of Charles. The king received him with great honour, and retained him longer than he would willingly have stayed. From the banks of the Moselle the longing thoughts of the monk turn to the peace and sweetness he had tasted amidst the majestic solitudes of Montecassino, and he writes to his abbot Theodemar in these words:—

"Although my body is separated from your company by a vast extent of territory, I am nevertheless joined to you by a tenacious affection which nothing will ever loosen; nor can I hope to express in a letter and within the brief limit of these pages, how constantly and profoundly I am moved by the thought of your affection and that of my elders and my brethren. For when I consider the leisure filled with sacred occupations, the delectable dwelling of my refuge, your pious and religious dispositions, —when I consider the holy band of so many soldiers of Christ zealous in all Divine offices, and the resplendent examples of individual brethren in special virtues, and the sweet converse respecting the perfections of our celestial home,—I tremble, I gaze, I languish, nor can I restrain my tears, while my breast is rent with deep sighs. I am living among Catholics and followers of Christian worship; I am well received; all show me abundant kindness for love of our father Benedict, and for the sake of your merits: but compared to your convent this palace is a prison; in contrast with the great calm which there is with you, life here seems to me a continual storm. I am only held in this country by my weak body, but with the whole of my soul I am with you. Now I seem to be in the midst of your sweet singing, now to be sitting with you in the refectory where the reading even more than the food satisfies, now to consider the works of each one in his special duty, now to inquire into the condition of those oppressed by age or sickness, now to wear away the tombstones of the saints dear to me as heaven itself."

He goes on in his letter to ask for their prayers on his behalf, that he may soon be restored to them; but his return was not to be as soon as he hoped. At that very time Charlemagne, by assembling at his court from every country all those in whom still survived some ray of a culture which had now almost entirely died out, was trying to infuse fresh life into Roman civilization, just as he aimed in the domain of politics at resuscitating the name of Rome and the authority of the Empire. Paulus Diaconus could not remain a stranger to this work, and was easily induced to take his share in it, as appears evident from the verses which Petrus Pisanus addressed to him in the name of Charles, in which his talents and his knowledge are exalted, and he is compared to the greatest writers of antiquity. "My daughter," Charles is made to say in these verses, "is to be married in Greece, and it is my desire that Paul may instruct in the Grecian tongue those who are to accompany her to Constantinople." Paul, answering likewise in verse, accepts the office, but modestly declines the royal praises, and at the same time denies that he attempted the conversion of Sigfried, king of Denmark, which Charles in another poem by Petrus Pisanus attributed to him. About this time Paul composed the epitaphs of Ildegard wife of Charlemagne (d. 783), of his sisters and daughters. Besides, also at Charles's request, he finished a valuable collection of homilies, already begun at Montecassino, and which doubtless was of great assistance to the clergy, who at that time were almost without exception exceedingly ignorant. Nor were these the only literary labours of this monk, who had now become a celebrity among the men of letters of his day. He made an extract of the famous Essay of Festus Pompeius, *De Verborum Significatione*, preserving thus for posterity a document which is still of great value to students of Roman Law. At the request of Angilramnus, bishop of Metz, Paul wrote the history of the bishops of Metz, and so began the series of episcopal histories on this side of the Alps which have done such good service in every country in completing the general history of the Christian Church and of its gradual development. In this work he gave a diffuse account of the life of St. Arnulph, a member of the Carolingian family, and did not omit this opportunity of celebrating the glory and the virtues of Charlemagne. It must have been at the court of Charles that Paul formed ties of warm and intimate friendship with Adalard, abbot of the famous monastery of Corvey, a relation of Charlemagne's, and one of the most important personages of that age. This friendship also bore literary fruit, as, at the wish of his friend, Paul undertook to look through and revise the letters of Gregory the Great, whose life he also wrote, but, being taken ill, was not able to complete more than a short part of the whole work, which he sent to Adalard together with a letter full of affection.

It appears that Paul, during the many years that he remained there, visited the greater part of France and its principal monasteries; but the attractions of that country were not enough to make him forget his own beloved land, nor were the many friendships that he formed able to retain him permanently at the court of Charles. Perhaps, as Wattenbach observes, the growing enmity between Charles and Arechis, the Lombard prince of Benevento, which finally broke out into open warfare, may have ended in making that residence a painful one for him, although these events did not in any way disturb his personal relations with the king. At any rate, in 787 we again find Paul at Montecassino, where he composed a fine epitaph for Prince Arechis, who died that very year; and thus gave a last pledge of his faithful friendship for the husband of his pupil Adelperga. The yearning aspiration of the monk was at length satisfied. After his long wanderings amidst the turmoil of the world and the pomps of courts, he finally returned to enjoy that undisturbed peace of which certain spirits feel more imperiously the need, the longer and more repeatedly it has been denied to them. From the summit of that mountain where so many centuries of holy memories are accumulated, and where St. Benedict sowed a seed which bore such civilizing fruit, this solitary monk, free at last from all worldly cares, was able to lift his thoughts from the observation of secular events, to the calm contemplation of the Divine Source of all. Thus in that tranquil retreat he employed the remainder of his days in composing the last two labours of his pen, a commentary on the Monastic Rule, and that history of the Lombards which secured him a lasting place among the best writers of the Middle Ages.

Paul seemed destined for an historian by his birth and the circumstances of his life. Born in Italy of Lombard parentage, when the Lombard rule was drawing near its fall, attached to the people from whom he sprang, and the friend of their princes, and on the other hand educated by Italian masters in the traditions, doubly Latin, both of classical and ecclesiastical studies, Paulus Diaconus was both Italian and Lombard. Hence that kind of patriotism which in him combined the two races, and seemed to symbolize a fusion between them which could not ever be complete, and was only partially reached when the Lombard oppressor, conquered by the Franks, found himself in this common misfortune on a nearer level with the oppressed race. Paul had already, when working at Eutropius, narrated the history of Rome, and now he seemed only to have changed the title of his work, and in the history of the Lombards to be writing the continuation of the former. The primitive Germanic races, without letters or culture, entrusted the preservation of their genealogies and of their daring deeds to tradition, which handed them down in songs and legends. The office of the historian was to extract from these the life of the people whom they celebrated, when the accumulation of events and the dawn of civilization created an almost unconscious wish for a more trustworthy and lasting narrative. Hence this continual interweaving of real and legendary facts, which gives a special character to the history of the Lombards, who, indeed, rough but chivalrous by nature, often acted in a romantic manner, and influenced more by a wish to show off their prowess than by reasons of state or prudence. A great Italian historian, Cesare Balbo, has very justly remarked that from the times of King Authari and Queen Theodolinda (that Theodolinda who was the friend of Gregory the Great), "in Italy the days if not the name of chivalry may be said to date,—days more agreeable to the imagination than in reality, more admirable in romance than in history,—days not without their virtues, but virtues lavishly thrown away." And indeed no tale of chivalry of a later age tells us of a more romantic or poetical adventure than the following one which we translate from Paul's words :—

"And afterwards King Authari sent ambassadors to Bavaria, to ask for the daughter of the King Garibald in marriage. He received them graciously, and promised to give his daughter Theodolinda to Authari. So when the ambassadors returned with this answer, Authari wished to see for himself what his bride was like, and taking with him a few chosen Lombards, and one especially in whom he had great confidence to act as elder of the party, proceeded to Bavaria without delay. And when they had been conducted, after the manner of ambassadors, into the presence of King Garibald, and when that one who had come as elder had, after the first greetings, made the customary harangue, Authari then came forward, knowing that he could not be recognized by any of that country, and approaching the king, said, ' My lord King Authari, has specially sent me hither that I may see and be able to describe to my lord your daughter, his bride and our future lady.' Then the king, hearing this, sent for his daughter ; and Authari, seeing that she was of most graceful appearance, long contemplated her in silence, and being charmed with her in every respect, turned to the king, saying, ' Since we see your daughter to be such as appears to us to deserve that she should become our queen, we would ask, if it please your mightiness, that she may hand to us now the wine-cup, as she will do hereafter.' And when the king had agreed that this should be done, she, taking the wine-cup, handed it first to him who seemed to be the elder. Then she offered it to Authari, whom she did not know to be her betrothed; and he, after he had drunk and returned the cup, touched her hand, without being perceived by the others, with his finger, and then drew his hand over his face from the forehead downwards. This she related to her nurse with shamefaced blushes; to which her nurse replied, 'Unless this man were himself the king and your betrothed, he would certainly not venture to touch you; however, in the mean time let us say nothing about it, nor even mention it to your father. For in truth he is most worthy both to govern a kingdom and to be joined to you in matrimony.' For at that time Authari was in the prime of his manhood, of noble stature, with a profusion of fair hair and of a very dignified appearance. Afterwards, having received an escort from the king, they set off on the return journey to their country, and hurriedly passed the frontiers of Noricum. For the province of Noricum, which is inhabited by barbarians, has Pannonia to the east of it, Suabia to the west, on the south Italy, and on the north the river Danube. And when Authari was already near the confines of Italy, and had still with him the Bavarian escort, he rose as high as he could in his saddle, for he was on horseback, and struck with all his might a small axe which he carried in his hand into a tree near him, leaving it hanging in the tree, and adding these words: 'Such are the wounds made by Authari.' And when they heard this, the Bavarians who were escorting him understood that he was himself King Authari."

Nor is it only in such facts that the story of the Lombards has so legendary a character. This chivalrous tendency spoken of by Balbo shows itself in many of the most important political events of the time, and leaves its impress on many real actions of the Lombard people. This tendency also is reflected as in a mirror in the simple and imaginative mind of Paulus Diaconus, and it is fortunate for posterity that it is so. He finds in it the inspiration of his narrative, which treats of historical facts with the vivid colouring borrowed from tradition, and does not spoil their effect by exhibitions of empty erudition or by attempts at criticism, which could not in his time have been other than imperfect. Thus he makes us intimately acquainted with that Lombard age, and his characters are painted with a vigour and richness of colouring which wonderfully help us to understand them, and to reconstruct those times, of which he alone has left us so general and lasting a record. Lombards, Greeks, Romans, from the reign of Albuin to that of Liutprand, all pass vividly before us. All these kings, their principal adherents, and their most determined foes, the heaven-inspired saints, the women of heroic virtues or of wicked wiles, all live again and pass before us in the pages of Paul. Open battles or conspiracies, the splendour of courts or the caves of hermits, sacrilege and miracles, the most devoted faithfulness and the darkest treachery follow each other and are woven together in lively contrast. We should gladly give many extracts in confirmation of what we say, but the limits of our space forbid our doing so, and we must content ourselves with one long and remarkable episode, giving it mainly as Paul himself relates it.

After the glorious reign of Rothari, the great Lombard legislator, and the very short one of his son Rodoald, Aripert, son of a brother of Queen Theodolinda, was called to the throne and reigned for nine years, of which the history tells us next to nothing. After his death his two sons, Godepert and Perctarit, divided the kingdom between them, the former fixing his residence at Pavia, the second at Milan. This division, quite a novelty for the Lombards, shows how unsettled general feeling was about the election, and how difficult any agreement was. Indeed, after a short time the brothers came to open discord, and Godepert, at the instigation of evil advisers, sent the duke of Turin to the south of Italy to Grimuald, duke of Benevento, then one of the most powerful princes, and held in high esteem for his personal qualities. The ambassador was commissioned to offer Grimuald a sister of Godepert's in marriage, and to ask his assistance against Perctarit; but he betrayed his master, and offered instead the crown to Grimuald, exhorting him to take advantage of the dissensions between the two brothers, in order to make himself king of Italy. When Grimuald betook himself to Lombardy, the duke of Turin, always intent on his project, succeeded so well in exciting suspicions in the minds of both, that their first meeting ended tragically in the murder of Godepert by the hand of Grimuald. As soon as King Perctarit heard of this, he found himself obliged to leave Milan so hastily, that his queen and his son Cunipert were left behind, and were both sent into exile to Benevento. Grimuald then married the sister of the murdered Godepert—a fact, though strange, not without its parallel in Lombard history,—and was confirmed king at Pavia, in the year 662. The vicissitudes of the dethroned King Perctarit during his exile until he regained his throne are thus narrated by Paulus Diaconus: "When therefore the kingdom on the Ticino had been assured to Grimuald, he not long afterwards married the daughter of King Aripert, who had been already betrothed to him, and whose brother Godepert he had killed. He also sent home, after having rewarded it largely, the army from Benevento, through the assistance of which he had made himself master of the kingdom, retaining, however, at his court some members of it, whom he enriched with large possessions.

"Later, when he heard that Perctarit had fled to Scythia, and was living there with a khan, he sent an embassy to this khan, who was king of the Avari, to let him know that if he allowed Perctarit to remain in his kingdom, he could no longer hope to be at peace, as he had been hitherto, with the Lombards and with himself. When the king of the Avari heard this he summoned Perctarit, and told him to depart in whatever direction he wished, in order not to create enmity between the Avari and the Lombards. On hearing this, Perctarit returned to Italy in order to appeal to Grimuald, of whose great clemency he had heard much. As soon as he reached Lodi, he sent forward a very faithful follower of his, to announce his coming to Grimuald. When Unulph came to the king he informed him that Perctarit was coming, trusting in his good faith; and the king hearing this, promised solemnly that no evil should happen to him since he put his trust in him. In the mean time Perctarit arrived, entered, and made an effort to throw himself at Grimuald's feet; the king, however, would not permit it, and graciously raising him, kissed him. And then Perctarit: 'I am thy servant,' saith he; 'and it is because I know thee to be so truly Christian and pious that I, who could live among the heathen, have come to thy feet, supported by the belief in thy clemency.' To him the king replied, sealing the promise with his usual oath, 'By him who begat me, since thou hast come trusting to my good faith, thou shalt surely suffer no evil, and I shall so provide for thee that thou mayest live honourably.' Then having appointed for him an apartment in a spacious palace, he desired him to rest after the fatigues of his journey, commanding that his food and all other requirements should be liberally supplied at the public cost. But Perctarit, when he had withdrawn to the dwelling provided for him by the king, was presently visited by large numbers of the citizens of Pavia, either from curiosity or because they were old acquaintances. But who is safe from slanderous tongues? For later, certain ill-natured flatterers, coming to the king, warned him that unless Perctarit were quickly made away with, he would himself soon lose both life and kingdom; for this they declared was the cause of his being visited by the whole of the city. Grimuald, too credulous in accepting these accusations, and forgetful of his promises, is inflamed with a sudden desire for the death of the innocent Perctarit, and holds counsel as to the way in which, it being already late, he should have him killed on the morrow. At length he sends him a variety of dishes for his supper, with choice wines and different kinds of drinks, in the hope of making him drunk, so that, spending the whole night in feasting, and oppressed by wine, he might not think of taking any measures for his safety. A certain one, however, who had been among the followers of his father, and being the same who brought now this royal banquet to Perctarit, bowed his head even below the table in act of homage, and informed him secretly of the king's intention to kill him. Perctarit then immediately desired his cupbearer to bring him nothing but a little water in a silver goblet. When, therefore, those who brought all these different kinds of drink from the king begged him in the king's name to drink the whole goblet, he, declaring he would drain it in honour of the king, in reality only sipped a little water from this silver cup. And when the messengers reported to the king how greedily he was drinking, the king replied, quite delighted, 'Let the drunken fellow drink; for to-morrow he will shed all this wine mixed with his own blood.' But Perctarit, having quickly called Unulph to him, told him of the king's designs against his life. Whereupon Unulph sent his servant immediately to his house to bring his bed-things, and to make him up a bed close to that of Perctarit. Nor was it long before Grimuald directed his satellites to guard the house in which Perctarit was sleeping, and not to let him by any means escape. When the supper was ended and every one had left, and only Perctarit and Unulph remained with the keeper of the wardrobe, of whose fidelity they were both sufficiently assured, they discovered to him the matter and implored of him, while Perctarit was escaping, to feign for as long as possible to be asleep in Perctarit's bed-chamber. He having promised to do so, Unulph loaded Perctarit's head and shoulders with the bed-things, the mattress and the bear-skin, and began to drive him out of the doors on purpose like a rustic servant, scolding him angrily, and not ceasing to whip and urge him on, so that often he fell to the ground from the violence of the blows. And when the royal satellites who were keeping watch asked Unulph what all this meant, he answered, ' This good-for-nothing servant of mine put my bed in the bed-chamber of that drunkard Perctarit, who is so full of wine that he lies there half dead. But now 'tis enough : I have endured his madness till now ; henceforth, while our lord the king likes, I shall remain in my own house.' When they heard this they were well pleased, for they believed it to be true, and allowed him to pass together with Perctarit, whom they supposed to be a servant, and whose head was purposely covered that he might not be recognized. When they had left, that most faithful keeper of the wardrobe, having carefully fastened the door, remained within alone. In the mean time Unulph let down Perctarit by a rope from the corner of the wall which is near the river Ticino, and collected round him as many friends as he could. They, having seized upon the horses which they found in the meadows, hurried on that same night to the town of Asti, in which some remained who were friends to Perctarit, and who were still in rebellion against Grimuald. Thence Perctarit, going on to the city of Turin with all speed, and crossing then the frontiers of Italy, reached the country of the Franks. And thus God Almighty, by the providence of his mercy, both saved an innocent man from death, and a king who in his heart desired to act aright, from a great offence.

"But in the meantime, King Grimuald, while he thought that Perctarit was asleep in his house, caused a body of men to be distributed between that house and the palace, in such a manner that Perctarit, being led through the midst of them, might not by any means escape. When those sent by the king to call forth Perctarit had come and had knocked at the door where they supposed him to be sleeping, that keeper of the wardrobe who was within prayed them, saying, 'Have pity upon him, and let him sleep a little, for he is still oppressed with a heavy sleep after the fatigues of his journey.' Which, when they had agreed to, they reported to the king, namely, that Perctarit was still overcome with a heavy sleep. To which he rejoined, 'He drank so much wine last night that he cannot yet wake.' However, he commanded them to arouse him now, and conduct him to the palace. So when they came to the door where they imagined that Perctarit was sleeping, they began to knock louder. Then the keeper of the wardrobe again began to beg of them to let Perctarit sleep a little longer. But they, calling out angrily that this drunkard had slept enough, break open the door with kicks, and having got in, look for Perctarit in his bed. Not finding him, they ask the keeper of the wardrobe what has become of him. To which he replies that he has escaped. Then immediately seizing him by the hair and striking him furiously, they drag him off to the palace. And having led him into the king's presence, they declare that he has abetted in the flight of Perctarit, and is therefore worthy of death. But the king desired them to loosen him, and inquired of him, in order, the manner of Perctarit's flight; and he recounted to the king everything just as it happened. Then the king asked those who stood around him, saying, 'What do you think of this man who has done such things?' Then they all replied with one accord that he deserved to die after many tortures. But the king exclaimed, 'By him who begat me, that man is deserving of good treatment who feared not to suffer death for the sake of his lord.' And then he commanded that he should be made one of his keepers of the wardrobe, admonishing him to be as faithful to him as he had been to Perctarit, and promising him many advantages. And when the king asked what had become of Unulph, he was told that he had taken refuge in the Basilica of the Archangel Michael. Then he sent to him, promising of his own accord that no evil should befall him, if only he would trust himself to him. And

Unulph, when he heard these promises of the king's, came to the palace, and throwing himself at the king's feet, was asked by him in what way and manner Perctarit had been able to escape. And when he had narrated everything to him in order, the king praised his fidelity and prudence, and graciously assured to him all his present possessions as well as any he might acquire in the future.

"And when, some time after, the king asked Unulph whether he still wished to be with Perctarit, he answered with a solemn oath that he would rather die with Perctarit than live anywhere else in the midst of the greatest delights. Then the king asked also that same keeper of the wardrobe whether he liked better to stay with him in his palace, or to follow Perctarit in his wanderings; and when he had answered just the same things as Unulph, the king, after listening graciously to what they had to say, and praising them for their fidelity, desired Unulph to take whatever he liked from his house—that is to say, servants and horses, and all sorts of household chattels, and to make all haste to Perctarit, and that no one should harm him. In the same way he dismissed the keeper of the wardrobe. So that having been able to take away through the king's kindness all that belonged to them, they departed with his assistance for the country of the Franks, in order to reach their beloved Perctarit."

The drama, however, was not yet finished. Five

years later Grimuald died from a wound which his doctors were suspected of having poisoned, and his chronicler thus sums up his character and appearance: "Powerful in body, foremost in daring, bald, with a prominent beard, gifted no less in mind than in bodily strength." At the very time of his death, Perctarit was preparing to sail for Britain, and had, indeed, already embarked when a supernatural voice called to him from the shore, bidding him return to his own country, for that Grimuald had died three days before. Obeying the Divine command he started without delay, and on reaching the Italian frontier found waiting for him the court officials and great dignitaries of the kingdom, and great multitudes of people. So he returned in triumph to Pavia and within three months of Grimuald's death was raised again to the throne by the unanimous wish of the Lombards. A son of Grimuald's, by a former marriage, reigned at Benevento as duke, but of the little Garibald, offspring of his later marriage with Perctarit's sister, we have little or no trace beyond the fact of his uncle having superseded him. Perctarit reigned for seventeen years, during the last ten of which he associated his son in the government, and of him also we have the following succinct description: "He was of goodly stature, corpulent in body, in all things gentle and gracious," which explains to some extent the devotion of his followers.

From the examples we have given, it will not be

difficult for the reader to comprehend the principal merits of Paul as a writer, as well as his defects. Born at a time when Latin literature had lapsed into complete barbarism, he wrote well as compared with his contemporaries, but certainly we must not expect from him that unerring purity of style which belongs to the Latin authors of another age. A sweet and often elegant poet, he handles the Latin language with the easy if not irreproachable grace of one who had spoken it from his boyhood. His style is very unequal, and the inequality arises often from the sources whence he draws his narrative. Generally he is clear, but sometimes we meet with passages in his book so intricate and obscure, that they still cause the desperation of the learned who have to interpret them. He loves truth with the fervour of a thoroughly honest man, but his credulity leads him to repeat in perfect good faith just as he finds them all the miraculous stories scattered in chronicles or preserved in traditions. Yet we should not be ungrateful to him for this, since his vast and at that time unusual erudition might easily have tempted him to spoil the simplicity of his narrative, which would have diminished both its charm and its historical value. As it is, his history is of immense importance, especially as we have the certainty that he made use of the materials, now irrecoverably lost, of an older historian of the Lombards, Secundus, bishop of Trent. Accustomed to interest himself in many places and countries, his canvas is a very wide one, and he has drawn largely upon other writers in order to give accounts of events which happened at a distance both of time and space from himself. Hence he often has recourse not only to the *Origo* and Bishop Secundus, but to Gregory of Tours, the Venerable Bede, the lives of the popes, the works of Gregory the Great, and other similar writers. The love of truth which animated him, the many things seen during his travels, his familiar intercourse with the Lombard and Frankish courts, gave him great facilities for collecting the traditions of the past; while his own ingenuous character added that "touch of nature" which gives life to his whole narrative. Whenever the *Historia Langobardorum* deals with real events, it is always worthy of the utmost consideration, and its testimony is important; when, on the other hand, it introduces legendary matter, we feel at least that it depicts the manners of the Lombards, just as the magic pen of Walter Scott has reproduced, better than any historian, the early history of Scotland.

CHAPTER III.

DECAY OF ITALIAN CHRONOGRAPHY—THE "LIBER PONTIFICALIS"—THE ACTS OF THE NEAPOLITAN BISHOPS—AGNELLUS OF RAVENNA—POLEMICAL WRITINGS OF AUXILIUS AND VULGARIUS—THE MONASTERIES AND THE SARACEN INVASIONS—FARFA : THE "CONSTRUCTIO"—LIVES OF THE SAINTS OF ST. VINCENT ON THE VOLTURNO—THE "DESTRUCTIO"—MONTECASSINO : CHRONICLE OF ST. BENEDICT—CATALOGUES—TRANSLATIONS OF RELICS—"HISTORIA" OF ERCHEMPERT—CHRONICLE OF SALERNO—ANDREW OF BERGAMO—PANEGYRIC OF BERENGARIUS—STATE OF LAY EDUCATION IN ITALY—POLITICAL CONDITIONS — LIUTPRAND — IMPERIALIST WRITINGS—BENEDIOT OF SORACTE—VENETIAN CHRONICLE OF JOHANNES DIACONUS.

THE *Historia* of Paulus Diaconus received several unimportant additions,[1] of which only passing men-

---

[1] *Pauli Continuationes* in the *Scriptores Rerum Langobardicarum et Italicarum*, sæc. vi.-ix. of the *Monumenta Germaniæ Historica*.

tion need be made in a work like the present, which does not regard the labours of the chroniclers exclusively as sources of history, but also as indications of the literary condition of the Middle Ages. We have come now to the time of greatest poverty in the Italian chronicles. After the last traces of classicism in the Gothic period, and the effort towards a revival made by Charlemagne, and which ceased with him, there followed a profound decline, and Paul's remarkable work is succeeded by scanty chronicles and historical memoirs of very secondary importance. "It is much to be regretted," writes Muratori in his Annals, when speaking of this age, "that Italian history should leave us for so long uninformed of the facts and events of the time, and only some faint light remains for us in the old ultramontane writers." And in fact, from the time of the Carolingians to that of the Othos, except when we are aided by indirect documents, such as inscriptions, diplomas, and similar remains, we are often obliged to have recourse to German and French sources, to gain some information respecting this obscure period of Italian history. Although the laity, as we shall see, had not lost all trace of literary attainments, the clergy on the other hand were too much mixed up in political agitations, and too much engrossed by them, to give their attention to historical writings. Generally ecclesiastical education seemed to be all directed to the management of state affairs, so that the documents most valuable, both for the vigour of their style and their historical importance, which we have at that time, are the collections of pontifical letters of Nicholas I. (d. 867) and of John VIII. (d. 882). Still this silence during the ninth century in Italy concerning contemporary events was not absolute. The events themselves sometimes necessarily produced documents, which, directly or indirectly, belong to history. Among these the *Liber Pontificalis* occupies a prominent place, as during the first half of the ninth century it is of great assistance towards tracing the history of the Church generally, and more especially of Rome. For a long time this work went by the name of a single author, Anastasius Bibliothecarius, a man of much learning, who translated several books from the Greek, and most probably compiled the life of the Pope Nicholas I. But to attribute the whole *Liber Pontificalis* to one author is to contradict the very nature of the work, which consists in a series of biographical notices of the popes, compiled more or less at length at various times and by various writers. The history of this book and of its compilations, the inquiries with regard to the authors of it, the criticism of its different manuscripts have occupied for long the learned, and have given rise quite lately to dissertations full of erudition and merit. But we must pass them over, and limit ourselves to hoping that a definite edition may soon be the result of these scientific discussions, while we briefly describe the first part of this book, which may be likened to the rising and course of a river, with its constant changes of form and scene. The need, continually felt for ecclesiastical purposes, of a familiar knowledge of the pontifical chronology first originated the book. So it was that about the fourth century, the *Liber Pontificalis* began to be compiled from the old catalogues of the names of the popes, from their sepulchral inscriptions, from mentions of them found either in letters or books. At first the biographies gave a bare mention of the name, the family, the country of the pontiff, the duration of his pontificate, the decrees made in his time, and the place of his burial. Between one pontiff and another was mentioned the length of time during which the chair was vacant. By degrees, however, this concise information gave way to fuller notices, which gradually took the form of complete biographies, rich in valuable details. Unfortunately in the last quarter of the ninth century, when we should have had greatest need of such assistance, it fails us almost entirely. The traditional custom of keeping these records being interrupted by political disturbances, the book falls back into its primitive bareness, and again becomes a mere catalogue. Later, in the pontificate of Leo IX., on the revival of historical culture, we shall again find it fuller in facts and more florid in style—in this also similar to a river which, after burying itself for a time,

Gesta Episcoporum Neapolitanorum. 95

reappears elsewhere unexpectedly with a stronger and a fuller stream.

When Paulus Diaconus wrote the *Gesta* of the bishops of Metz, he inaugurated a new kind of historical literature, which really supplied a want of the times, and met with imitators in many places during the following centuries. The same idea which had suggested the *Liber Pontificalis* also gave rise here and there in various dioceses to histories of the bishops, which often are of the more value for the general history of the Church on account of the importance of the sees, and the deficiency of other records. So the histories of the Neapolitan and Ravennese bishops, compiled in the ninth century, are documents of no slight moment for any one who is following carefully the vicissitudes of that age. Like the collection of the lives of the Roman bishops, the *Gesta Episcoporum Neapolitanorum* are the work of different writers, although also like them they were for a long time attributed almost wholly to one author, Johannes Diaconus. Waitz, in a recent addition of this book,[1] has shown how it must be divided into three parts. The first, compiled by an unknown author towards the end of the eighth century,

---

[1] *Gesta Episcoporum Neapolitanorum edidit G. Waitz*, in the volume *Scriptores Rerum Langobardicarum et Italicarum, sæc.* vi.-ix. of the *Monumenta Germaniæ Historica*. In what we say of the text of the *Gesta* we follow almost exclusively the authority of Waitz, whose edition is likely to remain the definite one.

begins with Christ, and descends to the year 763, adding with its dry records little or nothing to our knowledge. The second part belongs to that Johannes Diaconus to whom formerly nearly all the book was attributed, and to whom the credit still remains of having composed the larger and more important part. John began his work while a very young man, and taking up the history of the Neapolitan bishops from the year 763, when the other had left it, he brought it down to the death of the Bishop Athanasius I. (A.D. 872). The beginning of the life of this bishop's successor, written by a certain sub-deacon named Peter, forms the third part of the work, or rather the only fragment of it left, and it is so short that we need not stop to examine it. John has written his part with a fair amount of exactitude, nor can his Latin be accused of many errors. Considering the times, he is a writer of some merit, and is especially praiseworthy in the care with which he examines the truth of his facts, and the assurance of it which he gives his reader. This principal work of John's, as well as other minor ones, on the lives of some Neapolitan saints and the translation of their relics, owe their historical value to the numerous relations of Naples with other places, and especially with Rome, Greece, and the principality of Benevento.

Of greater moment is the pontifical book by Agnellus of Ravenna. The very great importance of this city at the time of the decline of the Empire not only continued, but, on account of its favourable position on the Adriatic, rather increased during the first centuries of the Middle Ages. After the war with the Goths, Italy being reconquered by the Greeks, and then again for the greater part lost through the invasion of the Lombards, Ravenna became the seat of the Imperial Government, and might be considered, far more than Rome, the capital of the Empire in Italy. While the exarchs were governing the Pentapolis from Ravenna in the name of the emperors, Rome, surrounded by the Lombard dominion, became less and less subject to the imperial influence, since the popes did all they could to strengthen their own, and sought to free themselves from their dependence on Constantinople. So it happened that from this importance of the city of Ravenna resulted the importance of its see, and the authority of its archbishops rose so high as to induce them sometimes even to withstand Rome herself, and to refuse to recognize her pretensions to supremacy. From this it is easy to understand how great the value must be of this book of Agnellus, dealing as it does with these powerful bishops. In form much the same as the Roman *Liber Pontificalis*, it has also the same title, although it often shows itself but little favourable to Rome. Contrary to the custom of those who compiled the papal Lives, Agnellus has not omitted to make considerable mention of himself in his book, and hence we have no difficulty in forming an idea of his life. Born about 805, at Ravenna, of a noble family, and destined from childhood for the Church, he was educated in the cathedral (*Ecclesia Ursiana*). While still a child, he had the benefice conferred upon him of the Abbey of St. Mary *ad Biachernas*, and later that also of St. Bartholomew. The latter, however, afterwards was taken from him for some time by the Archbishop George, who from being his great friend became his enemy, and according to Agnellus without any good reason. He was ordained priest by Petronax, the archbishop who ruled the see from the year 817 till 835. Not only did the birth and riches of Agnellus combine to place him in a high position, but he also was as greatly distinguished among the clergy for his talents and learning as for his merely external advantages. This indeed is not saying much, as the last editor of Agnellus justly observes, for the clergy of Ravenna at that time were completely uneducated, still it was enough to encourage him to undertake a work of no little utility for the distant future. A lover of the fine arts, and frequently commissioned to attend to the ornamenting and restoring of the churches of Ravenna, he does not omit to speak of them, and thus his book is also of use in tracing the history of those monuments which still make Ravenna among the most remarkable cities of Italy. He knew Greek, and often introduces Greek words into his writings, which, however, is quite natural in a country subject to the Greek rule. It appears that his reputation for learning led the other priests of Ravenna to persuade him to undertake the office of writing the history of their bishops. Having agreed to do so, Agnellus proceeded but slowly with his task, although urged on impatiently by his colleagues, to whom he apparently read his book bit by bit as he composed it. This work, completed about the middle of the ninth century, begins from the Apostolic times with the life of St. Apollinaris, and comes down to the bishops who were contemporaries of the author. It is a generally adopted opinion that it owed its original impulse to the Roman *Liber Pontificalis*, but we cannot see much foundation for this idea, which has grown out of the identity of name and out of some similarities in the arrangement; but such similarities seem to us unavoidable in a work of which the aim and materials were so similar. Besides, on this supposition how are we to explain why Agnellus never appears to have made use of the Roman Lives? In many instances he might have extracted from them notices which he would have found useful with regard to the bishops of Ravenna, and it is very unlikely that he would have failed to do so had he been acquainted with the book. But however this may be, one of the merits of the work of Agnellus consists in his having had recourse, not only to books, but to other sources of information. One of its similarities to the Lives of the Popes is its frequent mention of the public monuments, and the fact that much of its history is derived from them. As we have said, Agnellus had a knowledge of art which was of great service to him in his labours, and we constantly meet in his book with descriptions of the churches and of other buildings of the city, while his narrative is supported by the authority of epigraphs found in them. Neither does he neglect the personal appearance of the great men of whom he speaks, giving us descriptions of them taken from the numerous pictures then existing in Ravenna, of which there still remains a comparative wealth even after so many centuries and so many vicissitudes.

"And if any of you, who are reading this pontifical book, should be disposed to doubt, and should wish to inquire, saying: 'Why did he not recount the acts of this bishop as he did those of the others, his predecessors?' Listen, on this account: I, Agnellus, also called Andreas, a humble priest of this my humble Church of Ravenna, have composed this aforesaid pontifical book from the time of the blessed Apollinaris for about eight hundred years and more after his death, at the request and insistence of the brothers of this same see. And when I found what they had certainly done, it is presented to your view, and I have not defrauded your eyes of what I heard from the elders and ancient men; and when I have heard no history of them nor of what manner was their life, either through aged and long-lived men, or through some building, or through any other kind of authority, I have, God helping me through your prayers, composed their lives in order as one after the other held this see, that no interval should be left between the holy pontiffs; and I believe not to have lied, as they were men of prayer, chaste, charitable, and winners of men's souls for God. But if there has been wonder among you how I could know about their likeness, know that painting taught me, as portraits were always made in their likeness during their lifetime; and if there is any question as to whether I was right in describing their appearance from the pictures, Ambrosius of Milan, the holy bishop, in his Passion of the blessed martyrs Gervasius and Protasius, says of the appearance of the blessed Apostle Paul: 'Whose countenance a picture taught me.'"

As might be expected from this method of writing history, Agnellus mixes up many miraculous legends with his facts and the artistic details which he indirectly gives us. When in the older lives the assistance of positive information fails him and he knows little beyond the name of the bishop, he considers himself authorized to add on his own account meritorious acts and words of praise, comparing, with somewhat bitter reproaches, these ideal lives of the ancients, with the real ones of the modern bishops. Not only does this detract from his trustworthiness when relating distant facts, but also his impartiality towards his contemporaries is very doubtful, when we consider with what acrimony he expresses himself against the Archbishop George, who for a certain time took away from him his abbey of St. Bartholomew. He often uses great freedom of speech with regard to the popes, and shows them little favour, and this fact probably contributed to his being but little known in the Middle Ages, and to hinder the defusion of his book, there being now only one manuscript known which contains the whole of it. As a writer he exhibits the barbarisms of his time, and his rough and inelegant Latin is not even grammatical. His very unequal style has been aptly commented upon by Holder Egger in these words, with which we shall conclude our notice of Agnellus:

"His language, like that of all the Italian writers of that age, more similar to the plebeian tongue than to that of the classic authors, pays little attention to grammatical rules. But various parts differ much among themselves in style and manner. He writes sometimes correctly enough, and for him elegantly, sometimes faultily to an extraordinary extent, and quite neglectful of good composition or correct construction. Sometimes he speaks simply and concisely, but when he recounts stories which he has heard, he is verbose, excited, often highflown, and not seldom obscure. He principally imitates the Holy Scripture, his language being full beyond measure of its sayings, and also the fathers of the Church; but at times, when he is carried along by some description, you find him repeating phrases from Virgil. From which also he falls into the ridiculous habit of using ancient names, so that he calls the Greeks of his time Pelasgians, Danaids and Myrmidons. It is moreover to be noted that his language is full of unusual terms—ἅπαξ λεγομένων—of such especially as are derived from the Greek."[1]

The rapid moral decline which the Roman Church underwent towards the end of the ninth century, while it dried up the sources of the *Liber Pontificalis*, gave rise to some writings of a polemical character, which have had a continuous historical importance up to these latter times, on account of the numerous questions which have sprung up with regard to papal infallibility. The story is well-known of Pope Formosus, whose dead body was dragged from its sepulchre by order of his successor and enemy Stephen VI., and was tried and solemnly condemned by a synod. This sacrilegious assembly declared him guilty of having usurped the apostolic chair and of having offended the laws of the Church, and his election was therefore annulled and all the acts of his pontificate declared void. When Formosus had thus been degraded, his disfigured corpse was despoiled of the pontifical insignia, and after being mutilated was thrown with

---

[1] In the preface to the *Liber Pontificalis* by Agnellus, published in the volume *Scriptores Rerum Langobardicarum et Italicarum, sæc.* vi.-ix. of the *Monumenta Germaniæ Historica*.

contumely into the Tiber. The ever-increasing depravity of the times and the ferocity of party-feeling had brought the papacy down to this miserable condition, and Gregory the Great had now successors very different from him. But some writers raised their voice against the vile conduct of Stephen, and undertook the defence of the dead Formosus. One of them, Auxilius, Frank by origin, lived at Naples, and seems to have died as a monk at Montecassino. He had been ordained priest by Formosus, and the ordination being considered void, he, soon after this scandalous event, defended the cause of the condemned pope, which to a certain extent was his own, with much courage and, for that age, with much learning. The other who wrote on the same side was Eugenius Vulgarius, an Italian grammarian, also living as far as we know at Naples, and also author of a defence of Formosus, which was not only a defence but a panegyric. However, after his first writings, he leant for a time towards the opposite party, but again later, when John X. came to the papal chair, he showed himself favourable to Formosus by writing the *Invectiva in Romam*, if indeed he is the author of it, a point not yet quite cleared up. Although written in a heavy and artificial style, this pamphlet is almost eloquent from its tone of angry indignation. The *Invectiva* attacks the whole city of Rome, and accuses of the execrable crime the Romans who from ancient times were accustomed to repay their benefactors with death. Hence the holy, just, and catholic Formosus had now to suffer the violence formerly suffered by Romulus, by St. Peter and St. Paul. "You dragged from its sepulchre his corpse which had already been nine months buried. If it should be interrogated, what will it answer? If it answered, all that horrible assembly, struck with terror, would instantly disperse." So, in few words, he describes the synod which judged Formosus, and which was called *horribilis* also by the Roman council held in the year 898 in order to make amends for this barbarous insult.

From these polemical writings, which, notwithstanding their party tone, bear useful testimony to that extraordinary event, we must now turn to another kind of composition. As soon as St. Benedict had founded the first monasteries, the conventual system began immediately to take vast proportions. The spark lighted at Subiaco and Montecassino spread far and wide, and bands of Benedictines by this time were scattered over the country districts of Western Europe. As a response to this ascetic tendency many new monasteries were being constantly founded, which, favoured by circumstances, received privileges from princes and were enriched with gifts of land —a less-prized possession then than now—which they colonized, and by means of which they rapidly rose to a state of great wealth and power. The rule of St. Benedict, besides prescribing manual labour in the fields, imposed on the monks the duty of copying manuscripts, and this not only secured the inestimable advantage of preserving and multiplying books, but also helped to keep alive in the monasteries a faint trace of that intellectual culture which had then almost disappeared in Italy, being entirely neglected by the rest of the clergy. To this we owe various writings touching the origin and the early beginnings of some monasteries, which were nearly all composed in the ninth and tenth centuries.[1] Mixed with legends and miraculous stories, these writings contain a considerable mass of true facts, and many touches which the historian can make use of for filling in the picture of an age with regard to which we are singularly in the dark.

One of these works relates the origin of the monastery of Farfa in Sabina, which we shall later have occasion to mention more at length. The first foundation is quite uncertain, and involved in a legendary mist. A holy man named Lawrence, who came from Syria to Rome in the time of Julian the Apostate, is said to have founded this monastery, which was then destroyed on the

---

[1] In speaking of these monastic writings, we cannot always follow the chronological order as we have tried to do hitherto. In certain cases, for reasons of similarity which the reader will easily understand, we have found it necessary to group together writings which have a long interval between them, thus perhaps exceeding the chronological limit of this chapter.

coming of the Lombards, or, according to another version, even earlier, at the time of the Vandal invasion under Genseric. Later, with the assistance of Faroald duke of Spoleto, the pilgrim Thomas of Morienna rebuilt the monastery. Monks flocked in rapidly from all sides, and the abbey so prospered as shortly to become one of the first in Italy, having a vast extent of territory, and powerful connections with the dukes of Spoleto and with Frank and Lombard sovereigns. Hence the great interest which attaches to all that the *Constructio*, or *Liber constructionis farfensis* has to tell us from the year 705, to which the second and certain foundation of the monastery can be approximately assigned, till the year 857, when the record ceases. The work of an unknown monk of the ninth century, this writing has not reached us in the form which its author gave it, and there only remains of it a portion which was later interpolated into an old manuscript of the monastery containing lessons on the lives of some saints.[1]

---

[1] A fragment of the *Constructio* was published according to the only text which remains of it, by the Benedictine Caetani in the third volume of the *Acta. SS. Ord. S. Benedicti*, and reproduced in the collection of the Bollandists in the third volume for September. Bethmann was the first to publish the whole text in the *Monumenta Germaniæ Historica*, vol. xi., and thought that it contained the complete original of the *Constructio* as it was first written. The learned German, who has done much for the history of Farfa, was however mistaken, and it has recently been shown by Signor Ignazio Giorgi of Rome, in the *Archivio della Società Romana di Storia Patria*, Anno ii., that the original text has really been lost.

The fragments which remain are undoubtedly copied from the original, and bear witness to a purer Latin than is usual in contemporary writings. This perhaps is owing to the influence of the ties which always bound the monastery to the Lombard and Frank rulers, and made of it, from the beginning, the bulwark nearest to the walls of Rome which the royal and imperial authority had in its struggles with the apostolic chair. Governed by abbots of Frank origin, at a time when there was far more attention paid to ecclesiastical culture beyond the Alps than in Rome, the monastery never fell into a complete state of literary decay, and later we shall see come forth from its precincts the first beginnings of an historical renaissance, of which this *Constructio* gives in the mean time some indications. The life of the three founders of the monastery of St. Vincent on the Volturno is closely connected with this record, and has furnished materials for it. This monastery was founded in the first quarter of the eighth century, by three young noblemen of Benevento, through the counsel and assistance of that same Thomas of Morienna who had recalled to life the ruined monastery of Farfa. Autpertus, a monk, and later the abbot of St. Vincent, related the history of its founders not many years after their death. His narrative does not contribute much to our historical knowledge, and we only mention it on account of its connection with the history of Farfa, and as an ancient relic of the Lombard period.[1] More instructive, on the other hand, is the *Destructio Farfensis*, written at the beginning of the eleventh century by Hugo, abbot of Farfa. After the repeated invasions of the barbarians from the North, Italy had to undergo fresh invasions from Africa. The Saracens, having made themselves masters of Sicily, continued to extend their dominion in the south of Italy, and where they could not establish themselves permanently, they made temporary excursions, in which they slaughtered and plundered wholesale. They advanced or retreated according to the amount of opposition which they encountered, and which depended on

---

[1] Nevertheless we think it desirable to quote a passage where reference is made to the colonizing work of monasticism, which it appears to us was carried on in Italy, even in that time of profound moral degeneracy, of which we find traces in most monasteries towards the second half of the ninth century. It is the following passage, in which Thomas of Morienna exhorts the three young men to found their monastery on the banks of the Volturno: "But the place, beloved sons, whither I desire that you should go, is in the province of Samnium, on the banks of the river Volturno, about a thousand steps from where it rises. In which place is situated the oratory dedicated to Christ's martyr named Vincent, and on each side of the river is a thick forest which serves as a habitation for wild beasts and a hiding-place for robbers. But Almighty God, to whom you wish to do service, will both preserve you uninjured in that place, and will keep the road safe and tranquil from fear of robbers for all those going thither, and also will make it abound in fruitful trees when the thorns and brambles have been cut away. Go then, my sons, go and abide in that place without any manner of fear." (*Vita Padonis, Tasonis et Tatonis Vulturnensium*, in the volume already quoted of the *Scriptores Rerum Lang. et Ital.*)

the momentary political conditions of the peninsula. Rome herself, after having been frequently threatened, beheld the Saracenic hordes enter the church of St. Peter, and profane its altars. As was natural, the monasteries of or near the south of Italy, isolated in position and known to be wealthy, were the special object of the Saracens' greed. Their hatred of Christian temples and their rapacity combined, led to constant raids against these abbeys, which after pillaging they often destroyed. The monastery of Farfa, situated among the Sabine hills and in a sufficiently accessible position, shared the common destiny of destruction. For a long time it remained deserted, and the monks only returned when there was some hope of their doing so in safety. The abbey after its restoration underwent many vicissitudes, until the monk Hugo, having been raised to the dignity of abbot, succeeded, in the course of a long and glorious reign, in raising both the general condition of the monastery and its discipline, which had fallen very low. A remarkable man in many ways, he was not satisfied with reforming his monastery, and restoring to it its pristine splendour, but he also wished to be its historian, and to continue the work of the anonymous author of the *Constructio*. In the good Latin which was traditional to the school of Farfa, he took up the thread where the other had dropped it, and carried on the history to his own times, entitling it *Destructio* from the culminating fact related in it of the Saracenic incursion. For the history of these incursions, as well as for that of Rome and Spoleto in the times of Alberic, Marozia and Hugo, King of Italy, the *Destructio* is of great importance, and merits perhaps more attention than it has yet received from historians.

Previous to the destruction of Farfa, the Saracens had destroyed the monasteries of St. Vincent, on the Volturno and of Montecassino. This latter, no less flourishing than the others and more famous, before being finally pillaged by the Arabs, had long been menaced, in consequence of its position halfway between Rome and Naples, on the summit of a mountain which commands the valley of the Garigliano, on the banks of which there was an Arab colony. During this period of anxiety a short chronicle was written, which, after recapitulating with the help of Paulus Diaconus the early history of Montecassino, goes on to give many details of the events in those parts of Italy, from the middle of the ninth century to the year 867. This chronicle, called the chronicle of St. Benedict, is most valuable, both for the history of the Lombard principality of Benevento, as well as for that of the Arabs in Italy, and of their wars with the Emperor Ludovic II. Like the other chronicles of that time, it mixes up facts with legends, and is written in a Latin the rudeness of which could hardly be surpassed even in that barbarous age. In the following fragment is described the manner in which the monastery escaped on one occasion from the slaughter which threatened it; and the way in which the incident is related will show with what caution the historian has to examine these chronicles in order to separate the truth from the falsehood contained in them.

"In those days the Saracens, leaving Rome, devastated the whole oratory of Peter, the prince of the most blessed apostles, and the church of the blessed Paul, and they killed there some Saxons,[1] and as many more as they could without regard to sex or age. Then, taking the town of Fondi and plundering the neighbourhood, they quartered themselves in the month of September beyond Gaeta. Against these the army of the Franks advanced, but being beaten by the Saracens on the fourth of the Ides of November, took to flight. The Saracens followed them, and captured all their possessions till they came to St. Andrew, whose convent they burnt with fire. Then, when they came to the convent of the most blessed Bishop Apollinaris, called Albianus, and saw near it the holy mount of the most blessed confessor of Christ (Montecassino), they immediately desired to go there, but the lateness of the hour forbade their crossing; for then such was the cloudlessness of the heavens and the dryness of the earth, that any one could if he wished cross the river on foot.

---

[1] This seems to refer to soldiers stationed in Rome by the Frank emperors.

But the monks of the blessed Father Benedict, seeing that death was so near them, without loss of time gave each other absolution, imploring the merciful Lord that He would favourably receive their souls in peace, which they expected every minute should depart by a speedy death. And they turned to their blessed master, Benedict, with litanies, and barefoot, and with ashes sprinkled on their heads. Then, while the terror and fearful expectation was greatest, and copious prayer was being made to Almighty God, the Abbot Apollinarius his predecessor appeared in a vision to the Father Bassacius. 'What,' saith he, 'ails you, and why are you so sorrowful? And Bassacius in reply: 'Death is imminent, O father, and shall we not be afraid?' 'No,' replies he, 'be not afraid; for our pious Father Benedict has obtained your safety. Entreat God constantly with litanies and solemn masses, and God will hear the voice of those calling on Him; and we, joining with you in the church, do not cease in common with the citizens of heaven to implore our Lord Jesus Christ on your behalf.' So when the pastor Bassacius had awoke and had declared this thing to the brethren, they all together raised their voices and blessed God, who mercifully saves them who hope in Him. Then suddenly came on a tremendous rain, lightning, and loud thunder, so that the river Carnellus (Garigliano), rising, overflowed its boundaries, and where the day before the enemy might have gone over on foot, on the following day, constrained by the Divine repulse, they could not even reach the bank of the river. They made every effort to cross, and when no way of getting over to the convent was to be found, they ran about furiously hither and thither, such is their fierce barbarism, biting their fingers with rage and gnashing their teeth. And not to omit their usual crimes, they burnt with fire the convents of the blessed martyrs Stephen and George, and returned to their camp by the Two Lions. After some days, having killed their horses, they began their sea voyage; and when they approached their province, so that they already could discern the nearer mountains, they, as their manner is, expressed their joy in a nautical shout. Then appeared among them a small ship carrying two men, one having the appearance of an ecclesiastic, the other wearing a monk's habit. These said to them, 'Whence are you coming, and whither do you go?' And they answered, saying, 'We are returning from Peter; for we devastated all his oratory in Rome, and plundered the neighbourhood. We conquered the Franks and burnt the convents of Benedict. And you,' they add, 'who are you?' They answer, 'You will soon see who we are.' Instantly arose a violent storm and hurricane, and all the ships were wrecked, and the whole of the enemy destroyed, for hardly any one escaped to tell these things to others. And afterwards the venerable

Pope Leo surrounded the oratory of the blessed Peter with very strong, high walls, that such an event might never again occur in Rome."

To the chronicle of Montecassino is added a catalogue of the abbots of the monastery, with the years indicated in which they lived and ruled. And here, as we have mentioned this catalogue, appears to be the place also to speak of this other kind of historical document, not uncommon up to the end of the eleventh century, and very useful, especially for chronology. These catalogues generally consist in a simple list of names of sovereigns, bishops, abbots, and other personages, with a mention of the years in which they governed, and sometimes the record of some event. So, for example, in one catalogue the series of Lombard kings terminates thus:

"Ratchis reigned 5 years, 3 months.

"Aystulph reigned 8 years, 6 months.

"Desiderius reigned 18 years, 2 months, 10 days.

"And thus are completed the 201 years in which the aforesaid twenty kings reigned in the kingdom of Italy, as is set forth above in particular. In which time Pavia was captured, and the incarnation of our Lord Jesus Christ had at that time entered the year 775. But after these aforesaid twenty kings, the dominion of the kingdom of Italy came to the emperor Charles, who succeeded the above-mentioned Desiderius." And after a few more words the catalogue begins the series of the Carolingians, and continues through all the rulers of Italy up to the Henries of the eleventh century.[1]

When Montecassino was finally seized and devastated by the Saracens (A.D. 833), the monks were obliged to take refuge in the neighbouring towns of Teano and Capua, and there, in a sort of exile, wait for better days. The monk Erchempert went with others to Capua, and there wrote a history of the Lombards of Benevento, which begins with Duke Arechis, and extends to the year 889, as usual drawing on Paulus Diaconus and his followers for the older portion. Born at Teano, Erchempert entered the monastery as a boy, and shared its troubled destiny in that age of continual turmoils. Having left Capua for a time after the restoration of Montecassino (886), he appears to

---

[1] From the volume so frequently quoted of the *Rerum Langob. et Ital. Scriptores*, we take the names of a few catalogues, especially those which have an interest for Lombard history, such as the following: *Catalogus regum Langobardorum et ducum Beneventanorum, Catalogus comitum Capuan, Catalogus regum Langobardorum et Italicorum Brixiensis et Nonantolanus, Catalogus regum Langob. et Ital. Venetus, Catalogus regum Langob. et Ital. Lombardus, Catalogus regum tuscus, Catalogus regum Ital. Oscelensis, Catalogus imperatorum, regum Italicorum, ducum Beneventanorum et Spoletinorum Farfensis*. In the same volume are also published a short and interesting life of St. Anselm, founder of the abbey of Nonantola, and various accounts of translations of relics which are also noteworthy. As is well known, the passion for possessing the relics of saints was so eager in the rude and superstitious times of which we are writing, that they were being constantly carried about by fair or unfair means from one place to another. Under the generic name of *translationes* there are frequent accounts in the acts of the saints of these transportations, which have often indirectly an historical significance.

have returned there soon after, and to have lived habitually there, perhaps in some convent dependent on the mother abbey. During this second residence at Capua, being a Lombard by origin and connections, he was led, in consequence of the entreaties of his friends, to write his history, and to recount the vicissitudes of the Lombards in the south:

"Of whom in these days nothing honourable or praiseworthy is known that could be related by a truthful pen, hence I shall, while heaving deep sighs from my inmost heart, go on to recount briefly and rudely not their rule, but their destruction—not their good, but their evil fortune—not their triumph, but their downfall—not how they rose, but in what way they fell—not how they vanquished others, but how by others they were overcome and beaten. And I profess also, yielding to friendly entreaties, to narrate not so much what I have seen with my eyes, as what I have heard with my ears, imitating in part the example given by the Evangelists Mark and Luke, who described rather what they had heard than what they had seen."

Living in the midst of the scenes of which he writes, sometimes spectator or victim of the events, more often in direct relation with those who had witnessed them, his narrative flows on with the easy simplicity of one speaking of things with which he is familiar. Somewhat rude in style, but not without animation, he gives us many details with regard to the wars which were then weighing heavily on the south of Italy, and to the pillaging it underwent at the hands alike of Saracens and Greeks; and for these latter he entertains a profound contempt, and perhaps even a greater hatred than for the former. His work deserts us at the year 889, but had a sequel which very unfortunately is lost. For this loss we are compensated to a certain extent by the work of an anonymous writer of Salerno,[1] who gives us particulars about the history of the Lombard principalities up to the year 974. He makes great use of Paulus Diaconus and of Erchempert for his compilation, and can only be looked upon as original in the last part of his work. A lively but not very discerning writer, he is the only chronicler on whom we have to depend in these years for the history of southern Italy. This makes us regret all the more the work of Erchempert, who has certainly among the writers in the South the foremost place, nor are there any even in central Italy who can be compared to him, except those of the school of Farfa.

In northern Italy two writers, very different from each other, give signs of literary activity in the domain of history. One of them, the priest Andrew of Bergamo, made a *resumé* in the year 877 of the Lombard history by Paulus Diaconus, and con-

---

[1] *Chronicon Salernitanum. Mon. Germ. Hist. Scriptores,* iii.

tinued it up to his own time. This is perhaps the most barbarous of all the writings which we have yet mentioned, so that even its great accuracy, which makes it valuable for what regards the middle of the ninth century, does not prevent it from being exceedingly wearisome. On the other hand, a few years later, on the opening of the tenth century, we come upon an historical poem, which, leaving all other contemporary writings far behind, unexpectedly reveals to us a wide knowledge of the Latin language and of classic authors. Berengarius is the hero of this poem, which enlarges upon the exploits he performed in order to gain first the kingdom of Italy, and later the imperial crown. The poem, entitled *Panegyricus Berengarii*, is in truth a panegyric, and therefore, when taken as an isolated source of history, has not much weight. With great address the anonymous author tries to give a legitimate air to every pretension put forward by Berengarius, and to excuse with his verses the tyranny of might. But although this work must not be implicitly trusted, it is of great merit as a literary production. It was apparently composed at Verona, between the years 916 and 924, by a grammarian whose name is unknown. We cannot be sure whether the author was lay or clerical, but it seems more probable, considering the ignorance then prevalent among the clergy, that he was a layman. Proposing to himself the examples of Homer, Virgil, and Statius, he follows in their footsteps in relating the exploits of his hero up to his coronation in Rome. Notwithstanding many defects, such as involved constructions and artificial or obscure expressions, his hexameters — adorned with lines of classical poetry —are put together with sufficient ability, if we remember when they appeared. Intended to be read and studied in the grammatical schools, the panegyric was honoured by a contemporary commentary which explains the less easy passages. The commentary itself is also worthy of remark, on account of the excellent knowledge it shows of classical literature, but more especially for a certain way of treating the matter, which gives evidence of this knowledge, not only in the commentator, but also in those to whom he addressed himself.[1]

In presence of this work and of the other signs of learning that appear scattered here and there in Italy about that time, the question naturally arises, what was then the state of Italian education? Was Italy really sunk in the depths of barbarism,

---

[1] Some verses of two Scotch monks residing in Milan, composed almost entirely in praise of Tadus, archbishop of that city (860-868), and of the Emperor Lothair, prove the presence of foreign men of letters in Lombardy. Some other verses of an indirectly historical character were compiled by an anonymous author in the year 876, but are quite worthless. Of decided value, on the contrary, is a long poem in Saphic metre, dictated at Verona in praise of Bishop Adalard. (Cf. Wattenbach, op. cit. i. 251.) All the more interest attaches to this poem because it seems quite certain that the panegyric of Berengarius was also by a Veronese pen.

as would seem indicated by the scanty ecclesiastical writings which have reached us from those centuries? Professor Wattenbach has recently answered this question with such clearness and acumen that we should be defrauding our reader were we to withhold from him the following page of the learned German, or to give it instead in our own words:

"Here we meet with a culture which certainly does not originate in the Church, but is nurtured by those isolated grammarians whose activity never ceased in Italy. It is the merit of W. von Giesebrecht to have pointed out that these schools always existed in Italy, and spread a degree of education among the laity which was unknown on this side of the Alps. In Italy, says Wipo in the eleventh century, all the youths go regularly to school, and only in Germany is it considered unnecessary or unbecoming to have a boy instructed unless he is intended for the Church. The Italian laity read their Virgil and Horace, but wrote no books; while the clergy partly fell into a state of barbarism, partly were too much taken up with political affairs to share in the scientific efforts of the times. In this way we can explain the absence of literary productivity and the poverty of such literature as there was; while on the other hand, in this panegyrist, and somewhat later in Liutprand, a sudden and astonishing richness of classical learning, and great facility of expression, present themselves, especially in versifying, which was a principal point in the school education. For a few also of the clergy tasted of this forbidden fruit, though in general the Church was opposed to such pastime, seeing in it, and with truth, a pagan element. Science was not here taken into the service of the Church; it asserted its independence, but was almost entirely of a formal character, and therefore essentially unproductive."[1]

This arid historical era, the scanty sources of which we have tried here to place before the reader as they one by one presented themselves, closes in the year 961 with the rise of the dominion of the Othos. The feeble rule of Charlemagne's successors, by undermining the force of the monarchy, had so strengthened that of the nobles, that they, having become by degrees nearly independent, quarrelled among themselves in a struggle for supremacy. In this way grew up those haughty and powerful lords of Turin, of Friuli, of Tuscany and Spoleto, who aspired to the kingdom, no longer feeling any allegiance to the empire. To this

---

[1] Wattenbach, *Deut. Geschichtsqu.* i. 252 (ed. 1877). While we coincide in this opinion, we think it right to observe that long before Giesebrecht, the uninterrupted existence of Italian schools had been affirmed and proved by Tiraboschi in his History of Italian literature. On this subject there is an excellent essay by Ozanam, *Des Écoles en Italie aux Temps Barbares*, which takes also into account—perhaps even too favourably—the existence of ecclesiastical schools. A recent work by Salvioli, on public instruction in Italy from the eighth to the tenth centuries, is written in a less comprehensive spirit, but is valuable for its many details.

period belong the struggles of Berengarius, duke of Friuli, with Guido of Spoleto and with his son Lambert for the throne of Italy, and their disputes with each other and with the German and French princes for the imperial throne (A.D. 888-924); also the turbulent and tyrannical reigns of Rudolph, Hugo, and Lothair of Provence, and lastly of Berengarius II. who oppressed Italy, while in Rome the Alberics and the famous Marozia dragged through the mire the papacy of which they had made themselves masters (A.D. 924-961). At this point the darkness begins to diminish, and the age follows of the three Saxon Othos who held the empire and ruled Italy for about forty years, from the year 961 to 1002. This is not the place to examine the advantages and disadvantages of this rule, and how by it that bond between Italy and Germany was drawn so close as to unite the histories of the two nations from that time in a painful chain of events rife with misery and blood. We may mention, however, that Otho the Great, in order to restrain the unbridled power of the nobles, seconded the development of municipal liberty, and in the cities, by increasing the political attributes of the bishops, substituted to a certain extent the power of an elective nobility for that of an hereditary one. This was the cause of the many adherents whom the Othos numbered among the clergy, and especially among the bishops of North Italy. Pre-eminent among them is Liutprand, bishop of Cremona, who became the historian of those times.[1] Like the more ancient writers whose works we have examined, Liutprand played a distinguished part in public life. He was born about the year 920 in Lombardy, and according to some in the very city of Pavia. Having lost his father in infancy, he was educated with great care by his stepfather, "a man graced with dignity and full of wisdom," as he tells us in words which recall what we have just said of the education of the Italian laity. In the year 931, being recommended to King Hugo as a boy of much talent, and possessing a fine voice, he was admitted to the royal court, and gained the king's favour; later he entered the Church, and was inscribed among the deacons of Pavia. When in 945 Hugo had to fly from his kingdom, Liutprand succeeded in obtaining an honourable position in the court of the new king, Berengarius II. This monarch seems for some time to have appreciated his abilities and to have been glad to make use of them. In the year 949–50 he was sent to Constantinople as ambassador, for which position he seemed specially adapted by his education and family traditions, the

---

[1] *Liutprandi episcopi cremonensis opera omnia in usum scholarum ex Monumentis Germaniæ Historicis recusa. Editio Altera. Recognovit Ernestus Dümmler, Hannoveræ,* 1877. For all that refers to the life of Liutprand we owe much to Dümmler's admirable and concise preface, in which he recapitulates with great ability the many studies made in this century regarding Liutprand, though we think he sometimes treats him with rather too much indulgence.

same post having been filled both by his father and his stepfather. This journey was of the greatest use to him in learning the customs and institutions of the Greeks, as well as in gaining a thorough knowledge of their language and literature, which was destined to be of great service to him in after life. After his return home he fell into great disgrace, for what reason is not well known, with King Berengarius and his queen Willa, and was obliged to take refuge in Germany, where he was honourably received by the Saxon king Otho I. During his years of exile he familiarized himself with the German tongue, which also proved very advantageous to him later, in treating the State affairs with which he was entrusted when Otho, urged by his high destinies, descended into Italy. In the year 956, while he was still at the German court, he formed a friendship with Recemund, bishop of Elvira, who advised him to undertake a history of his own times. The advice was not given in vain, for after two years' reflection, Liutprand began his work at Frankfort. The hatred which he felt for King Berengarius and Queen Willa suggested a title for his work, and he called it *Antapodosis*, or the book of retribution, meaning by this that he would pay back good for good to his friends, and evil for evil to those who had driven him into exile. The six books of the *Antapodosis* were written in different places and with interruptions between 958 and 962. Beginning with the year 888—a date sufficiently recent for the author to be able to collect oral contemporary, or nearly contemporary evidence—he relates the history of the events as they had occurred throughout Europe. It is a very curious book, in which the vicissitudes of different countries follow and cross each other with an abundance of detail truly marvellous. Naturally Italian affairs occupy the greater part of the book, but its vast range embraces the most distant people and things. Italians, Germans, Saracens, types of every kind, from popes and emperors down to the common people, exploits of the purest virtue and indecent scandals, all are mixed up in this book, in which, moreover, it is remarkable how small is the part played by miraculous legends. The narrative reaches the year 950, but at that period the sixth book of the *Antapodosis* remains incomplete. Liutprand had intended to bring the work down to the time of his exile, but was hindered from doing so; partly no doubt by the mass of public business which weighed upon him, partly perhaps, as Dümmler thinks, because his anger was appeased by the fall of Berengarius. The year 961 had brought a great change in his fortunes, and Otho the Great, immediately after his descent into Italy, proposed him for the episcopal chair of Cremona. His quick and versatile talents, his decided aptitude for diplomatic posts, his familiar knowledge of various languages, made him specially fitted for the conduct of State affairs. From that time he was in the midst of everything that regarded Italy, and the relations of Otho with Greece. In the summer of the year 964 he went to Rome as ambassador to Pope John XII., and shortly afterwards was present at the council which deposed that unworthy pontiff, and there interpreted Otho's speech to the Italian bishops. He took part in the election of Leo VIII., and in the deposition of his rival, Benedict V. He wrote, at the command of the emperor, a history of all the events of which he had been eye-witness from 960 to 964, and called it *Historia Ottonis*. Perhaps the dignity of the high offices which he had filled, and his own share in the facts related, contributed to make the tone of this work much calmer and freer from that party feeling which rendered the *Antapodosis* so bitter against Berengarius and Willa. Nor did this only serve to render him less partial, it also added vivacity and colouring to his narrative. The deposition of John XII., for instance, is related in so lively and distinct a manner, that we seem, while reading, to be assisting at the council which decreed it. After describing the differences on account of which the emperor and the pope came to be on terms which admitted of no reconciliation, and telling how the pope not only paid no attention to his embassy, but, in defiance of the emperor, had received Adelbert, son of King Berengarius, within the very walls of Rome, Liutprand continues thus:

"While these things are happening, the oppressive constellation of the Cancer drives the emperor away from the Roman castles on account of the heat of Phœbus' rays. But when the constellation Virgo returning, brought a pleasant temperature, he came to Rome, having collected his troops, and been secretly invited by the Romans. But why should I say secretly, when the greater part of the Roman nobility proceeded to the castle of St. Paul, and invited the holy emperor, and even gave hostages? Why should I lose time with many words? The emperor having encamped near the city, the pope and Adelpert both fly from Rome. And the citizens receive the holy emperor into their town and repeat their promise of fidelity; adding, and firmly swearing, that they would never elect or ordain a pope against the consent and choice of their lord the Emperor Otho, their august cæsar, and of his son King Otho.

"After three days, at the request of the Roman bishops and people, a large assembly is held in the church of St. Peter; and with the emperor sat the archbishops: from Italy—for Ingelfred, patriarch of Acquileia, who as it happened was detained in that city by a sudden illness, the Deacon Rodalph; Walpert of Milan; Peter of Ravenna: from Saxony—Adeltac, the archbishop; Landohard, the bishop: from France—Otker, bishop of Spires: from Italy—Hubert of Parma, Liutprand of Cremona, Hermenald of Reggio."

Here follows a long list of bishops, almost all Italian, and of the cardinals and Roman priests who were present at the council, as well as the representatives of the nobility and people of Rome after which Liutprand resumes his narrative:

"These therefore being present, and keeping perfect silence, the holy emperor began thus: 'How right it would be that the Lord Pope John should be present at so distinguished and holy a council! But we ask you, O holy fathers, who have had life and business in common with him, why he refused to join such an assembly?' Then the Roman pontiffs and cardinal priests and deacons, with the whole populace, replied: 'We wonder that your most holy prudence should want us to inquire into this matter, which is not unknown to the inhabitants of Iberia, Babylon, or India. For he is not one of those who come in sheep's clothing, but are in truth ravening wolves. He rages so openly, he carries on so plainly his diabolical practices, that he uses no circumambient ways.' The emperor answered: 'It appears to us just, that the accusations should be set forth one by one; then what we should do can be decided on by common advice.' Then the cardinal priest Peter, rising up, bore witness that he had seen him celebrate mass without communicating. John, bishop of Narni, and John, the cardinal deacon, declared that they saw him ordain a deacon in a stable, and not at the appointed times. Benedict, the cardinal deacon, with other deacons and priests, said that they knew that he had for reward made ordinations of bishops, and had ordained a bishop of Todi ten years old. As to sacrilege, they said there was no need of information, since it could be witnessed by sight rather than by hearing. . . . They told how he hunted publicly; how he had blinded his godfather Benedict, who had afterwards died; that he had mutilated and killed John, the cardinal sub-deacon; they bore witness that he had been guilty of arson, and that he had worn helmet and cuirass with a sword girt round him. All declared —clergy as well as laity—that he had drunk wine in honour of the devil. They said that, in playing dice, he had invoked the assistance of Jove, Venus, and other demons. Finally, they declared that he did not even celebrate matins, or the canonical hours, nor bless himself with the sign of the cross.

"The emperor, having heard all this, and knowing that the Romans could not understand his language, which was Saxon, commanded Liutprand, bishop of Cremona, to express to them in the Latin tongue these things as follows. And rising, he thus began: 'It often happens, and we believe it from our own experience, that those placed in high dignities are defamed by the baseness of the envious; for the good are as displeasing to the wicked, as the wicked are to the good. And it is on this account that we hold in suspense this accusation against the pope which Benedict the cardinal deacon has just read and made with you, being uncertain whether it has arisen from a zeal for justice or from the malice of impiety. Hence, according to the authority of the dignity granted to me, unworthy though I am, I call upon all of you, by God whom no man can deceive though he may wish to do so, and by His holy and immaculate mother the Virgin Mary, and by the most precious body of the prince of the apostles, in whose church these things are being said, to fling no accusations against the lord pope of which he is not verily guilty, and which were not seen by men of the greatest probity.' Then the bishops, priests, deacons, and the rest of the clergy, with the whole Roman people, exclaimed as one man, ' If Pope John has not committed both these base crimes read aloud by Benedict the deacon, and others baser and greater than these, may the most blessed Peter, prince of the apostles, not absolve us from the chain of our sins, he who by his word closes heaven to the unworthy, and opens it to the just, but may we be entangled in a chain of anathema, and in the Last Day be placed on the left hand with those who said to their Lord God: "Retire from us, for we desire not the knowledge of Thy ways." Therefore, if thou dost not trust us, at least thou shouldst believe the army of our lord the emperor, to which he approached five days ago, girded with the sword and wearing a shield, helmet and cuirass, and only the Tiber which flowed between prevented his being captured by the army while thus equipped.' Then the holy emperor said: 'There are as many witnesses of this fact as there are warriors in our army.' The holy synod replied: 'If it please the holy emperor, let letters be sent to the lord pope, that he may come to purge himself of all these things.' Then letters were prepared for him to the following purport:

"'To the supreme pontiff and universal pope the Lord John, Otho, by Divine clemency august emperor, with the archbishops, the bishops of Liguria, Tuscany, Saxony, and France, in the Lord. Coming to Rome for the service of God, when we inquired of your sons, namely, the Roman bishops, cardinals, priests, and deacons, and moreover of the whole people, as to your absence, and what cause there could be why you should not wish to see us, the defenders of your Church and of yourself, they brought forward such things and so unseemly against you, that if they were said of actors we should feel ashamed. And lest these things should be hidden from your greatness, we mention some of them to you in brevity, since did we try to express them all one by one a whole day would not suffice to us. Know, therefore, that not by a few, but by all, of our order as well as of the other, you are accused of homicide, perjury, and sacrilege. . . . They also say, a thing horrible to hear of, that you have drunk wine in honour of the devil, and have implored the assistance, in the game of dice, of Jupiter, Venus, and other demons. We therefore earnestly entreat your paternity, that you should not refuse to come to Rome and clear yourself from all these things. If perchance you fear the violence of the impulsive multitude, we assure you with an oath that nothing shall be done against the sanction of the holy canons. Given the eighth of the Ides of November.'

"When he had read this letter, he wrote an answer as follows: 'John the bishop, servant of the servants of God, to all the bishops. We have heard it said that you want to make another pope; if you do this, I excommunicate you by Almighty God, that you may not have permission to ordain any one, or to celebrate mass.'"[1]

When this uncouth letter was read in the council, it gave as little satisfaction for its form as for its contents. They decided that the emperor, with the whole synod, should in reply bid John come to Rome to exculpate himself, threatening to depose him in case of his refusal. The letter was immediately written with the resolute vigour of phraseology and meaning with which it had been imagined. The excommunication threatened by

---

[1] "Johannes espiscopus, servus servorum dei, omnibus episcopis. Nos audivimus dicere, quia vos vultis alium papam facere; si hoc facitis, excommunico vos da deum omnipotentem, ut non habeatis licentiam *nullum* ordinare, et missam celebrare." It is curious that in the letter sent by the council in answer to John, they reproach him also with the grammatical error which he made in writing *nullum* instead of *ullum*.

the pope was set at nought, and his flippant treatment of the assembly was strongly censured, their authority for threatening him with excommunication in the case of his non-appearance was affirmed, and they finally compared him to Judas, whose treason had put an end to his apostolic authority. The letter was entrusted to the Cardinals Adrian and Benedict, with the injunction to convey it to him without delay,—

"Who, when they reached Tivoli, did not find him; for he had already gone armed into the country; nor was there any one who could tell them where he was. And when they could not find him, they returned with the letter to the holy synod, sitting for the third time. Then the emperor said: 'We waited for his coming that we might in his presence complain of his conduct towards us, but as we know with certainty that he will not come, we beg of you again and again to take diligent note of his perfidy to us. For we make it known to you, archbishops, bishops, priests, deacons, and the rest of the clergy, as also to the counts, judges, and the whole people, that this same Pope John, being oppressed by Berengarius and Adelbert, our rebels, sent messengers into Saxony to us, asking that for the love of God we should come into Italy and deliver from their fangs the church of St. Peter and himself. But it is not necessary to tell what by the help of God we effected, since you can now see it. But he, saved by my labours from their hands, and reinstated in the dignity due to him, forgot the oath and fidelity which he promised me on the body of St. Peter, brought the same Adelpert to Rome and defended him against me, stirring up seditions, and made himself a leader in the war in the sight of our soldiers, putting on helmet and cuirass. Now let the holy synod pronounce what it decides upon this.' To this the Roman pontiffs, the rest of the clergy, and the whole of the people answered: 'An unheard of wound must be cauterized in an unheard of manner. If he only injured himself and not all by his corrupt conduct, he should at any cost be tolerated. How many who were chaste before, have become immoral from imitating him! How many just men have from the example of his conversation become reprobate! We therefore beg your imperial greatness to drive away from the holy Roman Church this monster, unredeemed from his vices by any virtue, and to put up another in his place, who may merit by the example of a good conversation to preside over and assist us, who may himself live rightly, and give us an example of right living.' Then the emperor replies: 'What you say pleases us, and nothing will be more welcome to us than that such a one may be found, who may be placed at the head of this holy and universal see.'

"When he had spoken thus, all with one voice exclaimed: 'We choose for our shepherd, as supreme and universal pope of the holy Roman Church, Leo the venerable protonotary of the holy Roman Church, a proved man and worthy of the supreme grade of the priesthood; John the apostate being cast off on account of his reprobate conduct.' And when they had all said this for the third time, and the emperor had agreed, they conduct, with praises according to the custom, the said Leo to the Lateran palace, and, after a given time, raise him by holy consecration in St. Peter's church to the supreme priesthood, and promise with an oath to be faithful to him.

"When these things had happened in this way, the most holy emperor, hoping that he could remain in Rome with but few men, gave permission to many to retire, that the Roman people might not be oppressed by the great number of the army. And when John, who was called pope, heard this, knowing how easily the minds of the Romans are bribed with money, sent messengers secretly to Rome, and promised the money of St. Peter and of all the churches, if they would fall upon the pious emperor and the Lord Pope Leo, and impiously slay them. Why should I lose time in many words? Then the Romans, confiding in the smallness of the army, nay, deceived by it, and encouraged by the promise of money, try to hurry upon the emperor with the sounding of a trumpet, in order to kill him. And the emperor meets them upon the bridge of the Tiber, which the

Romans had barricaded with carts. And his strong soldiers, accustomed to war, and intrepid in courage and arms, rush out among them, and strike them down without resistance, as hawks among a crowd of birds. There were no hiding-places, no baskets, ships, or drains, which could protect the fugitives. They are slaughtered therefore, and as is customary in meeting with strong men, are everywhere wounded in the back. Who of the Romans would then have survived this massacre, if the holy emperor, moved by pity, of which he owed none to them, had not drawn and called back his men still thirsting for bloodshed?"

Unfortunately, the narrative of these events, written while they were happening, was not completed by Liutprand, and was interrupted soon after this exaggerated account of the Roman sedition. Public affairs pressed upon him. Returning to Cremona soon after the council, he did not remain there long, and on the death of Leo VIII. (A.D. 965), was sent again to Rome for the election of the new pope. In 967, he took part in two other councils at Ravenna and Rome, and in the latter city was present at the coronation of the young Otho II., whom his father had raised to a share in the Empire. With his thoughts fixed on the restoration of a western empire, Otho's actions tended to bring the papacy into a certain subjection to him, while appearing only to reform it, and he tried to appropriate the whole of Italy, by driving away from the south Arabs and Greeks. At the same time, and with the same object, he sought the friendship of the Byzantine court, and an alliance with it by means of the marriage of his son to a Greek princess, being desirous of surrounding his throne with the classic splendour of ancient traditions. The realization, however, of this plan met with hindrances in the susceptibility and suspicions of the Greeks, which certainly were justified by the growth of Otho's power in southern Italy. It was necessary to find the man fitted to conquer this diffidence, skilled in diplomatic intricacies and well acquainted with Greece. Certainly this man seemed to be Liutprand, who was sent to the Emperor Nicephorus Phocas, and commissioned to make a formal demand for the hand of Theophania, daughter of Romanus II. But the embassy proved fruitless. Liutprand was badly received, and with open contempt. Nicephorus, at the very first audience, complained to him vehemently of his master's occupation of Rome, of the title of emperor which he had assumed, and of the recognition obtained from the princes of Benevento and Capua,—all things which he considered injurious to his interests. The arguments and bold answers of the ambassador availed nothing, or only served to add fuel to the wrath of the Eastern potentate. After various audiences, all of which were useless, and after having been scornfully treated in a thousand ways, and kept a long time at Constantinople more as a prisoner than an ambassador, Liutprand was at last allowed as a favour to return to his own land without having succeeded in anything. He was very much vexed at this diplomatic defeat, and gave vent to his vexation in the report of his embassy which he addressed to the two Othos and to the Empress Adelaide. Notwithstanding the traces of personal vanity and partiality customary in Liutprand's writings, this *Relatio de Legatione Constantinopolitana* offers us a most interesting picture of the Greek court. Gregorovius, with his usual exuberance of fancy, says that "this charming pamphlet resembles an oasis which we meet with while crossing a literary desert," and adds, that since Procopius we have no writing to be compared to it. We, remembering Paulus Diaconus, should hesitate to subscribe to this judgment, but certainly the *Relatio* is among the most agreeable and instructive pieces of writing which the early part of the Middle Ages offers us in Italy. The description of the court of Nicephorus, the lively answers with which, according to his own account, Liutprand defended his sovereign and people from the accusations made against them, the treachery and greedy corruption of the Greeks, the difficulties he met with when he wanted to leave Constantinople, and also on his journey home, are all described with a vivacity which renders the book very attractive. Like all the other books of this writer, however, it also is incomplete, and the narrative of his return journey, at the beginning of the year 969 is interrupted. After his return to Otho's court, he continued to take part in public affairs. In 971, when the death of Nicephorus Phocas had made the relations between the two courts more amicable, it appears that he was again sent to Constantinople with the solemn embassy which went to fetch the princess Theophania, the destined bride of Otho II. But his career was now at an end, and he did not again reach his bishopric. The exact date and place of his death are unknown, but he seems to have died, either while still in Greece, or immediately after his return to Italy with Theophania, in the first months of 972, and when little over fifty years of age.

The life and writings of this remarkable man bear the impress of a keen and original intelligence, as well as of a lively and passionate character. Equal to the best writers among his contemporaries in Europe, he is incomparably superior to the other Italian writers of the day. He received an excellent lay education from a child, and soon learnt to know and value the best authors. Terence, Cicero, Virgil, Horace, Ovid, and the classics generally, were familiar to him, and he tried to introduce phrases from them everywhere into his writings; and though there was in this much ostentation, yet he did it at least with more judgment than other mediæval writers. Nor did he content himself with quotations from the Latin classics, but in all his writings took delight in showing off his erudition, by constantly interlarding his Latin with Greek words and phrases. As the model for his style he took principally Severinus Boetius, the influence of whose books was unlimited in the Middle Ages; and especially in his *Antapodosis* he followed the example of Boetius by mixing often tolerably good verses with his prose. But even this exaggerated spirit of imitation did not suffice to destroy the literary originality of a man so strongly imbued with a sense of his own personality. The *Antapodosis*, being the longest and most freely handled of his works, is the one perhaps which best reveals the character of the man and his contradictions. Talented and credulous, acute in his observation of facts, and rash in his judgments, desirous of good but too easily led to find fault, and a ready retailer of scandals, he takes bitter revenge on his enemies, especially Berengarius and Willa, while he is guilty of adulation when praising his benefactors; yet it is evident to the reader that he feels what he says, and paints in dark or bright colours according to his inmost convictions. His authority as an historian was formerly rated too low on account of these personal characteristics, and now we seem to note a modern tendency to rate him somewhat above his due. It appears to us that, although Liutprand's narratives, as far as they regard particular details, are of great use for confirming or explaining things related by his contemporaries, they must nevertheless be employed with more caution than is shown by some recent historians. But, on the whole, certainly no contemporary work assists us more than his does to form a general idea of the tenth century, and to give us in vivid colours a mental picture of it. With his varied experience of life, and his carefully cultivated talents, Liutprand, both as statesman and as author, was more than any one else in a position to seize and combine the facts which he witnessed, while his lively and ingenuous disposition is especially adapted to awaken in us those same impressions which the real events had made upon his mind.[1]

The chronicle of Benedict of Mount Soracte, written about this time, is very different, both in spirit and in form, from the works of Liutprand.[2]

---

[1] The imperial idea, revived by the Othos and so warmly supported in Italy by Liutprand, had already, before the descent of Otho the Great, found a champion in the author of a *Libellus de Imperatoria Potestate in urbe Roma* (published in the *Mon. Germ. Hist. SS.* iii. 719–722), which is not without historical importance. Also two poems, appearing in North Italy in the first years of the eleventh century, are of some value for history on account of the imperial sympathies expressed in them. One of them especially, which laments the premature death of Otho III., contains some striking verses.

[2] *Chronicon Benedicti de S. Andrea. Mon. Germ. Hist. SS.* iii. The life of St. Nilus, founder of the monastery of Grottaferrata, written in Greek by a disciple, and the letters of the famous Gerbertus, afterwards Pope Sylvester II., contain contemporary historical data regarding this period of the Othos. Two lives also of St. Adalbert are worthy of attention, especially the more ancient one, written in

The monk Benedict, with rude simplicity, tries to put together the history of the world from the coming of Christ, but the only value of his labours lies in the local history of Rome about the times of Alberic, on whom, as protector of his monastery, he lavishes great praise. The voice of the monk rises in tones of reproach, though without either hatred or malice, against the new monarchs from beyond the Alps, whose soldiery he saw from the solitary and poetic heights of Soracte, spread over the Roman campagna. In strong contrast with the adulatory exaggeration of Liutprand, and breathing a kind of inspired melancholy, these rude pages leave an impression of sadness on the reader, and their barbarous language rises to a funereal eloquence at the memory of the abandonment in which Rome was left after the ferocious acts of repression with which Otho stifled the rebellion of the Romans to his authority. "Woe to thee, O Rome!" he exclaims, "who art oppressed and trampled on by so many nations; who wert taken even by the Saxon king, and thy people put to the sword, and thy strength reduced to nought. Thou who in thy greatness didst triumph over the nations, didst trample on the world, and put to

---

Rome by John Canaparius, abbot of the monastery of St. Alexis on the Aventine. "This work," as Giesebrecht justly observes in his history of the German empire, "interesting for being the only noteworthy literary production of a Roman at that time, is moreover one of the most important sources of contemporary history."

death the kings of the earth, holding the sceptre and supreme power, thou art despoiled by the Saxon king and utterly exhausted. . . . Thou wert too beautiful; we can even now see all thy walls, with their towers and battlements. Thou hadst three hundred and eighty towers, forty-six castles, six thousand eight hundred battlements, and fifteen gates. Woe to thee, Leonine city! Thou wast but lately captured by the king of the Saxons, and art now already abandoned!"

Melancholy words truly, and a sad contrast between the present decline and the past splendour! But if the wretched condition of Rome inspired the rude lament of Benedict of Soracte, on the other hand from Venice Johannes Diaconus, chaplain and perhaps relation of the Doge Pietro Orseolo (991–1009), opens to us the first pages of one of the most wonderful histories of the world.[1] John had been sent several times as ambassador to Otho III. and Henry II., was a man of the world, and had much experience of life and of public affairs; of this we find evident traces in his narrative, which flows along easily and entertainingly, without any display of rhetoric or much attention to grammar. Beginning with the first origins of

---

[1] *Johannis Diaconi Chronicon Venetum et Gradense. Mon. Germ. Hist. SS.* iii. This chronicle was first known as the *Chronicon Sagornini*. The first books of the *Chronicon Altinate* also deserve to be mentioned, as they contain very ancient and valuable materials for the history of Venice.

Venice, it extends to the year 1008, full of omissions and errors in the older part, but affording valuable information about contemporary facts, especially regarding the relations between the emperors and Venice. With John we are outside the life of the cloister, and breathe freely the fresh air of the lagunes. A worthy predecessor of Andrea Dandolo, he first gives us glimpses of that glorious epoch of the communes, towards which Italy was tending throughout the period of laborious efforts that we are now about to examine.

CHAPTER IV.

INTELLECTUAL MOVEMENT IN THE ELEVENTH AND TWELFTH CENTURIES—REFORMS IN THE CHURCH AND THE CONTESTS REGARDING THE INVESTITURES—REVIVAL OF ECCLESIASTICAL CULTURE AND OF HISTORICAL RESEARCH IN THE MONASTERIES—MONASTIC REGISTERS AND CHRONICLES—THE MONASTERY OF FARFA AND THE WORKS OF GREGORY OF CATINO—THE "CHRONICON VULTURNENSE"—RENAISSANCE OF ARTS AND LETTERS AT MONTECASSINO PROMOTED BY THE ABBOT DESIDERIUS—THE MONK AMATUS AND HIS HISTORY OF THE NORMANS—LEO OSTIENSIS AND PETRUS DIACONUS, HISTORIANS OF MONTECASSINO — HISTORICAL WRITINGS OF SOUTHERN ITALY—LEGENDARY CHRONICLE OF THE MONASTERY OF THE NOVALESA.

AFTER the narrow defiles through which we have so long been wandering, wider horizons now open out to us. An age of giants begins, and the history of Italy returns to almost epic heights.

Many elements were working together at that time. The papacy, having struggled out of the degradation into which it had fallen, begins to assert its power with audacity, and, while exaggerating the Roman traditions of Gregory the Great, claims, under the name of a universal spiritual dominion, the supremacy of the Church over nations and kings. The empire, jealous of its rights, combats this excessive ambition, defends itself, partly by cavils, partly by violence, against the moral usurpation of the priesthood, and vainly tries to subjugate it. A band of Norman adventurers land in Sicily, and after clearing it of the Saracens, spread themselves over the south of Italy, where they lay the foundation of a kingdom which is sometimes hostile to, sometimes the champion of the popes, while these in the meantime are engaged in maturing with far-reaching care the vast conception of the crusades with which they electrify the world. In the midst of so many changes, the Latin instinct almost imperceptibly awakens, and sows the first seeds of a new life destined to give glorious results for Italy—and this is the life of the Communes. Fresh vigour is infused into letters. Church, empire, and people all labour in different ways for the renaissance of learning. The need felt of a reform in the Church, and the efforts made to obtain it, first by the Othos and then continued under the great popes of the eleventh century, bring back intellectual culture and a love of study into the ranks of the clergy. The clashing of parties gives frequent rise to vehement polemical writings, and the wish to find grounds in the past for the rights claimed on each side, leads to a study of Roman law. The renewed vigour of public and private justice inspires an interest in ancient documents; while the rise and growth of municipal life revives in the laity the smouldering traditions of literary activity. The iron age for Italian chronography is ended.

We may therefore infer that the reform which had made its way into the Church at the time of which we now write, was not solely the work either of the popes, the emperors, the minor clergy or the people. It was the result of a complex action. There was a regenerating breath stirring the world, and men's souls were unconsciously tending by different paths towards a reform which should satisfy their higher aspirations. Such a tendency, at first essentially religious in its tone, had of necessity to seek support from monasticism, which it carried along with it and made one of the principal instruments in this great movement. The second half of the eleventh century and the first half of the twelfth may be looked upon as the golden age of Western monasticism, both for the influence which it exerted on the Church in general and especially in the matter of reform, as well as for the influence and impulse which it received from the Church itself. In the preceding age the corruption of the monasteries was great everywhere, and, as we have seen, very great indeed in Italy. But when all seemed falling to ruin, we are met by a revival in the monastic rule at Cluny, which thence spread the beginnings of a universal improvement. Otho of Cluny, a wise and zealous reformer, did much good in spite of many obstacles, especially at Montecassino, and also, at the request of the famous Alberic, prince of the Romans, in the monasteries of Rome and Sabina. This missionary of monastic reform combined high attainments with his moral virtues, and in France had studied philosophy, grammar, and the art of poetry. Naturally one of his efforts was to bring back a love of study to the convents, and to reform their schools, and though these reforms took root slowly, they produced an abundant harvest within a century. The monastery of Farfa was at the head of this intellectual revival. We have seen in the former chapter how the Abbot Hugo was not content with restoring the abbey to its pristine splendour, but did his best also to perpetuate its records by dictating one of the most remarkable historical writings of his age. Nor was this good example without followers. When Hugo died in 1039, he left behind him in the convent a school capable of continuing his work. In this school was educated the boy Gregory, belonging to the family of the counts of Catino in Sabina. His father, according to the custom of the time, had offered this child to the monastery, as well as another son, who died soon after 1068. Gregory had been living humbly and unnoticed in the abbey for about thirty years, when towards the close of the eleventh century he proposed to the Abbot Beraldus II. a work of great magnitude, and was commissioned to carry it into effect. The invasions endured in the former century, the destruction and long abandonment of the monastery, the wastefulness of bad abbots, had necessarily produced great disorder and brought about many changes in the estates of the convent, whence arose frequent contests about rights, and lawsuits in the courts. On this account Gregory proposed to rearrange the archives, and after collecting all the documents on which the rights of the monastery were founded, copy them in their proper order into one book. This authentic copy would thus facilitate the use of them, and at the same time provide against any possible injury to the originals. Being entrusted with this undertaking, he immediately set to work, and continued at his fatiguing labour for fifteen years, only relinquishing it when advancing age and enfeebled sight rendered it impossible for him to proceed. But the larger and more difficult part of the work was done, and he could therefore safely confide what remained to a nephew of his called Todinus, also a monk of Farfa, who added the last documents and brought it to a successful termination.

The Farfa Register, or, as Gregory calls it, the

Liber Gemniagraphus sive Cleronomialis Ecclesiæ Farfensis, is certainly one of the documents possessing most importance for the Italian history of the Middle Ages from the Lombard times to the end of the eleventh century. The numerous and extremely ancient charters which it has preserved for us throw a special light on the history of law, and on the problem of the relations existing in the eighth and ninth centuries between the Latin populations and their Lombard and Frank rulers. The Register contains, belonging to these two centuries alone, nearly three hundred and fifty documents, which form one of the principal bases for the studies made in Italy and Germany touching this period of our history. In this collection there are hundreds of charters of popes, emperors, kings, and dukes, mixed with private papers, which also possess great interest for the indirect information they give with regard to history, law, and topography. For the early and remarkable history of the duchy of Spoleto, the Farfa Register is the only source which remains to us, while for the special history of Rome in the tenth and eleventh centuries it may be considered of primary importance.

We cannot, however, dwell long upon this unique document. Hitherto the scantiness of historical records has led to our mentioning collections which were not chronicles properly so called, but now, on the contrary, the great abundance which we meet with will oblige us generally to leave altogether on one side, or only to make passing mention of such indirect sources of history as diplomas and letters. Still we must pause for a moment over the Farfa Register, because it may be regarded as the most ancient collection, both large and complete, of this kind, and to a certain extent as the forerunner of the other registers, which appeared about this period, and which so wonderfully assisted to revive not only a taste for narrative, but also for historical criticism.[1] Then, as a natural consequence to the registers, or rather to the researches made in the archives, followed the monastic chronicles, and the critical spark was fired in those quiet monks poring over the records of their convents. In the meditative silence of their cells, while questioning and comparing these ancient documents, they found in them fragments of the history of their monastery, and were seized with the desire of narrating it to posterity. Gregory of Catino offers us an example of this kind of self-education, combined with a subtle sense of criticism. Alone and

---

[1] The only one of some importance which we know of prior to that of Farfa is the Register of Subiaco. It is not, however, a compilation made all by one person and at one time, but is the work of several authors, begun early in the eleventh century and finished towards the beginning of the thirteenth. It contains documents of great antiquity, and is valuable for the local history of Rome, but its general interest is not so great. Both the Farfa and Subiaco Registers were hitherto unedited, but are now being published under the auspices of the Roman Historical Society.

without the aid of example, he invented so true and simple a method for the compilation of his work, that we could hardly expect a more correct one in a critic of to-day. Well aware of the historical value of his work, he devoted himself to it with noble conscientiousness, and with an ideal of what historical aims should be—limited and deficient, it is true, but of a high moral standard. He seems to approach in this respect to Cicero's definition, when he shows that history should benefit posterity, and cites as examples the just of past generations. "On this account, therefore," he says in one place, "are the lives of the just especially described, that we may pass ours while they last in a careful happiness like theirs, and free from offence. For it is written that the example of the just should make us more careful; and if we follow in their steps we shall not stumble in the way." And animated with these thoughts he looked with affectionate diligence for what was true regarding the history of his abbey, rejecting what was merely fable, and verifying his facts by the documents found in the archives. For the first legendary story of the very ancient foundation of Farfa he has no other authority but the *Constructio*, of which indeed he makes use, and from which he quotes but very cautiously, and without affirming anything touching which he has not exact information. "Let it therefore be enough to know," he says, "that this holy convent was founded by that most holy man (Lawrence), but not at the public expense. And since we are ignorant of the time of its foundation, we prefer rather to be silent with regard to it than to say something untrue or without sufficient reason. For if it is unlawful to us to listen to a falsehood, how much more is it unbecoming in us to tell one." A noble maxim, worthy of an historian, and too often, alas, neglected by the writers of ecclesiastical history! But if, on the one hand, he was saved from credulity by the scrupulous fear of being mistaken, he does not hesitate, on the other hand, to seek assistance in his conjectures from critical comparisons, and so in this case, starting from a passage in St. Gregory's dialogues, and following out a close line of argument, he brings the foundation of the monastery to a date not to be exactly determined, but certainly anterior to that pontiff. However, the path he followed in his work is well indicated in the following page of his preface to the Register, which seems to us valuable if only for the signs it affords of the new intellectual movement which was beginning to make itself felt at that time in the convents:

"For I hope nothing from my own strength, but from the love of God, and trusting in His assistance through the intercession of our most glorious lady, I attentively studied to carry out as faithfully and truly as I could this very pious and most profitable work. And though I am not equal to correcting the corrupt parts in the matter of rhetoric, yet according to the littleness of my poor knowledge I have tried to correct what was confused beyond measure; not, indeed, too fully, lest it should appear to the simple that the order of the first edition made of the papers had been altered. And especially because I could not sit far aloof from the crowd in order to devote greater attention to this quiet work, but, placed in public, could hardly ever enjoy a little tranquility, whereas this work requires the concession of solitude. Nor do I either consider that I was sufficiently fitted for this work, for I am not trained in the schools of the poets, nor learned in the deep knowledge of the grammarians, but almost from my cradle was brought up to Divine exercises in the school of this holy convent, and fed upon the faithful wisdom of the milk of the mother of God, and therefore would rather refer to it whatever I may have learnt that was useful during my labours. Hence, as it was commanded to me by the aforesaid abbot, and by my other religious elders, I have diminished nothing of what I have seen in the order of the papers, and have increased nothing in the narrative of the facts, but have tried to transcribe what I saw with my eyes while writing, and could understand to be the true order, except some prolix and useless repetitions of words—as, for instance, some terminated obligations—lest, being already wearied by the corruptions in many parts, if kept still longer at my writing I should complete the volume much later, and it should be tedious, unfit for reference, and of immense size. Contenting myself, therefore, only with the truth of the facts and of those causes useful to be known, I have tried to carry out this work with ready and subtle sagacity and free from fraud, under the favour of Christ and assisted by the prayers of His mother, the perpetual Virgin, who is the cause of it. For we have been careful to insert the names of the witnesses into the copy of each charter, as we found them written in the originals. And those which we found worn from their great age, or eaten by worms, and therefore very difficult to decipher, we have left untouched for the same reason, being unwilling to insert into this unpolluted work anything but what we could clearly discern with our eyes, or understand by our truth-seeking intelligence. Thus, as I have striven to make a true and faithful copy, so may I deserve to receive pardon of my sins from Almighty God by the intercession of our lady, and also a perpetual reward for my relatives. For this did we put the name of *Gemniagraphus* to this book, that is, *A Memorial of the Description of Lands*, because in it we have inserted the lands of this convent from whomsoever or in whatsoever way they were acquired, and have comprehended them in one volume that they might ever be remembered. It also pleased us to call it *Cleronomialis*, that is, *Book of Heredity of the Farfa Church*, since it shows plainly the settled possessions belonging to her from the beginning. And we have prefixed the names of all the places, to each of which we have added its own number, and have noted very exactly in which documents you may find them."

This passage seems to us clearly to indicate with how much discernment Gregory carried on the compilation of his great work, and the complete dispersion at this day of the originals increases our debt of gratitude to him for his wise forethought. Nor did the learned monk limit all his activity to this collection, but undertook and completed three other works—the *Largitorium*, the *Floriger*, and the *Chronicon Farfense*. The first of these works, like the Register in its arrangement, contains the papers connected with the lands given by the monastery on long leases to those who undertook their cultivation. Thus, while the Register authenticated the fixed possessions of the monastery, the *Liber Largitorius*, or, as Gregory also called it, *Liber Notarius sive Emphiteuticus*, registered all its temporary contracts, and decided their circumstances and value. It begins with a document of the year 792 and ends about the beginning of the twelfth century, with documents of the time of the compiler. An index and a preface explain the object of this collection, which is still almost unknown, although of great value for the history of landed property and of the state of agriculture in Italy in the Middle Ages. Of the other two works of Gregory, the

Floriger Cartarum is a copious topographical index of the Register arranged in alphabetical order, and is of minor account. Very important, on the other hand, is the third book, which was published by Muratori under the name of *Chronicon Farfense*. This compilation, made half in the form of a register, half in that of a chronicle, recapitulates the contents of the Register, and extracting from it the history of the convent, reproduces its principal documents. Following the guidance of the *Constructio* and *Destructio*, of which we have already spoken, Gregory of Catino relates in this book the most remote events, critically comparing those two works with the documents found in the archives, and seeking the confirmation of the facts they relate. This book, full of information and papers taken from these archives, can be described in the same words as the Register, of which it may to a certain extent be regarded as both a compendium and a commentary. But the *Chronicon Farfense* in its scope and order has not really the form of a history; and this might astonish us more were it not evident that, notwithstanding his sufficiently good Latin, Gregory was entirely deficient in the art of composition. His merits are of a different order, and his having before others, and more thoroughly than others, opened the way to a critical examination of documents, his turn for erudition, and his sincere love of truth, give an incalculable value to his work, and render him deserving of a far higher estimation than that in which he has been hitherto held.¹

About the time that the archives were being put in order at Farfa, the same thing was happening to those of other monasteries, and was giving rise to other chronicles and registers. The monastery of St. Vincent on the Volturno, which had from its foundation a sort of similarity to Farfa, also has its chronicle to show, composed and enriched with documents by a monk called John. John, having been exhorted to the work by his abbot Gerardus, had the satisfaction of showing it when considerably advanced to the Pontiff Paschal II. (A.D. 1099–1118), who encouraged him with the words : " Well done, my son ; thou hast begun a great work, and study to accomplish still better what thou hast begun so well." This chronicle, which starts from the narrative of Autpertus touching the origin of the abbey,² and continues up to the year 1075, was finished later, when Gelasius II. was already pope (A.D. 1118, 1119). It may also be considered more as a register than a chronicle, and its real importance consists in the charters which form the basis and larger portion of the work. The antiquity of these charters—granted for the most part

---

[1] A certain polemical treatise is also generally included among Gregory's works ; it is entitled *Orthodoxa Defensio Imperialis*, and its object is to maintain the rights of the emperor against the papal pretensions. We, however, have not mentioned it among his writings, as we are strongly inclined to believe that he is not the author of it. [2] See the preceding chapter, p. 108.

by kings—makes this book very useful, not only for the history of Southern Italy, but also for that of the whole peninsula, as well as for the history of law. John's Latin is tolerably good in those passages in which he joins one document to another, but he has none of Gregory's critical discernment, and the valuable information which he gives is often mixed up with fabulous stories of miracles accepted by him without the least hesitation.

If Farfa may be said to have initiated in the eleventh century a new historical movement, Montecassino, on the other hand, must be admitted to have produced the best monastic histories written at that time in Italy. After the Abbot Aligernus (A.D. 949–985) had rebuilt that famous convent which the Saracens had destroyed, its intellectual life gradually revived, and little by little developed and increased, until between 1058 and 1087 it reached its period of greatest vigour under the Abbot Desiderius, afterwards Pope Victor III. This is the most glorious era in the annals of Montecassino up to our present days, and all the more remarkable is this light of renaissance when compared with the dark and stormy period upon which it shone. Descended as he was from the princes of Benevento, aristocratic in all his tastes, of versatile talents, and of even too mild a disposition, the pious, learned, and refined Desiderius seemed born to encourage arts and letters, and to give them efficacious support. To this also contributed the journeys undertaken by him, especially one to Constantinople, whither he was sent as *apocrisarius*, together with Frederick of Lorraine, destined also to become pope under the name of Stephen IX. "The Lorraine monk and the Lombard one," remarks Father Tosti of them with great truth, "when they returned from their Byzantine missions, brought back with them the seed of Greek civilization, and a description of what the St. Sophia of Justinian was like; and on this account later Desiderius called together colonies of workmen to build and decorate the basilica and the convent, of which he truly became a second founder. And, indeed, it appears to me as if this Desiderius had almost natural leanings towards the East, whence he sought to evoke a beam of sunshine, which should gild and revive the disturbed regions of the West, and should warm the roots of the old Latin trunk into giving forth new shoots of civilization. Hence he was the first of the Roman pontiffs who raised his voice to collect armies against the Moslems of the East. The crusades were a pious folly; but there is no doubt that from that disordered upheaving of all the West and its pilgrimage to the East, there resulted great benefits to science and art through the exchange of ideas between the long-divided generations."[1]

---

[1] *La Biblioteca dei Codici Manoscritti di Montecassino*, per D. Luigi Tosti. Napoli, 1874.

Under the influence of these inspirations, Desiderius rebuilt a great part of the monastery and the church, collecting into the latter all the most exquisite creations of the art of those days, and it is most unfortunate that this grand monument was entirely ruined by an earthquake a few centuries later. But it was not only art which was cultivated at Montecassino. At the same time that all kinds of artists summoned from Lombardy, Amalfi, and Constantinople formed a school of art while working at mosaics, sculpture, and painting, there arose also a school of letters which spread its roots far and wide. The library was enriched with precious manuscripts, which, by order of Desiderius, were written and illuminated in the abbey; the documents in the archives were put in order, and history opened a way for itself among the theological and polemical writings. Just as Farfa sided with the empire in the great struggle of the investitures, Montecassino took part with the pope. Thence, as from a fortress, the monks often sallied forth like champions, and no sooner had they quitted the peace of the cloister, than they threw themselves heart and soul into the whirl of political and religious warfare, fighting their battles with tongue and pen. The only power which could really give the victory to the papacy was moral force, and the principal means of obtaining it was the learning which the monks instinctively strove to acquire and to keep possession of. Placed not far south of Rome and well secured from imperial violence, Montecassino soon became the head-quarters of the most learned and zealous ecclesiastics of the time, and a centre of a political as well as of a literary movement. Among many other men of merit belonging to Montecassino were Pandulphus, of the family of the princes of Capua, who wrote in verse on mathematics and astronomy; Constantinus Africanus, the founder of the medical school at Salerno; Oderisius, belonging to the counts of Marsia, a writer of note and later abbot of the convent; Guaiferius, a poet; and Alfanus, also a poet and a celebrated man, who, when he became archbishop of Salerno, gave hospitality to the fugitive Gregory VII. and received his dying breath. Naturally history was benefited by these learned tendencies, and the Abbot Desiderius himself, in composing a book of dialogues on the miracles of St. Benedict, has preserved many most important historical facts, especially in connection with the pontificate of Leo IX., with whom he had lived intimately, and many of whose vicissitudes he shared. In the same way, the poems of Alfanus have not only a literary but also an historical interest,[1] as is also the case with those of

---

[1] Especially the *Versus de situ, Constructione et Renovatione Cænobii Casinensis*, on the rebuilding of the abbey as completed by Desiderius, are very valuable for the history of art in the eleventh century, and should be compared with what Leo Ostiensis wrote on the same subject in the history of which we are about to speak.

Guaiferius, and generally with many other writings coming to us at that day from Montecassino. But we have direct as well as indirect historical testimony, and the monk Amatus, a native of Salerno, dedicated to his abbot Desiderius, in appropriate words, his history of the conquest of Italy by the Normans, and of the earlier period of their rule. This history goes back to the origin of the Normans, and after treating of their invasions in Spain, England, and Italy, concludes with the death, in the year 1078, of Richard, Prince of Capua, one of the sons of Tancredi. The narrative is divided into eight books, and each of these into several chapters, which have short headings containing their respective contents. Unfortunately the manuscript of Amatus is lost, and we only know of it through an ancient French translation discovered in the present century, and published by Champollion Figeac.[1] All search after the original has hitherto proved fruitless, and it may be that it is irrevocably lost; happily this loss is compensated for, not only by the French translation, but also by our knowing that the work of Amatus, a few years after it was written, was drawn largely upon by a far greater historian in the composition of a work which still exists.

About the year 1060, the Abbot Desiderius

---

[1] *L'ystoire de li Normant et la Chronique de Robert Viscart par Aimé moine du Mont-Cassin*, publiées par M. Champollion Figeac, Paris, 1835.

received into the monastery a lad of fourteen named Leo, intended for the cloister. He was carefully educated in the schools of Montecassino, and among his masters was Aldemarius, who, as he tells us, before being a monk had been "a prudent and noble cleric of Capua and the notary of Prince Richard." Leo soon attracted the attention of the monks and gained the affection of Desiderius, who before long took him into his confidence, and began to make use of him in the many weighty matters which occupied his thoughts. This daily intimacy bound Leo to Desiderius with affectionate gratitude and veneration, feelings not diminished by the death of Desiderius at Montecassino after having been pope for two years. Urban II. succeeded him in the Roman pontificate, and Oderisius in the post of abbot; the latter was probably a relation of Leo's, and certainly showed him the same confidence and good will as his predecessor. It was the new abbot who commissioned him to write the life of Desiderius, and soon after enlarged the scope of the work by desiring him instead to write the whole history of the abbey from the earliest times. He could not have made a better choice than Leo for such an undertaking. He was specially fitted for it by his office of keeper of the archives, which gave him great facilities for acquainting himself with all the historical documents of the convent; also by his learning, and by his having always lived in the midst of monastic and state affairs, as well as by his intimate acquaintance with all the principal men who lived at Montecassino, or were in the habit of meeting there. He undertook the work at first with hesitation, but continued it earnestly, and related its origin and purpose in a dedicatory letter to the Abbot Oderisius.

"Thy beatitude, O most reverend father, had already commanded me to devote myself to writing for the remembrance of posterity the glorious deeds of thy predecessor, the Abbot Desiderius of holy memory, a man very remarkable, and in these days quite alone of his order. For thou didst judge it unworthy to imitate the sloth of the ancients of this place, who of so many abbots did not think of leaving any literary memorial, either of their deeds or times; and if by chance any one wrote about these things, it was so completely unmeaning and composed in so rude a style as to give more weariness than information to the readers. But thy paternity, striving anxiously to avert this from Desiderius, has been pleased to choose me for this work, imposing on me a burden certainly beyond my strength, so that; overcome by this consideration, I have already shrunk for a year from attempting it. Lately, therefore, when I was accompanying thee, according to my office, on thy return from Capua, thou didst remind me on the way of thy excellent command, asking me with interest whether I had fulfilled thy desire by writing out the deeds of Desiderius. But I, surprised by this sudden inquiry, was forced to answer according to the fact, that I had done nothing whatever. Then, regaining a little courage, I said: 'And when could I have obeyed thy command, when I have hardly been eight days following in the monastery for almost the whole of this year, sometimes by thy command in the service of our apostolic lord, sometimes occupied with thee in various matters? But does not this work demand no little leisure? nor is it possible for one who is busy to give himself to such a vast matter, but rather for one freed from all cares.' Then thou, having patiently listened to my arguments, and scolded me very gently for my negligence, didst say: 'And now take what leisure thou wishest, and add no further delays in writing about Desiderius. Nay, I also desire and command, since this matter has been delayed till this day, that now, making thy beginning from our Father Benedict, thou shouldst diligently inquire into the series, times, and deeds of all the abbots of our place up to this same Desiderius, and that thou shouldst compose a history in the form of a chronicle, very useful for us and for our successors, by scrupulously searching out the charters of emperors, dukes, and princes, as well as the documents of all the rest of the faithful, through which the lands or churches which we now see belonging to the monastery came into its possession, and under what abbots. Besides this, thou wilt not regret to note briefly in their proper places the destruction as well as restoration of this convent, which occurred on two separate occasions, besides whatever noble memories remain as to the works or deeds of distinguished men belonging to these parts.' After I began to meditate more attentively the importance of this command, there began also to increase in me many thorny thoughts as to whether or how I might fulfil it worthily, and not well comprehending from the poverty of my understanding, I did not know whether I had better choose to undertake or to decline so great a work, since in accepting it I felt guilty of rashness, and in declining it of disobedience. Besides, I remembered that my aforesaid lord, Desiderius, had formerly imposed this very work on Alfanus, archbishop of Salerno, the most learned man of our times, but that he, understanding well the great labour involved, had saved himself from such a danger. But if he who was incomparably superior in knowledge and eloquence was afraid of submitting to this burden, what was I to do, who possessed neither any knowledge nor any eloquence whatever? Moreover, it grieved my conscience that this work should not be committed by thee to some other of our brethren who are both far more learned than I am, and more accustomed to writing; such, namely, as the diligence of that same holy predecessor of thine had collected together into this place from different parts of the world, or had caused to be most carefully instructed in this same convent. So I was agitated by the uncertainty of these and similar thoughts, since the matter was certainly higher than I could reach, and more abstruse than I was capable of understanding. Yet, since from the attachment which I had always specially felt for thy paternity, I had long decided never to refuse thee anything, I at length made up my mind; and I who formerly had a cowardly fear of attempting only the deeds of Desiderius, now undertook to write in some manner those of all his predecessors, trusting in the assistance of God, and thus hoping to conclude everything by myself. Then I sought out such little writings as seemed to treat of this matter, composed in a ragged style and briefly, and chief of these the chronicle of the Abbot John, who was the first to construct our monastery at Capua Nova; also I collected the books necessary for this task, namely, the history of the Lombards, and the chronicles of the Roman emperors and pontiffs; likewise searched diligently for privileges and charters as well as concessions and documents with various titles (such as those of Roman pontiffs, of various emperors, kings, princes, dukes, counts, and other illustrious and faithful men), that were left to us after the two destructions by fire of this convent, although I could not find even all of them; lastly, I questioned scrupulously all who had either heard of or seen any deeds of modern times or of abbots: thus, according as the smallness of my judgment permits, I am attempting to do what thou hast commanded, more certainly from the obedience which I owe to thee as father and lord, than presuming on any knowledge of mine. May God be with me, and the grace of His Spirit, that I may fulfil this as efficaciously as thou didst diligently deign to command me; so may this little book be most pleasing to thee, and profitable to many. In the mean time I have thought it well to mention these things in this sort of little preface, providing for myself lest I should be accused by uninformed people of rashness or presumption, so that if I be accused heedlessly, the authority of him who commanded me may be my excuse."

Having thus begun his history, he carried it from the earliest beginnings of the abbey up to the year 1075, but could not continue it beyond that date, although he did not cease working at it even after being named cardinal bishop of Ostia by Paschal II., from which circumstance he has also been commonly called Leo Ostiensis. However, he was prevented by the interruptions of public affairs and of those troubled times from giving it his continued attention. He was in Rome at the time that Henry V. (A.D. 1111), having forcibly seized upon Pope Paschal in St. Peter's, carried him off as a prisoner into Sabina. Leo and John, cardinal bishop of Tusculum, were able to escape captivity by disguising themselves; and there seems no doubt that Leo, as well as John, sought to arouse the Romans to the determined resistance which they made to Henry's German troops. But although he was not taken prisoner, and did not sign the convention regarding the investitures extorted by force from the pope, still he found himself obliged by the exigencies of the times to yield, however unwillingly, and to join those prelates who, like the pope, preferred conciliatory measures to the system of "no surrender" upheld by others. Among these latter one of the principal was Bruno, bishop of Segni, and abbot of Montecassino, a man of great learning and of most blameless life, but steadfastly opposed to any reconciliation with the empire. The pope thought it dangerous to have such a centre of opposition at Montecassino, and therefore sent Leo there, who succeeded in bringing about the abdication of Bruno, and his withdrawal to his not distant bishopric of Segni. When Leo returned to Rome he took a great part in the Lateran Council of 1112, after which there remain but few traces of his life. We know indeed that he died on a twenty-second of May, but it is uncertain whether in the fifteenth, sixteenth, or seventeenth year of the twelfth century.

Besides the large supply of documents in the archives, Leo could also use in the compilation of his work the library of Montecassino, which furnished him with a rich supply of writings, bearing in some way on the history of the monastery.

The greater part of the writers of whom we have had to speak in these chapters were known to this learned monk, and he made copious use of them, besides drawing sometimes on sources now lost to us; while, in the later period of his narrative, he was able to add his personal testimony of what he had heard and seen of contemporary history. For superiority of mind and natural impartiality, Leo is one of the most trustworthy writers in that age, which was a time of strong partisan tendencies, and if he had had leisure to carry the work on to the last years of his life, perhaps we should to-day have to regard him as the greatest Italian historian of the earlier Middle Ages, next to Paulus Diaconus. Nor is the work of Leo less remarkable as a literary production, than as a contribution to history. We again quote with pleasure, on this point, the great living historian of Montecassino: "Then as to the form, we think that in the midst of much barbarism this Leo of Montecassino is the first to recall to us the Latin historians, and to give promise of those who would arise in Italy after the renaissance of letters. Neither in Italy, nor out of it, do we find any one who in those times approaches Leo, either for a certain connecting together of the facts, or for the reasoning and order in his manner of writing, whereby history is distinguished from the rude chronicle, which is nothing else but a material reproduction through writing of successive and incoherent notices of facts, dropping from the mind of the writer without a suggestion as to how or why they entered it. He himself feels that he is not a common writer of chronicles, for when deputed by the Abbot Oderisius to write the deeds of his predecessor Desiderius, he tells how they had thought it blameworthy that there had never been any one in the past who had undertaken to hand down in writing the labours of the ancient abbots, or if there was any one, he did it in so rude and uncouth a style as to cause the reader more weariness than instruction. He goes over the ground from St. Benedict to his own times; prepares himself studiously for the narrative he has undertaken; alludes to the sources whence he drew his information;... and under a veil of religious humility reveals the consciousness of having done more than others in this narrative which the very Alfanus would not undertake when called upon to do so by Desiderius; therefore he considers the title of chronicle unworthy of his work, and ventures to call it *historiola*. Hence, both for its truthfulness and for its form, this chronicle throws much light upon the history of the Middle Ages."[1]

---

[1] Tosti, *La Biblioteca dei codici manoscritti di Montecassino*. See also what the learned father writes about the times of Desiderius in his history of Montecassino. And to mention other judgments, Baronius calls Leo Ostiensis *scriptor sui temporis integerrimus*, Muratori speaks of his *magnæ gravitatis et auctoritatis*, and Wattenbach, who edited his works for the *Monumenta Germaniæ*, regards him as most trustworthy.

This work of Leo's, which breaks off with the account of the consecration of the restored abbey, was taken again in hand by Petrus Diaconus, and continued up to the year 1138. Peter was a descendant of the illustrious family of the counts of Tusculum, and was born about 1107, son of the Roman Egidius, grandson of the Patrician Gregory, and great grandson of Alberic and Marozia. Offered as a child in 1115 to the monastery under the Abbot Giraldus, he was educated there with care, studying principally under the superintendence of the monk Guido—a man, by his pupil's account, of great reputation, and the author of several historical works now lost, and of a "Vision of Alberic," which has remained famous from some people finding in it the idea which may first have inspired the "Divine Comedy." In 1128 the hostility of the counts of Aquino, with whom Peter's father had joined himself in close alliance, led to the Abbot Seniorectus sending the young monk away from Montecassino. Peter then retired to the neighbouring Atina, where, at the request of Atenolfus, the count of that city, he wrote the history of St. Mark's martyrdom, that saint having been the first bishop of the see of Atina in the apostolic times. During Peter's exile, his uncles, from whom his father had separated in order to join the counts of Aquino, wrote asking him to try if he could induce his father to become again their friend. Nothing is known with certainty about it, but it appears that Peter agreed to the wishes of his relations; certainly, not long after, we find him on amicable terms with them, and back at Montecassino in favour with the Abbot Seniorectus, who later deputed him to continue the history of the abbey, giving him many details regarding it of which he had himself been eye-witness. But in the meantime, before being entrusted with this work, he had gained a reputation by other writings. Being nominated, like Leo, keeper of the archives and librarian of the abbey, his quick and versatile talents, combined with his southern vivacity, led him soon to enter on a wide course of literary activity. At different times, and amidst many occupations, he copied a number of manuscripts, wrote lives of saints, stories of miracles, verses and letters, compiled a large register of the documents kept in the archives, related the lives of the more illustrious monks of the monastery, and continued the work which Leo Ostiensis had left unfinished. Peter was less mixed up than Leo in the political events of his day, and his numerous cares were almost all limited to the narrow circle of his convent, which explains both the number of his writings and the considerable size of some of them. The descent of Lothair into the south of Italy (A.D. 1137), constitutes the most eventful period of his life, which he relates to us with boastful self-complacency. In his day, the struggle about the investitures being at an end

Montecassino showed, as far as was possible, an inclination to look to the Empire for support against the frequent pretensions of the Norman princes and the Roman court. The abbey found that dependence on a distant emperor was far less disturbing than her temporal and spiritual relations with powerful neighbours. When Lothair and Pope Innocent II. were together near Melfi at Lago Pesole, Peter accompanied his abbot thither, and was there deputed to sustain, in the presence of the emperor, the rights of the monastery against the claims put forward in the Church's name by the Cardinal Gerardus. His easy and subtle eloquence carried off the victory after a dispute of several days, and the emperor was so astonished at such learning and eloquence, that he took the monk into high favour, heaping honours upon him and expressing a wish to take him back to Germany. This at least is Peter's account, and it really does appear that he would have followed the emperor, had not many causes combined to prevent it, and to keep him in Italy and in his convent. The date of his death is uncertain, but there is great probability in Wattenbach's conjecture which would fix it soon after 1140. The fact is that after that year we have no further notice of him, and it does not seem natural that so fertile a writer, who in the course of about ten years had begun and completed so many works, should have suddenly ceased writing and become absolutely silent.

Without taking into account his minor works, we find that the claims of Petrus Diaconus on our attention rest on several historical works full of good and bad points. His books on the illustrious men of Montecassino, and on the lives and deaths of the holy men of that monastery, contain a mixture of miraculous legends and of most valuable historical information, especially concerning the period nearest the author's lifetime. But his two most important works are the Register of Montecassino and the continuation of its chronicle. If the honourable love of truth which distinguished Gregory of Catino and Leo Ostiensis had also animated Petrus Diaconus, certainly the value of these two works, and especially of the chronicle, would be incalculable, but unfortunately this was not so. The doubts which he constantly inspires in us are very different from the security with which we can trust ourselves to the narrative of Leo. This latter is simple, impartial, truthful; Peter vain, passionate, and insincere. His compilation of the Register is a great work and very useful, although most of the original documents still exist in the archives of Montecassino. This book, written in a beautiful Lombard hand, is very nearly as large as the Farfa Register, but differs from it in the arrangement of its contents. The documents do not follow each other simply in the chronological order, but are divided instead into various groups according to their various characters, and, as appears from some words in the preface, according to a plan already initiated by Leo. "But in this work," says Peter, "the history of the venerable Leo, bishop of Ostia, was of the greatest service to us; for he, beginning from our most blessed Father Benedict, wrote a book most valuable for everything relating to the convent of Montecassino, in which he showed such a profusion of knowledge, that he hardly omits anything which happened in that convent. So that, following in the footsteps of so great a man, I shall not indeed be able to reach to him with my poor faculties, yet have I retained the order of the oblations just as he determined them." This work of Peter's has been often and profitably consulted by the learned, and it would be desirable that the monks of Montecassino, when they have finished the splendid description which they are making of their manuscripts, should undertake the publication of a *codex diplomaticus*, of their original documents, compared with the Register of Petrus Diaconus and completed from it. But if his work is valuable, it is not, however, to be received without much reserve. Both his own disposition and a tendency of his day contributed to render it untrustworthy. The constant contests about monastic property, often also as to the origin and authenticity of relics preserved in the convents, not only led the monks to compile Registers, but led also too often to fabrications and unscrupulous alterations of documents. Nor was Peter free from this fault, to which his vain disposition rendered him specially liable, from the desire to find imaginary nobility of origin and circumstance for his monastery which was already so noble and famous in reality. Even if we cannot affirm that he actually fabricated false documents, there is certainly no doubt that he sometimes wittingly altered with interpolations the originals which he copied into his Register. And the same want of honesty is an ugly blot on his chronicle, which, starting as we said from the point where Leo had stopped (A.D. 1075), continues up to the year 1138, and thus embraces the most remarkable historical period of that momentous age. Moreover, in this latter work, to the vanity of the monk for his monastery, is added the boastfulness of the man with regard to his lineage and himself; so that, wherever his book refers to the interests of the abbey or to his own person, whom he never fails to mention, its authority cannot be ever implicitly relied upon. Nevertheless the importance of the times gives a special value to his narrative, and in spite of these failings, we find it pleasant reading in consequence of the off-hand outspokenness of his style, which is attractive and often lays bare the mind of the writer, who was a strange mixture of ingenuousness and craft. Another thing in which he also differed from Leo was that, while the latter, though taking his information from many sources, always composed the narrative himself, Peter, on the contrary, often copies whole passages from other writers, and transfers them in the very same words to his own book, from which results a great inequality of style. But the original part of his work, though sometimes too hastily and carelessly written, is always graphic, full of life and colour, and, notwithstanding his defects, Petrus Diaconus always remains a curious and entertaining writer, whom any one, anxious to be familiar with the historical literature of this age, will find it worth his while to read.[1]

The great artistic and literary revival at Montecassino was associated with a similar movement in the whole of southern Italy, where, in consequence of its immediate contact with the Greeks and Arabs, the fertilizing influence of two civilizations had succeeded in penetrating. The instincts, resembling those later exhibited by the Medicis, which Desiderius had carried with him into the cloister, were the instincts of the Lombard princes from which he sprang. The great Lombard nobles of that part of Italy, who had already in the times

---

[1] Another register, called that of St. Placidus, noteworthy though of less importance, is still kept at Montecassino, and is also the work of Petrus Diaconus. There as well are preserved two other interesting registers of the same age, belonging to convents connected with Montecassino, that of St. Angelus *in Formis*, a monastery in the territory of Capua, and that of the monastery of St. Matthew, the ruins of which still exist on a mountain very near the mother abbey.

of Paulus Diaconus shown themselves protectors of literature, now having gradually grown into greater harmony with the native tendencies, had, in doing so, imbibed both the virtues and faults peculiar to them, as well as to the elements which remained of Greek rule. This was how it happened that those regions awoke so readily to new civilizing life, and exercised such useful influence for some centuries to come on general civilization. And witness is borne to this first awakening, not only by the monastic labours of Montecassino, but also by various other works of an historical character, which we shall now mention in order to be free to turn to other subjects in the next chapter.[1] Lupus Protospatarius has left us some accounts of the city of Bari on the Adriatic up to the year 1102, and later the *Anonymus Barensis* has done the same till the year 1152. Benevento possesses annals which reach the year 1130, and a chronicle which unfortunately is in-

---

[1] *Annales Barenses* and *Annales Lupi Protospatarii*, in Monumenta Germaniæ Historica. Script., vol. v. *Anonymus Barensis*, in Muratori, Rerum Italicarum Script., vol. v. *Annales Beneventani* and *Chronicon Ducum Beneventi*, in Mon. Germ. Hist. Script., vol. iii. *Falconis Beneventani Chronicon*, in Muratori, op. cit., vol. v. *Annales Cavenses*, in Mon. Germ. Hist. Script., vol. iii., and more recently an important edition in the *Codex Diplomaticus Cavensis*, vol. v. *Chronicon Normanicum Breve*, in Muratori, op. cit., vol. v. *Guillermi Apuliensis, Gesta Roberti Wiscardi*, in Mon. Germ. Hist. Script., vol. ix. *Gaufredi Malaterra Historia Sicula*, in Muratori, op. cit., vol. v. *Alexandri Telesini, de Rebus gestis Rogerii Siciliae Regis*, ibid.

complete and rudely written, but of great historical value. In the same way there are the annals of the famous monastery of the Trinity at La Cava, near Salerno, which had been rebuilt about that time, and solemnly consecrated by Urban II.—an account of the consecration having also come down to us. We find information about the first Norman invaders in the *chronicon normannicum breve*, of Taranto. Of the monk Amatus, who wrote at more length about the Normans, we have already spoken, and where his work breaks off there comes in to complete it the epic poem of William of Apulia, who celebrates Robert Guichard and the exploits of his Normans. A tolerably good poet for his day, and sufficiently acquainted with the classical writers, he sings the deeds of his hero in hexameters sprinkled with quotations from Virgil. His work, undertaken at the desire of Urban II., and dedicated to Roger the son of Robert, in addition to the merit of having been written at times and in places near the events, shows a good knowledge of preceding writers, and, among these, of a biographer of Robert's of whom we have to-day no traces left. A contemporary of the poet William, Godfrey Malaterra composed at the command of the great Count Roger a most valuable history of the Normans in Sicily, written in a fluent style, and full of information, also, regarding the mutual relations of the Normans and Pope Urban. The abbot Alexander of Telese related the deeds of King

Roger with great partiality and affected elegance, while showing considerable knowledge of the subject. We see, therefore, that the great Norman epic was not without writers to celebrate it, and the newly awakened historical spirit found in those exploits such wide ground as no longer to yield to the legendary tendencies of a former age.

And it is certain that the imagination began now to turn to human interests, with their living truths and strong ideals, so that the twilight of legendary story gave way to the full daylight of historical research, and took refuge in popular tradition, or in some obscure monastic writing destined to receive unexpected attention centuries later. And so it was that, far distant from the scenes of which we have been speaking, in the valley of Susa on the slopes of the Mont Cenis, a monk belonging to the monastery of the Novalesa was collecting the traditions concerning the descent of Charlemagne into Italy, and so preserved memories of a cycle of legends which later inspired the medieval troubadours and poets, threw a glamour over Ariosto's fancies, and in our day added grace to the thoughtful muse of Manzoni, who in the tragedy of "Adelchi" combined them with historical facts. The real history of this convent of the Novalesa is the same as that of so many others of that time. Founded in the year 726, destroyed by the Saracens in 906 or in 916, restored about the year 1000, it had, towards the middle of the eleventh century, among its monks one belonging to the territory of Vercelli, who wrote the chronicle of the monastery.[1] This strange and fragmentary work has come down to us in the same old parchment roll on which the author wrote it, with interruptions, at long intervals, and without ever completing it. It begins almost immediately, drawing upon popular traditions for its inspiration, with the fabulous legend of a gardener monk of royal birth called Walter, who achieved wonderful exploits in defence of the convent; and this is the same Walter, son of a king of Aquitania, and taken as hostage by Attila, whose story belongs also to the Niebelungen, the Scandinavian Wilkina-Saga, and the whole cloud of heroic traditions which surround Attila. And after these follow other legends concerning Charlemagne, which have this great importance that they relate what in less than three centuries the popular imagination had created regarding the facts which had taken place among those very mountains where the monk collected them. The vision of Charlemagne, the hospitality he met with at the Novalesa, the *jongleur* who taught Charles the pass by which he might cross the Alps and surprise the rear of the Lombards, the taking of Pavia, the sufferings of the Lombard king Desiderius, and the extraordinary prowess of

---

[1] *Chronicon Novaliciense*, in Mon. Germ. Hist. Script., vol. vii.

his son Adelchi, are all so many legendary episodes full of poetry and feeling. A special value of this chronicle of the Novalesa, in which it differs from the learned chronicles of the monks of Southern Italy, is that it has preserved the impressions of the people, impressions which long outlast their original causes. Going backwards to the Lombard age where Paulus Diaconus leaves us, we can, by the light of this old parchment, give some colouring to the scanty notices which we succeed in extracting from vast registers and unadorned chronicles; for if this writing, born at the foot of the Alps, is rather poetry than history, it is certainly poetry which recalls the life of past ages, and repeats it to us after centuries of silence, just as the mountains which form a majestic circle round the ruins of the Novalesa, repeat the long and solitary echo of a sound that is hushed.

CHAPTER V.

THE LATER CONTRIBUTIONS TO THE "PONTIFICAL BOOK"—BRUNO OF SEGNI—WIBERT OF TOUL—PAUL OF BERNRIED—"ANNALES ROMANI"—PETRUS PISANUS—PANDULPH—BOSO—POLEMICAL WRITINGS—ST. PETER DAMIANI—BONIZO'S "LIBER AD AMICUM"—THE LIFE OF ANSELM OF LUCCA—DOMNIZO'S LIFE OF THE COUNTESS MATILDA—THE LETTERS OF GREGORY VII.

"THE blessed Pope Gregory (VII.) used to relate to us many things touching this man (Leo IX.), and it is from him that I remember having heard most of what I have been telling hitherto. Now one day when speaking of him (Leo), he began to reprove us, and me especially (so at least it seemed to me, since he kept his eyes fixed on me), for not commemorating the deeds of the blessed Leo, and not writing what would redound to the glory of the Roman Church, and be an example of humility to many hearers."[1] These words of Bruno, bishop of Segni, show how, on the revival of authority and vigour in the Roman See, the need of a pontifical book was again felt, and the popes themselves sought to encourage the undertaking. And in fact in the eleventh century we find the lives of the popes, beginning with that of Leo IX. (d. 1049), related at great length by writers of some merit who often had been eye-witnesses of the events or nearly so, and connected with them in some way. Thus, for instance, the words which we have just quoted, occur in the life of Leo IX., written by that very Bishop Bruno, who was also abbot of Montecassino, and who in the former chapter showed himself so zealous and active a partisan in the struggle of the Investitures. But this work of his has little value, and was surpassed by others which were composed about the same time, such as a pathetic account of Leo's death, written in Rome by the priest Libuinus, the guardian of his tomb, and full of real facts as well as of miraculous legends. Also the life written by a monk of Benevento, which is very important for what it tells us of the imprudent expedition of Leo's against the Normans, and of the imprisonment

---

[1] The importance of these words has been already pointed out with great judgment by Watterich, in the preface of his work on the lives of the popes, a collection which has been of great use to us in writing this chapter. *Pontificum Romanorum Vitæ, ab æqualibus conscriptæ*, edidit I. M. Watterich, Lipsiæ, 1862.

which followed his defeat. Of still greater importance are two other works by two Germans,[1] Wibert of Toul, and Paul of Bernried, who wrote very diffusely, the first on Leo IX., the second on Gregory VII. Wibert, who was an intimate of Leo's when this latter was bishop of Toul, especially abounds in details of his early history, but of the remainder, although meritorious, he does not give us so complete an account as not to oblige us to look elsewhere for further materials towards his life.[2] Turning to the history of Gregory VII., left by Paul of Bernried, we find that it was written when the struggle of the Investitures was at an end, and in it we still hear the echo of the old dissensions, while the moral power of Gregory is magnified as if to admonish his adversaries of the risk they would run in renewing that great struggle. Having embraced an ecclesiastical career in 1102, Paul was ordained priest in 1120, but owing to his persecution by the Emperor Henry V., he took refuge in the following year at Bernried, in the diocese of Augsburg. In 1122 he proceeded to

---

[1] We should here notice that many German annalists of the eleventh century and beginning of the twelfth are of great use for the history of the papacy, which at that time was so intimately connected with the history of Germany. As it is beyond our province to examine them here, we content ourselves with mentioning that among the most important of these annalists are Berthold, Bernold of Constance, and Lambert of Hersfeld, whose writings deserve careful attention from the student of Italian history.

[2] Ap. Watterich, *Vitæ Pontificum*.

Rome, and there perhaps he first thought of writing the life of Gregory VII., for which no doubt he then collected materials, studied the register of the Gregorian letters, and made inquiries touching his hero's vicissitudes of the eye-witnesses who survived, and among the rest of the pope himself, Calixtus II. After his return to Bernried, he applied himself to his work, and completed it in 1128. He tells his story simply, and without displaying much critical ability, but his sources of information are generally good, he makes free and constant use of official documents, and he writes of what occurred fifty years before his own day with a tone of firm and ingenuous conviction which has a reassuring effect on the mind of his reader. He often has recourse to the supernatural for the explanation of his facts, to which he frequently adds legendary episodes, but he does it with so much simplicity and good faith that the modern critic has no difficulty in distinguishing between them and the trustworthy portion of the narrative, in which, taken as a whole, we find that dramatic age wonderfully reproduced. Villemain, an artistic historian who has painted in brilliant colours the life of Gregory VII.,[1] made large use of this biographer in order to add vivacity to his picture, especially in describing that stormy Christmas night in which a noble Roman, called Cencius,

---

[1] Villemain, *Histoire de Grégoire VII.*, Paris, Didier, 1872.

entered St. Maria Maggiore, tore Gregory from the altar, and dragged him wounded and a prisoner to his tower. We give here part of this scene as related by the old chronicler, whom it is interesting to compare with the modern historian, since it shows us how the vivid impressions of this simple priest of the Middle Ages have served to inspire one of the finest pages of French historical literature in this century.

" The night has come in which the son of darkness attacks the minister of light. First he sends out an exploring party to make inquiries, and they, calling together a certain set who lived in the street near the church, and hearing everything from them, sent notice of all that they heard to that villain, who lost no time in putting his men into armour and so disposing matters that each man might find a horse ready, in case any one should think of rising against them, after they had been successful either in compassing his death or in carrying him off alive. At last they came to the church, where the pope with great solemnity was chanting the midnight mass before the manger, according to the teaching of the Church, and received the Lord's body, he and all the clergy with him, the others also who were present partaking of the same sacrament, when suddenly a great noise and shouting arose and filled the whole church. Then searching everywhere and striking all they met with their drawn swords, they made for the place of the manger, where the pope was enthroned high above all, and there, having struck some of those near and broken the doors, they were able to touch with their violent hands a small portion of the manger of the Eternal King and His Mother. Then they laid hands on the pontiff and seized him; and one indeed, brandishing his sword, tried to cut off his head, but the Lord was pleased to prevent him. Yet was he struck on the head and severely wounded, and finally they dragged him with violence from the church before the mass was finished, dealing out on all sides slaughter and blows. But he, like an innocent and gentle lamb, raising his eyes to heaven, returned them no answer, complained not nor resisted, nor did he ask that they should have mercy upon him. At length, having divested him of the pall and chasuble, the dalmatic and tunic, and leaving him only the linen vestment and stole, they dragged him like a thief and placed him behind a sacrilegious fellow on horseback. But that other who had struck him on the forehead with a sword was seized by the devil, and for a long time rolled, foaming at the mouth, before the vestibule of that very church, while his horse fled away, nor was it ever again found.

"... So all the clergy, their shepherd being struck down, ran hither and thither, and dismantled almost all the altars, nor were Divine services held in any of the churches on that day, except what had preceded this event. But the elements, which up to that time had been so disturbed, became calm in order not to hinder the people who were zealous in the zeal of the Lord, and the earth absorbing nearly all the water which had collected during that heavy downpour, showed a dry surface to all who were ready to avenge this deed. So the whole night through signals and trumpets were sounded, and the soldiers patrolled all the roads, lest by any subterfuge he should be carried out of the city, but no trace of him could be found. Then while all were in doubt and ignorance even whether he were alive or dead, certain persons made it known to the crowds gathered together in the Capitol, that he was held captive in a certain tower. Then all the people began to raise their voices to the skies, and as soon as daylight had returned to the earth, they encouraged each other, and made for the house of that antichrist in immense numbers. So the battle began ; but at the very first attack the hostile party took to flight, and the whole faction shut itself up in that same tower. Then fire was set to the whole of the fortifications, and engines and battering rams being brought, the wall was broken, and everything within the enclosure became the prey of the people of God. No one heeded his own danger, but each man, forgetful of himself, fought with might and main.

"But a certain man, together with a certain noble matron, had followed the Father Gregory, and they were of some comfort to him. For the man warmed him, suffering as he was from the length of the way he had been dragged and the cold of a winter night, with furs which he had brought, and cherished his feet in his bosom, while that matron fomented our father's wound, all wet from the great flow of blood, with medicaments, weeping and denouncing all those men as enemies of God and sacrilegious murderers; acting like another Mary, for as that one, bewailing her sins, had washed the Lord's feet with her tears, so this one, declaring the crimes of all those men, was bathing with her tears this great shepherd. . . .

"But great as was her courageous fidelity, equally great was another woman's perfidy of tongue. For as formerly, in the time of the Lord's Passion, the maiden who kept the gate had terrified Peter, so this one disturbed his vicar with biting insults. And she was the sister of that traitor, and for this reason did not hesitate to curse this great father. But there was another servant also and follower of the traitor who, holding a drawn sword, declared with blasphemies that he would, that very same day, cut off this great man's head. Yet the swift judgment of God was not slow in avenging his impiety. For a lance hurled from without and transfixing his throat, the passage of his cruel voice, flung him to earth dying and gasping, and thus despatched him to hell. . . .

"Finally the pious pope, standing in the window with outstretched hands, commanded the excited crowd to be calm, and to let some of the principal people come up to him in the tower. Some, however, fancying that he was urging them on to the work they had begun, made a great effort and broke into the tower. And so he was taken into the open air, the whole populace weeping for joy and compassion; for now they could see how he was covered with blood, which struck them with such horror that they all raised their voices to the skies. After this victory, following Pope Gregory to the same church of the Mother of God from which he had that night been dragged, they all congregated there, their hearts filled with no small joy. Then, at that same hour, their common father finished the mass which those ministers of Satan had stopped in the night, and gave them the blessing of God upon their victory.

"But the son of perdition had, in the meantime, escaped with all his family and his dependants, and, far from repenting, led a worse life than before, collecting around him many others like himself, and continuing, while he lived and when he could, to devise evil against him who had preserved him."[1]

Party contests now more than ever seconded the revival of history in connection with the papacy, each side hoping to find support in a narrative of

---

[1] Ap. Watterich, *Vitæ Pontificum*, i., p. 501, et seq. Paul of Bernried has also left us the account of the life and miracles of the blessed Herluca, a saintly visionary who died in 1142, and with whom he was on terms of close friendship.

the facts; and since it is but very rarely that men can judge of facts quite irrespectively of the persons who are responsible for them, the lives of the popes are very frequently represented in a favourable or unfavourable light according to the sympathies of the writer. In Rome itself some writings were produced by these contending parties, which have been published under the name of Roman Annals,[1] and exhibit the two contrary currents of thought in that day. The first of these writings, intended really to continue the old *Liber Pontificalis*, contains the lives of the various popes who followed each other at short intervals between the years 1044 and 1049. This writing, anonymous like all the others of this collection, is carefully composed, and full of details relating to the affairs of the town and of the noble families of Rome. Two other narratives follow this, which include the series of popes from Leo IX. to Alexander II. (1049–1072), written by partisans of the Empire, and consequently enemies to the papacy. On the other hand, the latter is favoured in another writing, which gives us a simple and graphic description of the violence to which Paschal II. was subjected in the Vatican, when Henry dragged him away from Rome as a prisoner. This writer was present at the occurrences which he relates, for he tells us: " We have written down the exact

---

[1] *Mon. Germ. Hist. Script.*, vol. v., and republished by Watterich, op. cit.

truth of these things just as we suffered them, saw them with our eyes, and heard them with our ears;" and he goes on to describe also the lives of the antipopes who set themselves up against Paschal II. and Gelasius II. The last continuation reaches later times, and embraces the short papacies which followed each other quickly between Lucius III. and Clement III. (1181–1188), and the controversies of these popes with Frederick Barbarossa. All these writings are biased, exaggerated both in praise and blame, and we find in all of them the party predilections of the authors, yet from having been composed on the spot, and while the events were happening, they are full of useful information, and, from a literary point of view, their rude and popular Latin is not without interest on account of its Italian forms of expression, suggesting the great change in language which that age of transformations was preparing for Italy.

Besides this collection of pontifical lives, which may to a certain extent be regarded as a popular continuation of the ancient *Liber Pontificalis*, there is another continuation of a more official character, written almost under the eyes of the popes, by two dignitaries of the Curia, Petrus Pisanus and Pandulph. The first of these writers, doubtless a native of Pisa, was already in the Curia in the time of Urban II., about 1094, while still very young, as notary of the apostolic palace, and continued in that office until he was named cardinal deacon, between 1104 and 1116, during the pontificate of Paschal II. When in 1108 the pope was obliged to go into Apulia, it appears that Peter was chosen to remain, together with Ptolemy of Tusculum, and Walfred, chief of the soldiery, in the territory of the lower Marittima round Terracina, in order to guard the rights of the Church. If this was so, the choice was a good one, for this was the only province which remained to a great extent quiet and loyal, while Rome and its neighbourhood were kept in a state of disturbance by the nobility opposed to the pope, and Ptolemy himself went over to the rebels. In the following year the pope returned to Rome, and Peter seems to have returned with him, but for some years we cannot follow his movements with any certainty.[1] When the crusaders from Pisa

---

[1] We think it prudent to speak hesitatingly of many details in the life of Petrus Pisanus. Watterich, who has devoted several most valuable pages to this author, appears to us to affirm with too much certainty as fact what is often only probable and ingenious hypothesis. And sometimes some of these hypotheses seem to us more ingenious than probable. For instance, not seeing Peter's name among those whom Henry V. made prisoners together with the pope in 1111, Watterich thinks that he may have escaped in disguise, like the Cardinals John of Tusculum and Leo Ostiensis, and may with them have incited the Roman people to take up arms against the Germans. But this does not appear to us admissible even as an hypothesis. Such a fact could hardly have passed unnoticed, and we think it more likely either that he was not in Rome at the time, or that he was not yet cardinal, and thus his doings did not receive so much attention as they were destined to receive later.

made a victorious expedition to the Balearic Isles against the Saracens (1114, 1115), he was apparently there with his country people, and has left us an account of their deeds, of which we shall have occasion to speak. He certainly was cardinal in 1116, and we find him again in Rome, commissioned by Paschal II. to quell a tumult; and when not successful, endeavouring at least to protect the old pope's life, which was menaced with danger by the Roman rebels. Afterwards, when the pope was compelled to fly, Peter, still in Rome, was one of those cardinals who refused to consecrate Henry V., who had returned to Rome to receive the imperial crown. He joined the sick pope later at Anagni, and took part in the election of Gelasius II., whose troubled destiny and exile he shared, remaining faithful to him and to his two successors, Calixtus II. and Honorius II. After the death of this last, there was schism in the Church, and Petrus Pisanus, being on the side of the antipope Anacletus against Innocent II., was for eight years regarded as the soul of the schism on account of his learning and eloquence. At last, after a warm and lengthy discussion, carried on at Salerno in presence of King Roger, St. Bernard prevailed upon him to desert the antipope (A.D. 1137). It is strange that although this was a conversion of the greatest use to his cause, Innocent II. should have tried to deprive Peter of his dignity as cardinal, and perhaps he would have really done so had not St. Bernard opposed with great vigour such an act of injustice, in a letter to the pope which well depicts the ardent nature of this apostolic man. "To you," he wrote to the pope—"to you I appeal, judge you between me and you! In what, I ask, has your son deserved so badly from your paternity that you should be pleased to brand and design him with the marks and name of a traitor? For did not your grace appoint me as your vicar in the reconciliation of Petrus Pisanus, if perchance God would deign to recall him through me from the filth of schism? If you deny this I will prove it by as many witnesses as were in the Curia at that time. And was not this man, after these things, finally received into his order and dignity according to the word of my lord? Who then has by counsel, or rather by fraud, obtained that things promised are withdrawn, and the words which proceeded from your lips made of no effect? And this I say, not in order to blame the apostolic severity and zeal which has kindled the fire of God against the schismatics . . . but . . . neither is it fitting that there should be involved in the same sentence he who abandoned his sin with those whom rather their sins abandoned. For His sake, who, to save sinners, spared not Himself, remove this ignominy from me, and by restoring him whom you established, consult also thereby your own sound and upright reputation." Nor was this letter written in vain. Petrus Pisanus continued to be cardinal, and in that character took part in the Lateran council of 1139, and died in this dignity at an advanced age, in the year 1144. The histories of the popes who governed the Church from Leo IX. to Calixtus II. (1049–1124), may be in a way regarded as so many acts of a drama which culminates in the pontificate of Gregory VII. All those pontificates had a single aim, and struggled for a principle, which the monk Hildebrand sustained before becoming pope, and, when he died, left as a legacy to his successors. From which we can easily understand why the pontifical book once more treats on a larger scale the lives of the popes, beginning with Leo IX., since with him also begins a new period in the history of the Church. In the words quoted above, according to which Gregory VII. exhorted Bruno of Segni to speak of Leo, we already catch a glimpse of this idea, and the same is followed out by Petrus Pisanus. Indeed, he has left us an almost uninterrupted series of the lives of the popes during that period, two of which, those of Gregory VII. and Urban II., are valuable for their many precise details; but superior to all, and showing a wide and searching knowledge of the facts, is that of Paschal II. What we have said of the personal experiences of Peter during this latter papacy will have sufficiently indicated the facilities he had for knowing the exact state of things, and the importance of his testimony. He was a man of great talent and eloquence, "of whom," says John of Salisbury, "there was hardly the equal in the whole Curia;" he was well acquainted with all the most important official documents with which he completed his narrative, quoting from them, and sometimes giving the whole of them. He thus depicts very vividly the course of that long and momentous pontificate, and writes in a pure style and with a serenity of judgment extremely rare in his day. In this last respect he may be compared to his illustrious contemporary and companion in the purple, Leo Ostiensis, to whom he is, however, very inferior; for Leo is a true historian and works upon a wide canvas, whereas Peter, as a biographer, has to remain within narrower limits. In another work, which we shall mention later, he gave more freedom to his imagination; but in this he wisely restrains it, for in a narrative of events which touched him so nearly he might easily have fallen into exaggeration, and lost sight of that just measure and sober treatment of the subject which should be the special care of all authors.

The very active personal part which Petrus Pisanus was obliged to take in the events of his day, forced him to discontinue the compilation of the pontifical book, which was then carried on by Pandulph, descendant of a noble Roman family and an officer of the Curia from the time of Paschal II. During the schism he, like Peter, took part with the antipope Anacletus, and by him was made cardinal, but, when the schism ceased, his rank does not seem to have been recognized, and we have no further record of him. He wrote the lives of Gelasius II., Calixtus II., and Honorius II., the two latter but briefly, the former more at length, and it is the best written and most important of the lives which we have from his pen. Unlike his predecessors, Pandulph does not bring forward documents to support his story, but draws upon his memory for the materials of his work. The story he has to tell is of things seen and suffered by himself in very anxious times. His pictures are vivid and graphic, and the dramatic force and feeling with which he depicts them, reproduces and fixes in the reader's imagination that agitated past just as he had himself experienced it. Thus, for instance, no one who has read it will forget the scene as described by him of the painful flight to Gaeta of the old and careworn Pope Gelasius II., escaping from a sudden attack made upon him by Henry V. (A.D. 1118).

There succeeded to this Roman Pandulph, in the compilation of the pontifical lives, an Englishman, Cardinal Boso, who held his title from the church of St. Pudenziana. He appears to have first belonged to the Curia about the year 1147, when Eugenius III. was in France, and continued in his office of apostolic writer until the elevation to the papal throne of Adrian IV., the only Englishman who ever filled the Roman See. Then Boso, as he himself tells us, "having been appointed his chamberlain from the beginning of his apostolate and ordained (cardinal) deacon in the church of the holy Cosma and Damianus, remained with him constantly and intimately until his death." Raised in this manner to the dignity of cardinal, he managed the papal finances with great care, reduced to subjection some rebellious vassals of the Church, and went as legate to England. After the death of Adrian he warmly supported the election of Alexander III., opposed by the Emperor Frederick I., and until the election was over protected the conclave sitting in St. Peter's from the armed threats which surrounded it. From Alexander he received the title of cardinal priest of St. Pudenziana, and shared with him in the famous struggle revived between Empire and papacy which, transformed into a national movement by the league of the Lombard communes, weakened the power of the Empire at the battle of Legnano. After the peace of Anagni, Boso was present at the meeting in Venice between pope and emperor, and followed the pope on his return to Rome, March 12, 1178. Soon after that, all mention of him in the pontifical registers ceases, and we may infer that his life closed about this time.

Boso's work embraces, with but little interruption, the history of the popes from Stephen VI. till Adrian IV. and Alexander III., but can lay claim to be original only in these two last pontificates.[1] For all the rest he reproduces almost verbally the old catalogues and what had been written by the pontifical writers before his time, and especially for the eleventh century by Petrus Pisanus, Pandulph, and in the *Liber ad Amicum* of Bonizo, of which we are about to speak. But if the first part of Boso's work is a mere useless repetition, the second and longer portion makes ample compensation for this. His intimacy with the two popes of whom he writes, his high position in the Church, the varied and arduous offices which he held, and which procured for him a personal acquaintance with all the principal men in Europe, made Boso an invaluable biographer. Less talented than Petrus Pisanus, less graphic than Pandulph, he is at the same time more diffuse, more precise than they are, and gives us in minute detail all the events which took place in the Curia at that time, and their connection with the general events of the age. The first disagreements between Adrian and Frederick Barbarossa, the death of Arnold of Brescia, the relations

---

[1] This work of Boso's, republished recently by Watterich in his *Vitæ Pontificum*, was preserved to us by Cencius Camerarius (later Pope Honorius III.), who in 1192 inserted it into his *Liber censuum Romanæ Ecclesiæ*, an ill-composed compilation but historically valuable, which was extracted from the archives and intended to serve as a register of all the sources of Church income. A fragment by another Englishman, John of Salisbury, very important for the history of Eugenius III., was published under the name of *Historia Pontificalis* in *Mon. Germ. Hist. Script.*, vol. xx.

of the pope with Southern Italy, the struggle of Alexander III. and the Lombard league against the Empire, and finally the interview between pope and emperor at Venice are the most salient features in the large picture which Boso has given us. His narrative, which may be said to close this older part of the pontifical book, makes us feel that we have entered on a new phase of history; the perusal of these two lives brings before us the rapid transformations which society was then undergoing, and we catch a glimpse of fresh and wide horizons disclosing the new destinies which we shall presently meet with in the municipal chronicles. And, indeed, Boso gives much important testimony to the relations of the papacy, not only with the Empire, but also with the Italian municipalities, both when he quotes from documents in the pontifical archives, and when he describes from memory things which he has seen. Especially for the study of the history of Rome itself, he appears to us worthy of more attention than he has hitherto received, as enabling us to correct the exaggerations of the imperial partisans too exclusively followed by some modern historians. Nor in this work of correction and comparison must we adopt all that Boso says without criticism, and it is only by weighing impartially the writings of the two parties against each other that we can arrive at that exact truth which can seldom be expected from one, however well intentioned he may be, who has taken an active part in the events of which he writes. And least of all could we expect it from Boso. Even without taking into account the personal affection he felt for both the popes whose lifes he wrote, it would not have been possible for any man to avoid all party feeling in that period of romantic struggles, when for a moment the national cause in Italy was interwoven with that of the Church, and the resistance made by the Lombards to a foreign foe seemed to take the proportions of a holy war.

But while following the course of the pontifical book we have left the eleventh century far behind, and we must now retrace our steps. The dispute regarding the Investitures, long, obstinate, and violent, gave rise to many polemical writings which have also more or less historical value, and of which some deserve the name of history. We have already mentioned the *Orthodoxa Defensio Imperialis*, a short treatise generally, but perhaps incorrectly, attributed to Gregory of Catino, and composed certainly at Farfa in the days of Paschal II. A temperate and able work, which may almost be said to be the best written at that time in favour of the Empire, and with the intention of giving canonical proof of its rights, it seems the precursor of Dante's *De Monarchia*, and merits special attention. There is another defence of the imperial rights based on the authority of the Roman law, and written by Petrus Crassus, besides some other

noteworthy writings in favour of the antipope
Wibert, especially one by Wido, bishop of Ferrara,
who after being attached to the cause of Gregory
VII. and writing in defence of it, changed sides on
the death of that pontiff and confuted his own
arguments in another work full of historical information.
Also of a polemical character and in
support of the imperial pretensions is a sort of
panegyric of Henry IV., written by Benzo, bishop
of Alba, in rhymed and rythmic prose, abject in its
adulation of the emperor and in the vile insults
directed against the Gregorian party; and still
worse than this is the libel entitled *Vita Gregorii
VII.*, which Benno, one of Wibert's cardinals, wrote
not only against Gregory but also against his predecessors
and Urban II. Both these abusive
writings have a certain value, not for the facts they
relate, but as an expression of the state of men's
minds and of the violence with which the two
adverse parties fought. For if, as Wattenbach
observes, this violence showed itself in Italy with
more bitterness and fewer scruples among the
imperial followers, while the Gregorian party had
the advantage on their side of greater culture and
a higher morality, still these latter by no means
exhibited much gentleness in their writings. Party
feeling is evident in all the literature of that age,
and as we have already found it in Bruno of Segni
and in the authors of the pontifical lives, so it shows
itself among other instances in the angry poem

which laments the imprisonment of Paschal II., and in a writing on the honour of the Church composed by Placidus, prior of the Abbey of Nonantola, as in another, but recently discovered, on the pope's right to excommunicate the emperor, attributed to Lambert of Ostia, later Pope Honorius II.[1] But we cannot here go minutely into all the polemical literature of this period, and as we have already mentioned sufficiently Bruno of Segni, it will be enough to speak only of two other writers of this kind, Peter Damiani and Bonizo of Sutri.

Among the papal apologists in the eleventh century, the first place certainly belongs to St. Peter Damiani, one of the most singular men of his age, always contending between the instinctive mysticism which drove him into solitude and rigorous penances, and the inflexible will of Hildebrand who forced him to come out of his convent and join in the warfare with all that passionate

---

[1] *Widonis ep. Ferrariensis de scismate Hildebranti*, in Mon. Germ. Hist. Script., vol. xii. *Benzonis ep. Albensis ad Heinricum IV.*, libri vii. Ibid. vol. xi. *Bennonis Vita Gregorii VII.*, ap. Goldast, Apol. pro Heinrico IV. *Placidi Nonantulani Liber de Honore Ecclesiæ*, ap. Pez, Thes. Anecd., vol. ii. *Tractatus de Investitura*, in Jahrbücher der Akad. gemeinnütz. Wiss. zu Erfurt, Heft VIII., 1877. Also noteworthy is the writing of Cardinal Humbert *Contra Simoniacos* in Martene et Durand, Thes. nov. Anecd. V., and that of Cardinal Deusdedit, *Libellus contra Invasores et Simoniacos et Reliquos Schismaticos*, ap. Mai, Patrum Nova Bibliotheca, vol. vii. Cardinal Deusdedit is also author of a kind of register, in which, besides a collection of canons, are preserved imperial diplomas and charters of great antiquity relating to the Roman Church. It was published by Monsignor Martinucci, at Venice, in 1859.

vehemence which characterized him. A nervous nature full of complex sensibilities, a strange mixture of tears and fire, of tenderness and violence, Peter Damiani left the mark of his own individuality on all his writings, which for the most part seek their justification in recent events, and contain arguments drawn from the state of society and, above all, of the clergy, for whose reform he worked with fiery zeal. He insisted on the celibacy of the clergy, and his treatises are our principal guides in following out the development of that question, so angrily contested and, notwithstanding all resistance, then definitely settled according to the wish of the Roman Church. Not only for this, but for all the burning questions of that day, Peter Damiani laboured, wrote and spoke, in councils, in courts, among the people, as theologian, ambassador, and agitator; so that it would be impossible to give the history of the Church and of Italy in the eleventh century, without taking into account the polemical works and still more the correspondence of this monk, in whom were so strangely blended the opposite characters of a vehement partisan and of a contemplative eastern mystic.[1]

Strange also is the life of Bonizo, whose *Liber*

---

[1] *S. Petri Damiani Opera*, ed. Const. Caetani, Bassano, 1783. This is a collection in four volumes of the works from this fertile writer's pen, which treats in prose and verse of every possible subject, whether in letters, homilies, lives of saints, political or religious treatises. Noteworthy next to the letters, and also very strange, are the writings entitled *Apologia* and *Liber Gomorrhianus*.

ad Amicum is more than anything else a history of the papacy in his times, written in the form of a polemical treatise. Born, as may be conjectured, in the second quarter of the eleventh century, he makes his appearance in 1074 as subdeacon at Piacenza, and as one of the most zealous chiefs of a popular party then formed in Lombardy, and called the *Pataria*, which, favoured by the pope and favouring him, was bitterly opposed to the imperialist tendencies of the higher Lombard clergy, and to the marriage of priests. At the head of his party, Bonizo soon entered into a struggle with Dionysius, bishop of Piacenza, which ended in the defeat of this latter, who was rebuked by Rome and driven out of his see by the Pataria, who would have no more to do with him. In 1078 Gregory VII. appointed Bonizo to the bishopric of Sutri—a town which, on account of its position near Rome and on the road to the north of Italy, required a thoroughly faithful bishop, one of determined energy in the temporal as well as in the spiritual struggle, and ready at need to take up arms in defence of the Church. In that same year, as things were looking bad in Lombardy, Bonizo was sent there by the pope as apostolic legate; and again we find him there in 1081, always among the most active leaders of the Pataria, and so formidable that Benzo of Alba, in the panegyric mentioned above, when congratulating the emperor on his having seized Runtius, the head of the Pataria in

Cremona, blinded and killed him, adds: "O Runtius, sleep in thy sightless deformity! Praise be to God that he who had dared to insult thee (the emperor) could not succeed in escaping from thy hands! It is known in the four quarters of the globe how thou, most dreadful power, didst avenge thyself on Runtius of Cremona, and on several others. But as to Bonizellus,[1] Armanellus, and Morticiellus, those three demons, the whole nation laments that the same did not befall them also." As soon as he had escaped from this danger, he left Lombardy and hastened to rejoin the pope when the emperor moved towards Rome; and afterwards, on the emperor's return northwards, he quickly went to his see of Sutri, where the following year Henry, when again in that neighbourhood, seized him and carried him off prisoner. But whether he was released or escaped by flight, certain it is that we find him, after a short interval, again on the scene as apostolic legate in Lombardy, in Tuscany, and with the Countess Matilda, to whom he was a trusty counsellor, always indomitably active and courageous. Perhaps to enable him to

---

[1] A contemptuous form for *Bonizo*. This habit of altering the names of their opponents in order to give them a humiliating meaning, common among these polemical writers, is especially so in Benzo. Thus, for instance, besides the three names quoted in this passage, that of Anselmus, bishop of Lucca and friend of the Countess Matilda, becomes *Asinelmus*, that of Alexander II. *Asinandrus;* and these examples of scurrilous hostility might be multiplied, nor was the opposite party free from it.

direct better the energies of the Pataria, of which he was the soul, he was transferred from the see of Sutri to that of Piacenza, where he had begun his career, and where—it is not known in what year, but certainly before 1092—he met with a tragic end and died a martyr to his cause. "Bonizo of pious memory"—such is the record of him by the annalist, Bernold of Constance—"bishop of Sutri, but expelled thence for his faithfulness to St. Peter, at last after many captures, tribulations and exiles, chosen as bishop by the Catholics of Piacenza, having had his eyes put out by the schismatics of that same place, and nearly all his limbs torn asunder, was crowned with martyrdom." Thus the ardour with which he fought excited revenge, and the fierce wish expressed by Benzo of Alba was triumphantly fulfilled.

To his activity in doing, Bonizo added equal activity in writing. As proof of his ecclesiastical erudition he left behind him a collection of canons, a book on the sacraments, and an extract from the works of St. Augustine. But the book which places him in the ranks of polemical and historical writers, is one entitled *Liber ad Amicum de Persecutione Ecclesiæ*, in which, with the assistance of the canons and of Church history, he answers two questions submitted to him by some friend, namely, why God had permitted His Church to suffer such calamities, and whether it was lawful to take up temporal weapons in her defence. "Thou askest me, thou my only support in the tribulations which surround me : How is it that in this storm the mother Church on earth groaning cries aloud to God and is not heard, she is oppressed and is not delivered, and the children of obedience and peace are lying prostrate, while the children of Belial exult with their king, especially since He who dispenses all things is also He who judges righteously? There is also another thing for which thou askest me the authority from the ancient examples of the holy fathers: Whether it was or is lawful for a Christian to take up arms on behalf of the faith? To which uncertainties of thy mind, if thou wilt lend the ear of a sound heart, it will be easy to answer, both because we have it ready and because I have seen the great necessity at this time of writing it. Therefore, trusting in the mercy of God, who makes the tongues of infants eloquent, let us begin our discourse." And to find the answer he goes back to the past, and searches for it in the first vicissitudes of the Church, condensing them briefly with great though confused erudition, down to those of his own time which he relates at length. He sees the plant of Christianity spring from the blood of the martyrs in the first persecutions, take root among the nations and continue to grow in the midst of a thousand heresies from Constantine down to the Lombards, flourish under the first Carlovingians, then decline, and again revive with varying fortunes until his own age. And here begins the valuable part of his book, which, leaving almost entirely on one side the questions proposed by his friend, relates at length, with much historical insight and, for the last years, with the knowledge of an eye-witness, the events which had occurred during nearly half a century, from the days of Leo IX. to those of Gregory VII. Not an elegant writer, yet without pretensions, he sets down the facts simply as he knows them without ever intentionally altering anything, but seeking in them, if not the cause, at least the justification for later facts, and thus inaugurating an almost philosophical study of history, at the same time that Gregory of Catino in his solitary cell was inaugurating the erudite side of that study. Bonizo's disposition is always to justify the facts he relates by canonical and scriptural examples, for we must remember that his narrative aims at showing that the action of the papacy in his times was correct, and in accordance with the traditions of the Church. For if his ill-digested learning often makes him confuse dates and facts which were far removed from him, yet gradually, as he comes nearer to his own time, he becomes more precise, until in contemporary history, and especially in the life of Gregory, there is an amount of knowledge shown throughout the narrative which gives it considerable authority. Watterich, who in republishing Bonizo's work has written his life with great care, points out very justly that this is quite natural. His eventful life had made him acquainted with all the principal men of the day, and he had had dealings with them in connection with the events of which he leaves us a record. Gregory VII. and his successor Desiderius of Montecassino, the Empress Agnes, the Countess Matilda, Bruno of Segni, the antipope Wibert, and many others, were all known to him personally, and with many he was on terms of intimacy, so that every new circumstance he relates suggests to us the thought that he may have had it related to him by an actor in the event, or at least by an eye-witness. For this reason we select from his work the account of one of the most striking episodes of the Middle Ages—the famous Canossa episode (A.D. 1077)—which he tells just as he must have heard it from the principal persons who took part in it. The history of this scene and the causes which led to it are so generally known, that it is superfluous to add any explanation to Bonizo's exceedingly clear narrative.

"Meanwhile, when the excommunication of the king had reached the ears of the people, our whole Roman world trembled, and the Italians and Ultramontanes judged differently of these things. For the Italians, after Easter, held at Pavia a council of malignants, in which all the Lombard bishops and abbots, under the direction of Wibert, and imitating Fotius and Dioscorus, joined in excommunicating the lord pope of ancient Rome—a thing unheard of in the world that all at once the enemy of mankind should arm so many possessed bishops against the holy Roman Church. While these things were happening in Italy by the persuasions of the devil, the Ultramontane princes meet together, and with wise counsel constitute both parties into a sort of tribunal, that they may clearly see whether the pope can excommunicate the king or not, and whether he can himself with justice be excommunicated. For they did not wish to destroy their law, which prescribes *if any one has not been absolved from excommunication within the year and day, let him lose all the honours of his rank.* Therefore the most prudent bishops, abbots, and clergy of that kingdom, having taken counsel according to the decrees of the holy fathers and the examples of the elders, decreed that the king could be excommunicated by the pope, and had been justly excommunicated, on account of his imitating Fotius and Dioscorus. What else? Finding nothing better at the time, after taking the sacrament, and followed by the Dukes Rudolph, Guelph, and Theodoric (for Godfrey, the husband of the most excellent Matilda, had died a few days before), and the rest of the bishops of the kingdom—they resolved that, if the king would acquiesce in their advice, they would bring the pope within the year's term beyond the Alps, who, unforced, would absolve him from the chain of excommunication; and they obliged the king to swear with his own mouth, after taking the sacrament, that he would await the pope's presence and sentence. After which they all again unanimously swore that, if the king would observe the sacrament taken, they would make the expedition into Italy with him, and would, having raised him to the imperial dignity, attack the Normans and deliver Apulia and Calabria from their yoke; but that if, driven by his sins, he took the sacrament in vain, they would never again accept him as king and lord.

". . . In the meantime the venerable Gregory, for the sake of peace, was journeying towards Augsburg under great difficulties, for there was then raging a most severe winter. But the king, little heeding the sacrament, entered Italy. And some say that he desired to seize on the pope unexpectedly, which seems probable enough; for Gregory, the bishop of Vercelli, his chancellor, who was commanded by the princes to conduct the pope over the Alps, when he had crossed the Apennines, heard that he (Henry) had secretly entered the city of Vercelli, and told the pope of this, who then went to Canossa, a strong fortress of the most excellent Matilda.

"Meanwhile the king, seeing his machinations discovered, laying aside, as it seemed, all fierceness, and putting on a dove-like simplicity, goes to Canossa, and for some days remaining barefoot on the snow and ice, deceives all the less cautious, and receives from the venerable Gregory the absolution which he craved in the sacrament during the celebration of the mass, in the following manner: For he made him partake of the holy table in the presence of the bishops, abbots, monks, priests, and laity in this manner, *that if he humiliated himself in spirit as in body, and believed that the pope was the rightful one, and that he had been excommunicated on account of his imitating Fotius and Dioscorus, and believed that he could be absolved by this sacrament, then might it be given him for his salvation; but if otherwise, might Satan enter into him, as into Judas, by his mouth.* What else? During the celebration of the mass they took the communion together. Then it is commanded to all who are absolved from excommunication that they should keep aloof from the society of the excommunicated. But there are some who say that he swore to the pope by his life, and limbs, and honour: I, however, will affirm nothing of which I am quite ignorant.

"Then the king, after he had been absolved from the ban, seemed in appearance sufficiently devoted and obedient to the pope; for he separated himself from the society of all those bishops, considering them to be excommunicated, agreeing, however, at night, in all their wicked plans, and resolving that in his mind which afterwards was made clear by the result of the matter. And so he acted all the time that he remained at Piacenza, fearing especially the presence of his mother, the most religious empress, who happened to be there.

"At the same time that Cencius,[1] hateful to God, whom we have mentioned above, came to him, whom in the day time he refused to see as being excommunicated, but at night gave himself wholly up to his pestilent counsels; and when he saw that the pope could in no way be torn from the fortress of Canossa, he went to Pavia. There Cencius, hateful to God, died by a bitter death, and Wibert, with other excommunicated persons, celebrated his funeral with great pomp."[2]

After completing the history of Gregory VII., Bonizo's book returns to the point whence it started; and from the teachings of the past he comes to the conclusion that, in spite of all its persecutions, the Church is indeed dear to the Lord, and is growing in grace in the midst of difficulties which sometimes oblige her to take up temporal arms, and make it lawful for her to do so. "Therefore," he concludes, "let the glorious soldiers of God fight for the truth, strive for justice; let them fight with true courage against heresy, which is raising itself in opposition to all that is said or worshipped. Let them emulate in good the most excellent Countess Matilda, a daughter of the blessed Peter, who, with a manly soul and despising all worldly goods, is prepared to die rather than infringe God's law, and is ready

---

[1] The same that seized Gregory in St. Maria Maggiore, and carried him off to his tower. See above, p. 190.
[2] Watterich, op. cit. i. 327-331.

to combat the heresy now raging in the Church, as far as her strength permits. Into whose hand we believe that Sisera will be betrayed, and, like Jabin, will be lost in the river Kishon, because he has destroyed the Lord's vineyard and devoured it, so that it has become as the filth of the earth. But we pray, as befits our office, that heresy may speedily perish, burned with fire and abashed at the rebuke of Thy countenance." Such is the conclusion of this book, of which Bonizo wrote a sort of continuation in a work directed against Hugo, a cardinal of Wibert's, the loss of which is much to be regretted as, from what we know of it, it appears to have contained valuable information regarding the first years of Urban II.'s pontificate.

One of Bonizo's friends and companions in these party struggles was Anselm, bishop of Lucca, nephew of Pope Alexander II., and beloved by Gregory VII., who had proposed him as counsellor to the Countess Matilda, with whom he remained till his death. We have a biography of him, which is not without importance on account of the times and persons it mentions, written by a priest named Bardo, an intimate of his, who collected with affectionate fidelity the records of his virtues and of the miracles said to occur frequently at his grave.[1] Better known, and of greater value, is a curious

---

[1] *Vita Anselmi cp. Lucensis, auctore Bardone*, in Mon. Germ. Hist. script., vol. xii. Anselm himself was the author of several works, partly polemical, most of which are lost.

poem written by Domnizo, a Benedictine monk, belonging to the church of St. Apollonius in the Castle of Canossa, at the time of the Countess Matilda.[1] In extremely rude and often obscure verses, he describes the deeds of his liege lady, moved to do so by his profound attachment and admiration for that remarkable woman. This devotion naturally weakens the authority of his statements, and his official position constrains him sometimes to a prudent reserve, while the confused rudeness of his style makes him tedious and often difficult to understand. This notwithstanding, as a recent admirer of his observes,[2] "All those who write about Matilda and her times are obliged to have recourse to him, and find him very useful." Incorrect when relating distant events, passing rapidly or in silence over what he fears may offend Matilda, he abounds in sufficiently exact details of the matters in which he has personal experience; and the affection which he retained for his heroine after her death gives a certain eloquence to his rough verses, as in the following passage at the end of his work, when he addresses Canossa, exclaiming, "O white stone ... once thou wert happy and glorious when the great Matilda was with thee; her illustrious forefathers

---

[1] Domnizo, *Vita Mathildis*, ed. Bethmann, Mon. Germ. Hist. script., vol. xii.

[2] A. Ferretti, author of a careful little treatise, entitled *Canossa*. Reggio Emilia, 1876.

loved thee with ready affection, and built aloft thy walls; the noble race which repose in thee are no more; ... No more breathes the great Matilda, but in thee her memory lives, and while she is blessed in new regions, everywhere resounds the glory of her lofty name."[1]

These were generations rich in remarkable men, but Gregory VII. towered above them all, and was doubtlessly the animating spirit of his age. A great man in the true sense, and superior to all the other successors of the first Gregory, he was both pope and monk, living in the world and with the world, and yet so separate from it in rigid strength of character, as to seem other than human in his nature. This extraordinary man, while he was carving out with iron hand a wonderful historical scheme, was at the same time its unconscious annalist, and marked the milestones of his progress in the register of his letters. From the earliest times, and during the whole of the Middle Ages, the Roman Curia adopted and continued the practice of copying all the acts sent out in its name, and of keeping them in registers for that purpose,

---

[1] The following verses which describe the meeting of Henry IV. with Gregory VII., will give an idea of Domnizo's versification. He happened to be himself at that moment in the Castle of Canossa :—

"Ante dies septem quam finem Ianus haberet,
Ante suam faciem concessit Papa venire,
Regem cum plantis nudis a frigore captis.
In cruce se iactans, Papæ sæpissime clamans :
Parce, beate pater, pie, parce michi, peto plane !

arranged chronologically into books, and divided by years. This wise forethought would have prepared an inexhaustible mine of historical wealth, but that all the registers between that of Gregory the Great, and this of Gregory the VII., with the exception of a few letters of John VIII., were lost in the course of time and circumstances. And unfortunately, not even the register of Gregory VII. has reached us entire, eight books only having survived, so that his assistance fails us wholly for the last four years of his pontificate. Philip Jaffè, who has given us the best and completest edition of the Gregorian letters,[1] tried partially to supply this want by collecting every other letter he could find, whether published or not ; but even so, what remains relatively to this last period is very scanty and unsatisfying. Still, fragmentary though it is, this historical document, more than any of the others which appeared at that time in Italy, throws immense light on the events of that age, and reproduces for us with statuesque distinctness the austerely majestic figure of Gregory, and shows him to us as he was in his intercourse with his contemporaries, and in his daily struggles with the difficulties unceasingly presenting themselves against his vast designs. An admirable book, which merits careful study, and can only be compared to

---

[1] *Monumenta Gregoriana*, edidit Ph. Jaffè, Berolini, 1865. A few more letters have been discovered since. We have here limited ourselves to mentioning the letters of Gregory only, but those which still exist of the popes near his time are also of great value.

the letters of the Great Gregory, from which, however, it differs in many respects. A comparison of the books is equivalent to a comparison of the authors. Both blessed with the strength which springs from unbounded faith, and moved by an impersonal desire to assure the victory to this faith, both gifted with genius, and each of them superior to his age, yet following and bounded by many of the prejudices inseparable from it, these two popes still differ from each other in character, and in their ideal of the Church, an ideal which naturally varied with the change of times, events, and inspirations. In the first of these men, born on the threshold of the Middle Ages, there still breathes the life of the past, and his mind is formed amidst the traditions of ancient Rome and of the apostolic age—amidst the echoes of the Palatine and the Catacombs. Of an intelligence both far-seeing and flexible, of a heart disposed to indulgence and thirsting for affection and sympathy, of a character essentially human, he stands out as the most perfect figure in the whole course of medieval history. The other appears at the height of those dark ages, after a long night of corruption and barbarism, a monk from his childhood, not hardhearted, but little disposed to tenderness, calm, severe, unyielding, a born ruler. To reform the Church rotten to the core in consequence of past sins, to transform an enervated clergy into an austere order without worldly interests or affections, to render the episcopate independent of royal authority and devoted to a pontiff, shepherd of nations and kings, supreme leader in the paths of righteousness and peace; such is the ideal of this seventh Gregory, as it reveals itself in these letters which, if not written by his hand, are certainly inspired by him, and all express in different circumstances the same tendency. And if this ideal, exceeding the limits of possibility and of justice, did not reach its object, but soon giving way to new ideals was partly transformed, the personality of Gregory does not lose in grandeur on this account, and he still remains in history like a solitary eagle dominating the vast horizon from his lofty eyrie, and looking downwards in majestic indifference.

CHAPTER VI.

NEW PHASES OF ITALIAN THOUGHT FROM THE TWELFTH TO THE FOURTEENTH CENTURIES —SOUTHERN WRITERS OF THE NORMAN AND SUABIAN TIMES — SABA MALASPINA — HISTORIANS OF THE SICILIAN VESPERS—LIVES OF THE POPES—LIFE OF COLA DI RIENZO—LOMBARD MUNICIPAL WRITERS OF THE FIRST PERIOD—OTHO OF FREISING—GENERAL HISTORIES—FRA SALIMBENE OF PARMA—CHRONICLERS OF VARIOUS CITIES OF CENTRAL AND NORTHERN ITALY — CHRONICLERS OF LOMBARDY AND OF THE MARCA TRIVIGIANA —ALBERTINUS MUSSATUS.

DURING the struggle of the Investitures between Church and Empire, a great change was gradually growing up in the political and intellectual condition of Italy, so that, on the cessation of that struggle, the literary history of the country is found to have passed unexpectedly into a new phase. The kingdom founded in the South by the Normans took deep root, became for a moment the seat of the Empire, and, in spite of many vicissitudes and changes of dynasty, remained up to our own days the only stable monarchy in Italy. The Roman Church, after rising so high under the powerful influence of Gregory VII., and widening immensely the circle of its spiritual and political influence, also occupied itself in increasing and strengthening its temporal patrimony, till, in the days of Innocent III. (d. 1216), the summit was reached of a dominion which began to decline with Boniface VIII. (d. 1303). In Central and Northern Italy the communes, after a laborious season of latent preparation, suddenly blossomed out on all sides, and rapidly grew strong, rich, and free. Milan, Venice, Genoa, Pisa, Florence,—at every step we meet with a city, and each city is a power. After the dawn which in the former century scattered much of the intellectual dimness, there now breaks forth the full radiance of Thomas Aquinas, Giotto, and Dante. In the midst of such abundance of life and energy, the laity begin to emancipate themselves from their sacerdotal leading-strings; nay, democracy, after invading the State, attempts also to invade the Church. Everywhere there is a quick ardour of thought and of action, while the new-born philosophical spirit begins to initiate new reforms, and under a thrilling impulse first given by Arnold of Brescia, boldly criticises the Church doctrines, which are defended by St. Bernard and later by the Dominicans. At this time also various heresies insinuate themselves among the masses, and with the introduction of new observances, give rise to religious enthusiasms and to strange excesses, promoted partly by tendencies not varying from those which gave their first impulse to the democratic order of St. Francis of Assisi. These altered conditions alter the aspect also of the German Empire, which in the days of Frederick Barbarossa enters upon a national struggle, is Italianized for a moment under Frederick II., and then, being again transplanted to Germany, loses all its influence in Italy, and is completely enervated when Henry VII. crosses the Alps at the invitation of the Ghibellines. The names of Guelph and Ghibelline become a pretext and a password of Italian discord, which increases with the increase of vitality, and prepares for the nation every conceivable misfortune in the shape of strife, anarchy, and tyrannical rule. Nevertheless, amid these contests, the true expression of Italian thought and character is developed in the growth of art and still more of language, which makes its first poetic efforts in Sicily at the court of Frederick II., sings among the people the spiritual songs of the Franciscans, and after seeking perfection throughout all Italy, at last establishes its home in Tuscany, and there awaits the approaching muse of Alighieri.

Such is the period whose historians we now have to examine. Just as the sources of history dried up on the decline of the Roman Empire, so now the chronicles multiply in number, and become veritable histories, with the increase and fruitfulness of popular life. The materials begin to crowd upon us in so much greater number and importance, that it is no longer possible, nor would it answer any purpose, to follow individually all the hundreds of chroniclers who spring up on all sides between the twelfth and fourteenth centuries. It is necessary to be brief. And to begin with Southern Italy, in addition to the chroniclers of the first Norman period, already mentioned in the fourth chapter, we must notice others who flourished under the last kings of that dynasty, and who are more or less connected with the chroniclers of the Suabian period (A.D. 1194–1268) which followed.[1] The monastic chronicles also revived. To this age belong the *Annales Casinenses* (A.D. 1000–1212), a compilation of the history of Montecassino, derived by various monks from the historians already mentioned, and for the later years completed by facts which these monks had themselves collected. The monasteries

---

[1] For the southern writers, in addition to our study of the originals, we have had frequent recourse to the excellent work published by Capasso, and entitled, *Le fonti della storia delle provincie napoletane* in the *Archivio storico delle provincie napoletane*, An. 1876. Some other publications in the *Archivio storico Siciliano* have also been of great service to us, and so have the works of two Sicilian historians, La Lumia and Amari. To this latter, the illustrious author of the Sicilian Vespers and of the history of the Moslems in Sicily, we owe special thanks for information given to us personally, and which proved most useful.

of St. Clement of Casauria and of St. Bartholomew of Carpineto, both situated in the Abruzzi and of very ancient origin, also had their chronicles which, like that of Farfa, were enriched with valuable documents, and were compiled about the end of the twelfth century, the first by John, the second by Alexander, each a monk of the monastery whose records he collected. Of a wider character were the *Annales Ceccanenses*, first published under the name of *Chronicon Fossæ Novæ*, from the monastery in which they were found. They are composed in the form of a universal history, beginning with the Christian era and continuing down to the commencement of the thirteenth century, when they were written by a native of Ceccano. The first part is a useless piecing together of old writings, but later it becomes more diffuse and circumstantial. There is added to it by a different author (A.D. 1192) a rude poem against the Emperor Henry VI., who by his marriage with the Norman Princess Constantia had set up the Suabian dynasty of the Hohenstaufen in the South, and had made himself hated both for the German influences he introduced, and for his cruelties towards the party of the Normans identified now with the Sicilians. Still more universal is the chronicle of Romuald Guarna, archbishop of Salerno and a celebrity of the medical school there, which begins with the creation, and comes down to the middle of the twelfth century where it breaks off. Romuald bore high offices in

the Norman court under the two Williams of
Sicily, with whom he was allied by birth, and took
a large part in the many turmoils which disturbed
the last reigns of the Hauteville dynasty. He
went to Venice as the representative of William II.,
surnamed the Good, and assisted in the name of
his master at the meeting and treaties of peace,
which took place there between the Pope Alexander III. and the Italian communes on the one
hand, and the Emperor Frederick Barbarossa on
the other. Being received by the emperor with
great consideration, and having been successful in
his negotiations, he speaks with lengthy com-
placency of this meeting at Venice in his chronicle,
which naturally is of great importance in its account
of contemporary events. Nevertheless a certain
partiality, easily explained in a man constantly
engaged in violent party struggles, leads him often
to colour his facts, or to pass them over in silence,
according to the interests of his own party, which
was that of the government and monarchy, opposed
by the feudal party of the barons impatient of the
new men, who had seized the reins of power to
their disadvantage. On the other hand it was to
this feudal party that belonged Hugo Falcandus, a
powerful and elevated writer, who with his history
of Sicilian matters gained for himself the honourable title of the Tacitus of the Middle Ages. His
birthplace is disputed, but the truth seems to be
that he was born in France, went while very young

to Sicily, and remained there a long time, meeting, as he himself tells us, with assistance, favour, and an honourable position. Having returned to France, (or perhaps to England), he then wrote his history, and completed it about 1169; later, in 1189, he took up the subject again in a letter to Peter of Blois, and touched once more on Sicilian affairs, at the time when William II. had died, and Tancred de Hauteville, placing himself at the head of the Norman party in Sicily, and being proclaimed king, tried to oppose the claims of the German Henry VI., and indeed continued to oppose them for four years until his death. Falcandus was the partisan and friend of the feudal Norman nobility established in Sicily, and he identified their interests with those of the kingdom to which he was much attached, notwithstanding the sharp words which he every now and then addresses to the Sicilians and Apulians,—words arising, however, rather from party antipathies than from dislike to their nation. He differs from Romuald of Salerno in hardly ever speaking of himself, and it is owing to this reticence that we know so little of his life. Another difference between him and the archbishop is that, whereas the latter has a tendency not to mention at all circumstances which are unfavourable to his party, Falcandus on the contrary is more courageous and faces the difficulty; explaining in accordance with his own point of view all the facts with which he is acquainted, either from having himself seen them, or from the accounts furnished him by his friends among the Norman nobility. And although his information is derived from interested sources, and he himself is a partisan in his heart, yet he shows more impartiality than one could expect; while his great sagacity also told him that a bare narrative of the facts does not exhaust the duties of the historian's office, and he therefore has preserved for us a number of details which we should not otherwise know, respecting the political constitution of the monarchy, the condition of the feudal lords, of the municipality, and of the people. Gibbon, notwithstanding some slight inaccuracies, speaks of Falcandus with his usual insight, and says that "Falcandus has been styled the Tacitus of Sicily; and after a just, but immense, abatement from the first to the twelfth century, from a senator to a monk, I would not strip him of his title; his narrative is rapid and perspicuous, his style bold and elegant, his observation keen. He had studied mankind, and feels like a man." And in relating the last vicissitudes of the Norman kingdom, and how Henry VI. made himself master of it by force, "against the unanimous wish of a free people," Gibbon quotes the prophetic words which Falcandus, on completing his history and when the struggle was beginning, wrote in his letter to Peter of Blois,—words which we give here in the English historian's rather free translation, that however reproduces faithfully the colouring and profound melancholy of the original.

"Constantia, the daughter of Sicily, nursed from her cradle in the pleasures and plenty, and educated in the arts and manners, of this fortunate isle, departed long since to enrich the Barbarians with our treasures, and now returns with her savage allies, to contaminate the beauties of her venerable parent. Already I behold the swarms of angry Barbarians: our opulent cities, the places flourishing in a long peace, are shaken with fear, desolated by slaughter, consumed by rapine, and polluted by intemperance and lust. I see the massacre or captivity of our citizens, the rapes of our virgins and matrons. In this extremity how must the Sicilians act? By the unanimous election of a king of valour and experience, Sicily and Calabria might yet be preserved; for in the levity of the Apulians, ever eager for new revolutions, I can repose neither confidence nor hope. Should Calabria be lost, the lofty towers, the numerous youth, and the naval strength of Messina might guard the passage against a foreign invader. If the savage Germans coalesce with the pirates of Messina; if they destroy with fire the fruitful region so often wasted by the fires of Mount Etna, what resource will be left for the interior parts of the island, these noble cities which should never be violated by the hostile footsteps of a Barbarian? Catania has again been overwhelmed by an earthquake: the ancient virtue of Syracuse expires in poverty and solitude; but Palermo is still crowned with a diadem, and her triple walls enclose the active multitudes of Christians and Saracens. If the two nations, under one king, can unite for their common safety, they may rush on the Barbarians with invincible arms. But if the Saracens, fatigued by a repetition of injuries, should now retire and rebel; if they should occupy the castles of the mountains and sea-coast, the unfortunate Christians, exposed to a double attack, and placed as it were between the hammer and the anvil, must resign themselves to hopeless and inevitable servitude."[1]

We may say that with Hugo Falcandus closes the series of historians belonging to the Norman period, from which we pass to those of the Suabian rule, beginning with a poem by Peter of Eboli, who related in well-turned verse the struggle between Tancred and Henry VI., writing of the latter what is more a panegyric than a history. This period is not very abundant in local chroniclers for Southern Italy, although it is in it that appears the striking personality of Frederick II., who exercised such fascination over his contemporaries in Italy, and whose court became a centre for all men of learning and letters, and almost the cradle of Italian poesy. The anonymous chronicle *De Rebus Siculis*, the *Annales Siculi*, and the *Breve Chronicon Lauretanum* are writings which the historian is glad to consult, but which in themselves

---

[1] Gibbon, *Decline and Fall of the Roman Empire*, chap. lvi.

are of little value; and the only really important Southern chroniclers of that age are Richard of St. Germano, Nicholas of Iamsilla, and Saba Malaspina on the continent; and in the island of Sicily, Nicholas Speciale and Bartholomew of Neocastro. The first of these writers, born in the town of St. Germano at the foot of Montecassino, was imperial notary, and served Frederick II. in many matters. All that he had seen, his long acquaintance with public life, and perhaps the traditions of historical studies preserved in the great Abbey near which he was born, inspired him with the wish to write the history of the years from the death of William the Good until 1254. This accurate and simple work, written with impartiality, full of facts related frankly and without rhetorical effort or much vivacity of colouring, is really a chronicle, not a history, and is the surest guide we have for Frederick II.'s reign, and for the Neapolitan provinces in his time.

The two others, whose names we have coupled with his, are also well-meaning and honest, but both of them passionate partisans in the struggle, now renewed for the third time, between Church and Empire, the last vicissitudes of which struggle they describe. Of the Ghibelline Nicholas of Iamsilla we know nothing except his name, and even this with some uncertainty; but from his work we may infer that he also was a notary, the secretary of King Manfred, and his familiar follower from 1253 to 1256. This we gather from the very minute and exact information which he gives us of that chivalrous sovereign, especially during those years. His style is elegant and dignified, and his Ghibelline tendencies do not detract from his fidelity as an historian, since his party sympathies bring into play a natural disposition to compare events, and to judge of them synthetically, a disposition which he has in common with Saba Malaspina. We have also but scanty notices of this Saba, who was born in Rome of an ancient Roman family, became dean of the Church of Miletus in Calabria, and a member of the Curia in the time of Pope Martin IV., during whose pontificate (A.D. 1281-1285) he wrote his history, which he dedicated to a college of officials belonging to the papal court. In this history he declares his intention to relate those facts of whose truths he could bear witness, or which, being generally received, seemed to him trustworthy. This work, divided into two parts, treats of the events of the kingdom from the death of Frederick II. to that of Charles of Anjou (A.D. 1250-1285). It is the history of a period of great disturbance and full of sudden changes, and embraces the adventurous reign of Manfred, who inherited from Frederick, together with the royal crown, the deadly hatred of the Guelphs against his family, as also the hostility of the papacy, which by its support advanced the designs of Charles of Anjou, until at the battle of

Benevento Manfred lost both life and kingdom And after Manfred's death Saba continues to tell how Charles strengthened his position, and of his complex relations with the Guelph party in the whole of Italy, and especially with the pope and Roman municipality, of which he was senator. He also relates the tragic fate of the handsome and unfortunate Conradin, of Hohenstauffen, who as a boy of sixteen came from Germany in the vain hope of regaining the kingdom of his ancestors, but was vanquished at Tagliacozzo, and, by command of the fierce Anjou lord, the graceful young head rolled like a stricken flower on the scaffold, to be, however, later avenged in Sicily at the sound of that terrible vesper bell (A.D. 1282). Although Guelph in feelings and belonging to the Curia, Saba renders full justice to the characters and misfortunes of both Manfred and Conradin, and makes no effort to disguise the faults of King Charles, while extolling exceedingly in him those qualities which had enabled him to conquer the kingdom, and to establish in it his own dynasty. Notwithstanding his pompous, affected style, and his bad Latin, he is not without a certain expressive vigour arising from the importance of his subject, and from the impression made upon him by all these changing fortunes.[1]

---

[1] It is no longer possible for us to notice any sources of history other than chronicles. We can only mention here in a note the letters of Petrus de Vinea, Frederick II.'s great chancellor, who

Saba treats the unexpected outbreak, which led to the revolution of the Vespers, and the establishment of the house of Aragon in Sicily, with much historical acumen and honesty, recognizing, in spite of his personal feelings, the causes which led to it, and the consequences resulting from it; and like him in this are the other two principal historians of that event, Bartholomew of Neocastro and Nicholas Speciale, both Sicilians. Bartholomew, a lawyer and native of Messina, republican magistrate of that town during the revolution of 1282, then fiscal advocate, and in 1286 ambassador of John I. of Sicily to Pope Honorius IV., is perhaps the best witness we have of that movement. His narrative begins in 1250, and terminates in 1293, becoming more diffuse in the latter years, and describing minutely the events still fresh in the author's memory; showing also an honest desire to be

---

inspired Dante with one of the finest episodes in the *Inferno*. These letters are amongst the most valuable literary monuments of that age, and have the greatest historical merit. There are also existing other contemporary collections of letters written by men taking an active part in public life, but they are mostly unedited, though they deserve to be published either entirely or in part, as it is also most desirable that there should be a complete and definite edition of Petrus de Vinea's letters. For information with regard to them, an essay of the Neapolitan De Blasiis, may with advantage be consulted, as well as one by Huillard Bréholles, *Pierre de la Vigne, sa vie et sa correspondance*. We should further make passing mention of the great collection in ten volumes, prepared by Huillard Bréholles, and entitled *Historia Diplomatica Friderici Secundi*, as also another by Bartolomeo Capasso, *Historia Diplomatica Regni utriusque Siciliæ ab anno* 1250 *ad annum* 1266.

impartial, although occasionally his excessive affection for his native town of Messina prevents him from doing full justice to Palermo, and the part she took in freeing the island from French tyranny. The *Historia Sicula* of Nicholas Speciale embraces a later period, and beginning with the Vespers, reaches the year 1337, thus giving the reigns of the first princes of Aragon in Sicily. A distinguished statesman and a refined man of letters, Nicholas was on terms of friendship with Frederick II. of Aragon, who sent him in 1334 as ambassador to Pope Benedict XII., and from this friendship we have, to quote the words of Amari, both an advantage and a disadvantage; the former because he was in a position as to time and place, to know exactly, and not as an outsider, what he was writing about, since he had seen it with his eyes and studied it closely; on the other hand there is the disadvantage which may always accrue to the truth from a courtier's caution.[1]

---

[1] *Annales Casinenses*, in Mon. Germ. Hist. Script. vol. xix. *Chronicon Casauriense*, in Muratori Rer. Italic. Script. ii. 2. *Chronicon S. Bartholomæi de Carpineto*, in Ughelli, Italia Sacra, vol. vii. *Romualdi Salernitani Annales*, ibid. *Hugonis Falcandi Historia de Rebus gestis in Siciliæ Regno*, in Muratori, op. cit. vii. *Petri de Ebulo Carmen de Bello inter Heinricum VI. et Tancredum*, ap. Dal Re, Cronisti e scrittori sincroni napoletani, Napoli, 1845. *Ricardi de Sancto Germano Chronica*, Mon. Germ. Hist. Script. xix. *Nicolai de Iamsilla De Rebus gestis Friderici II.*, Muratori, op. cit. viii. *Sabæ Malaspinæ Res Siculæ*, ibid. and better in Dal Re, op. cit. *Nicolai Specialis Hist. Sicula*, Muratori, op. cit. x. *Bartholomæi de Neocastro Hist. Sicula*, ibid. xiii. Of the writings

Leaving now this celebrated island and returning to the mainland, we shall pass by the writers of the first Anjou period, who are few and of little interest for our subject, and turn immediately to the Roman writers. They also are scanty, and Gregorovius remarks with truth that the best materials for the municipal history of Rome are furnished by the English chroniclers, William of Malmesbury, Roger Hoveden, and, above all, Matthew Paris, whose works are treasures of Italian history in the thirteenth century. We have already mentioned that Saba Malaspina, being a Roman, treated at the same time of Neapolitan and Roman affairs, which were then closely connected. The lives of the popes after those written by Cardinal Boso were resumed again by an anonymous priest, who related the doings of Innocent III. (A.D. 1198–1216), and describes that famous pontiff's position respecting the East and Sicily, with the accurate though diffuse knowledge of a contemporary writer, but without either clearness or elegance of style; while by another contemporary is the life of Gregory IX. (d. A.D. 1241), written with great partiality, and in a spirit

---

recognized as apocryphal, such as the *Diurnali* of Matthew Spinelli da Giovinazzo, and among the Roman chronicles that of Monaldeschi, we do not speak; omitting likewise the *Rebellamentu di Sichilia*, a sort of historical romance, as Amari calls it, written in the Sicilian dialect, and proved, as we think satisfactorily, not to have been of the same period as the Vespers.

hostile to the Emperor Frederick II. Of much greater merit is the history of the succeeding pope, Innocent IV. (A.D. 1243–1254), composed by his chaplain, Nicholas of Curbio, a laudatory writer, who is, however, well informed and careful, and reminds us of the best writers of the Pontifical Book, while he is superior to them in the facile grace of his style, and in a purity of language which makes us feel that we have entered upon a new and improved period of Latin letters—a period of rapid and extraordinary progress. After Nicholas of Curbio we have no more actual biographies of popes, only dry notes which later were collected when, in the fourteenth century, historical studies took a wider character, from which resulted compilations such as the absurd chronicle of Martin of Troppau, famous under the name of Martinus Polonus, and others, less well known, but much better, by the Dominicans Bernardus Guidonis, and Ptolemæus Lucensis, who, both starting from the Christian era, stop in the early part of the fourteenth century.[1]

The transfer of the papal court to Avignon led naturally to a falling off in Roman historical writings. The municipalities of Central and Northern Italy represented so many States, and had a political importance which was quite wanting to Rome, absorbed as it was in that of the

---

[1] *Ptolemæi Lucensis Historia Ecclesiastica*, Muratori, op. cit. xi. All the other pontifical lives, ibid. iii.

Popes. When they are not taken into account, the historical importance of the actual city of Rome was not greater than that of any other of the secondary communes, from which it was only distinguished by its ancient renown and its unique associations. And so true is this, that no sooner does the fantastic apparition of a singular man, emerging from the ruins of the Forum, and dreaming the return of past glories, ascend to the Capitol, and, after a short splendour, vanish again into the darkness, than a chronicle immediately appears, recording the passage of the meteor; but the life of Cola di Rienzo comes alone, and remains a solitary instance of its kind, as solitary as the hero whose deeds it commemorates.

Among a few fragments of little value, this life of Cola di Rienzo is really the only noticeable historical work produced by Rome in the fourteenth century. Some doubts have been raised as to its authenticity, which has even been positively denied, nor can we say that we feel complete certainty on the point. Yet so strong do the reasons seem for considering it authentic, that when a careful examination of the remaining manuscripts, and an historical and philological study of the text make it possible to come to a definite conclusion, we think that the verdict will be a favourable one for the chronicle, and the result will be a genuine edition free from the errors and interpolations which deform the present one. But even now, with all its imperfections, this life is very attractive, written as it is in the Roman dialect, interspersed with dialogues and ingenuous exclamations, simple, clear, full of movement and life. The great admiration of the chronicler for Cola is tempered by his sincere patriotism and his love for Rome, which is stronger than any other feeling, nor does he fail to represent the Tribune in all his strange contradictions. That mixture in him of wisdom and caprice, of a classical grandeur of aims in a man who seemed almost inspired, and the childish vanity of one who had suddenly risen from a humble estate to unlimited power; every impulse, every characteristic is so vividly described that he seems to rise before us, and live over again his life of turmoil. And with him we see those papal legates and proud barons now caressed, now threatened by Cola, trembling before him with fear and anger, and meditating vengeance the while; here also are seditions boiling up suddenly, and as suddenly settling down, and those turbulent Romans armed and fighting in the public squares, then momentarily tranquilized to flame up afresh, and pass again through all the stages of indignation, shouts and tumults. This book is a romance far richer in imagination and vivacity than that of Bulwer, and is at the same time a history, just as the Tribune himself is one of those types, which arrest both the attention of the historian and the fancy of the poet.[1]

If in Rome there was a great scarcity of chroniclers, it was very different in other parts of Italy, especially in Lombardy, where the municipal life was a very vigorous one, the liberty of the citizens was spreading, and with it their commerce, their ambitions, and the contests of arms, sometimes raised against the German invaders, more often in fratricidal wars between neighbouring cities, and even within the walls of the same city. In the eleventh century, when Rome was striving for supremacy, Milan was already beginning to trace the outline of her history according to the new tendencies, and a popular lay element penetrated into it, and introduced a special character of its own. Thus even the historian Arnulph, although a partisan of the ecclesiastical aristocracy of Milan,

---

[1] *Vita di Cola di Rienzo*, Bracciano, 1624 and 1631, ap. Muratori, Rer. Italic. Script. vol. iii., and another with notes by Zefirino Re, Forlì, 1828, reprinted at Florence by Le Monnier. All imperfect editions, and the last the most imperfect of all. We should mention here that historical studies owe much to Cola, who may be said to have inaugurated Roman archæology, by searching in ancient writers and inscriptions for the history of those monuments, which fired his imagination, and which up to that time had hardly any other record but the mediæval legends, which are contained in the *Mirabilia*, a characteristic book of which we should very willingly have spoken, had we not feared to exceed the limits of our work. Some annals of Rome and the places near, published in the nineteenth volume of the *Monumenta Germaniæ*, also have a certain interest; and important too are the *Cronache Viterbesi* of Nicola della Tuccia, published in Florence by Ignazio Ciampi.

is also unconsciously influenced by this element in his *Gesta Archiepiscoporum Mediolanensium* (A.D. 925–1076). In them he relates a disturbed period of perplexity and contest. On the one hand were the higher Milanese clergy, traditionally hostile to the pretensions of Rome, jealous of its riches and its prerogatives, and opposed to the rule of celibacy; on the other hand the majority of the lower clergy and of the people, who, drawn into the current of the new ideas of reform, joined that party of the Pataria of which Bonizo of Sutri was, as we have seen, the champion, and afterwards the martyr, at Piacenza. Arnulph introduced the municipal chronicle at Milan, as at Venice we have seen it inaugurated by John the deacon, and "in the pages of Arnulph," as a recent writer well says, "we are no longer in the cloister, we are in the city, in the midst of its tumults and contentions.[1] And while the Pataria of Milan also had its martyrs in Ariald and Erlembald, of whose lives we have a narrative, several writers arose to preserve for us the history of both the religions and the civil struggles; among others the two Landulphs, the elder and the younger, the former belonging to the archiepiscopal party, and violently partial, the latter far better, more moderate and truthful, and of greater learning and accuracy. Born about the end of the eleventh century, this younger Landulph was carefully

---

[1] Adolfo Bartoli, *Storia della letteratura italiana*, vol. i., Firenze, 1878.

educated, and for the sake of further instruction went to Paris, where at that time young men from all parts of Europe congregated for study. On his return to his native town he was attached to the church of St. Paul, which had been rebuilt by his uncle Liprand, an eloquent, zealous and persecuted head of the Pataria; and notwithstanding his high reputation, Landulph did not either escape persecution in the course of his life. The history of Milan from 1095 to 1137, which he wrote, contains according to Muratori all the more important events occurring during those years in Milan, and describes graphically to what excesses the greed for power could lead in those, as indeed in all, days; nor does Landulph confine his narrative within the walls of Milan, but extends it to a considerable tract of Italian history.

Two contemporaries of Landulph are a Magister Moyses, who celebrated in verse the praises of his native Bergamo, and another, but anonymous poet, who deplored the laying waste of Como by the Milanese, and the long and cruel war which preceded this misfortune from 1118 to 1127. But the rapid succession of events prepared plenty of materials for new chroniclers, among whom we first find a Milanese known as Sire Raoul, or Radulph, to whom we are indebted for a good history of the wars sustained by the Milanese against Barbarossa.[1]

---

[1] This chronicle has been generally attributed to Sire Raoul, of

That solemn moment for Milanese history, when, after being levelled to the ground and furrowed by the plough of the conqueror, she suddenly rose up again unconquered and more implacable than ever against Frederick; the terrible cruelties of that desperate struggle; the deadly enmities between some cities, and between others that honourable harmony, by which in the victory of Legnano Italy was saved (A.D. 1176, May 29th); all this finds in Raoul the testimony of an eyewitness, who relates the facts with calm severity and with a desire of benefiting future generations by these examples: " Those things which I have seen and have heard from truthful sources, I shall try to describe; for posterity may derive the greatest benefit from them, if they learn through what has gone before to guard against the future." And the same sympathies animate the pen of another chronicler, Boncompagnus Magister Florentinus, who, from the Adriatic coast, describes, though with much more warmth, an episode in this contest, namely the siege of Ancona, which, when hemmed in by Frederick's soldiers under the leadership of a warlike priest, Christian Archbishop of Cologne, made a vigorous resistance, and obliged the Germans to raise the siege.

Taking a very different view of matters, and

---

whom we know nothing except the name, but it appears that he had only collected and written down the notes of some other writer whose name has not reached us.

passionate partisans of the emperor, were Otho Morena and his son Acerbus, who have left us a record of Frederick's doings in Italy, and of the vicissitudes of their native place of Lodi. Otho, who was Judge and *Missus Imperialis* under Lothair and Conrad III., carried his work down to 1162, and it was continued afterwards to 1167 by his son Acerbus, a favourite with the Emperor Frederick, who made him Podestà of Lodi. On his death at Siena in 1167, an anonymous writer continued his history for a few years longer, and wrote in a somewhat more national spirit than the two Morenas, who, influenced by their great affection for the Empire, and by the hatred of long standing between Lodi and Milan, betray a violent animosity against this latter town; yet in spite of their partiality, their power of reasoning and expression is such, and so varied is their information, that they must be considered among the best sources of our knowledge concerning that memorable period.[1]

The grand figure of the Emperor Frederick Barba-

---

[1] *Arnulfi Gesta Archiepiscoporum Mediolanensium*, Mon. Germ. Hist. Script. vol. viii. *Landulfi Historia Mediolanensis*, ibid. *Landulfi Junioris de S. Paulo Historia Mediolanensis*, ibid. xx. and Muratori, op. cit. v. *Andreæ Vita S. Arialdi*, Acta Sanctorum, June 5, *Moysis Magistri Bergomensis De Laudibus Bergomi*, Muratori, op. cit. v. *Anonymi Poema de bello et excidio Urbis Comensis*, ibid., *Radulfi sive Raul de Rebus gestis Friderici I.* ibid. vi., and *Annales Mediolanenses*, Mon. Germ. Hist. Script. xviii. *Boncompagni Magistri Florentini De Obsidione Anconæ*, Muratori, op. cit. vi. *Otto Morena, Acerbus Morena, Anonymus, De Rebus Laudensibus*, Mon. Germ. Hist. Script. xviii.

rossa evoked in Germany an historian, who must not be omitted from these pages. This was Otho, bishop of Freising, who was born from a second marriage of Agnes, daughter of the Emperor Henry IV., with Liupold, marquis of Austria, and hence was half-brother of King Conrad III., and uncle of Barbarossa, whose faithful counsellor he became, and sharer in State affairs. In mind quick and versatile, melancholy and mystic in disposition, Otho inclined to monastic life, and indeed after some time passed in study at Paris, he turned Cistercian monk in the Abbey of Morimund, and became its abbot, but later was raised to the episcopal see of Freising, without however abandoning either the dress or the feelings of a monk. He accompanied his brother Conrad during the second Crusade, and led against the Saracens in Palestine an army which was destroyed, he himself escaping with difficulty, and after visiting Jerusalem he returned to Europe. There seems to have been little harmony between him and King Conrad, but when Frederick ascended the throne he took more part in public affairs, and remained with the emperor till 1158, when on Frederick's preparing to return to Italy, he obtained permission to remain behind in his native country, on account of his failing health. There he died soon after in that same Abbey of Morimund where he had been monk and abbot, and to which he was bound by many ties of affection, as he also was to his diocese of Freising, whose cathedral, after long neglect in those troubled times, was restored by his munificence to riches and splendour.

Otho, naturally inclined to meditation, and drawn to it still further by his serious philosophical and theological studies, was prompted by the scenes in which he was both spectator and actor to write a book of history, wherein to philosophize sadly on the vanity of human things and to seek comfort in the thought of immortality. The *Chronicon*, or, as Otho preferred to call it, the *Liber de duabus civitatibus*, is a synthetical study of the various ages of the world, beginning, as usual, with the Creation, and coming down to his own times, divided into seven books, and containing, in an eighth, a treatise on the last judgment and the world to come. He drew his historical information from Paulus Orosius and his philosophical opinions from the works of St. Augustine, and perhaps is the first who, in that early dawn of the renaissance, tried to connect the whole story of humanity into a foreordained system of causes and effects. Hence the value of this work for any one who is inquiring into the progressive development of historical research, and also, for a minute study of German history, the value of those books of the *Chronicon*, in which Otho treats of the times nearest his own. But the book of his which has greatest interest for Italian history is another concerning Barbarossa's earlier enterprises, and entitled *Gesta Friderici Imperatoris*. An impartial examiner of the differences between the Church and Empire, this bishop-monk, uncle of the emperor, eye-witness of many events, and minutely informed on many others, would be beyond all comparison the best historian of the day, did not certain grave defects obscure his merits. The same philosophical tendency of his mind which enables him to take in facts with a glance, and judge of them with sufficient fairness from a distance, makes him often careless in the details and not very reliable. Moreover, a love of showy phrases, a wish to increase the rhetorical effect by strong contrasts of light and shade, frequently induce him to alter in such a way the circumstances of his narrative that, even when it is on the whole truthful, many of its incidents become quite incredible. An instance of this is where, in his account of the sudden rising of the Romans against Frederick's army (A.D. 1155, June 18th), of the long and obstinate resistance, and the slaughter which ensued, he affirms that, while of the Romans there were a thousand killed, two hundred prisoners, and innumerable wounded, only one of the Germans perished, and another was taken prisoner, an assertion whose incredible nature he softens with a classical *mirum dictu*.[1] But if this defect, and a

---

[1] "Prælium hoc a decima pene diei hora usque ad noctem protractum est. Cæsi fuerunt ibi vel in Tyberi mersi pene mille, capti ferme ducenti, sautiati innumeri, cæteri in fugam versi, uno tantum ex nostris, mirum dictu, occiso, uno capto. Plus enim nostros intemperies cœli æstusque illo in tempore maxime circa Urbem im-

certain mixture of national boastfulness with a courtier's adulation, often make him untrustworthy in details, he is nevertheless, taken all in all, of great importance as an historian, and often, when accounting for facts, he shows remarkable insight in discovering their historical and political causes, and with great sagacity explains the present by the past. Thus, in the passage we are about to quote, we find a striking instance of this, especially if we take into consideration the fact that it was written by a German imperialist at a time when the will of Barbarossa, and the renewed study of Roman law were calculated to exaggerate the rights of imperialism beyond all limits.

"Nevertheless the Lombards had laid aside all the bitterness of their barbarous ferocity, in consequence, perhaps, of their marriages with the Italians, so that they had children who inherited something of Roman mildness and intellect from their maternal parentage, or from the influence of the soil and climate, and retain the elegance of the Latin language and a certain courtesy of manners. They also imitate the activity of the ancient Romans in the management of the cities and in the preservation of the State. Finally, they are so attached to their liberty that, to avoid the inso-

---

moderatior, quam Romanorum lædere poterant arma." Nevertheless, "finito tam magnifico triumpho," the emperor drew off his army the following morning, and encamped at a respectful distance from Rome.

lence of rulers, they prefer to be reigned over by consuls than by princes. And since, as it is known, there are three orders among them, of captains, vassals, and the commons,[1] in order to keep down arrogance, these aforesaid consuls are chosen, not from one order, but from each, and, lest they should be seized with a greed for power, they are changed nearly every year. From which it happens that that territory is all divided into cities, which have each reduced those of their own province to live with them, so that there is hardly to be found any noble or great man with so great an influence, as not to owe obedience to the rule of his own city. And they are all accustomed to call these various territories their own *Comitatus*, from this privilege of living together. And in order that the means of restraining their neighbours may not fail, they do not disdain to raise to the badge of knighthood, and to all grades of authority, young men of low condition, and even workmen of contemptible mechanical arts, such as other people drive away like the plague from the more honourable and liberal pursuits. From which it happens that they are pre-eminent among the other countries of the world for riches and power. And to this they are helped also, as has been said, by their own industrious habits, and by the absence of their princes, accustomed to reside north of the Alps.

---

[1] Capitanei, vavassores, plebs.

In this, however, they retain a trace of their barbarous dregs, forgetful of ancient nobility, that while they boast of living by law they do not obey the laws. For they seldom or never receive the prince reverently, to whom it would be their duty to show a willing reverence of submission, nor do they obediently accept those things which he, according to the justice of the laws, ordains, unless they are made to feel his authority, constrained by the gathering of many soldiers. On this account it frequently happens that, whereas a citizen has only to be restrained by the law, and an adversary must be coerced with arms according to the law, they find him, from whom as their proper prince they should receive clemency, more often having recourse to hostilities for his own rights. From which results a double evil for the State, both that the prince has his thoughts distracted by the collecting of an army for the subjection of the citizen, while the citizen has to be compelled to obedience to his prince, not without a great expenditure of his own substance. Whence, for the same reason that the people are in such an instance guilty of rashness, the prince is to be excused, by the necessity of the case, before God and man.

"Among the other cities of that nation, Milan, situated between the Po and the Alps, now possesses the supremacy. ... And it is considered more famous than other cities, not only on account of its greater size and its large number of armed men, but also because it has added to its jurisdiction two other cities placed in the same region, namely Como and Lodi. Then, as happens in human affairs, through the blandishments of a smiling fortune, it swelled out into such daring of pride, being elated with success, that it not only did not refrain from attacking all its neighbours, but ventured even without alarm to incur the recently offended majesty of the prince."

It is to be regretted that a premature death prevented Otho from continuing his history beyond 1158, when the conflict between Frederick and the Communes may be said to have only just begun. Doubtlessly his experience of the facts, his intimacy with the emperor, and his easy access to official documents would have increased the value of his book with the progress of events. Nor are we compensated for this loss by the continuation of his work down to 1160 by his faithful chaplain Ragevinus, also an eye-witness and perhaps a more accurate narrator than his master, but as incomparably inferior to him in talent and learning as in position. Besides this continuation, the *Gesta* gave rise to the poem of Guntherus Ligurinus, entitled *Carmina de Rebus gestis Friderici I. Ænobarbi*, which has latterly led to many controversies regarding its authenticity, called in question by some of the learned to the extent of declaring it to be a fabrication of the sixteenth century. This conclusion, however, appears exaggerated, and it is far more reasonable to hold, with Gaston Paris, that this poem is a sort of literary exercise, written about the end of the twelfth century, almost entirely on the lines of Otho of Freising's *Gesta*, so that historically speaking it is little more than a paraphrase in verse. Nor of much greater value are the *Gesta Friderici* by Godfrey of Viterbo, who treated of the same subject, but rudely and confusedly, without saying almost anything new. He wrote several other works, among them one well known, called the *Pantheon*, and also to him is attributed a poem on the exploits of Henry VI. against Tancred in Sicily, but it does not seem to be really his. It is disputed whether he was born at Viterbo or in Germany, and most critics regard him as German, but we cannot say that the reasons for one opinion seem to us better than those for the other. Certainly when a boy he was educated at Bamberg, and belonged later as chaplain to the court of Frederick, whom he served zealously, following him in his campaigns and travelling for him, as he tells us, " twice in Sicily, three times in Provence, once in Spain, often in France, and forty times to Rome from Germany." He died at Viterbo, which, if not his birthplace, was certainly his adopted home during the last years of his life. It was rather the gift than the opportunities which were wanting on his part, to enable him to become one of the more distinguished historians of his time.[1]

Of a very different value, on the other hand, is another poem lately discovered by Professor Monaci in the Vatican library, and which is about to be published by the Roman Historical Society. The anonymous author, apparently a native of Bergamo, and probably disciple of that Magister Moyes whom we have already mentioned, was an imperialist and admirer of Barbarossa, whose exploits in Lombardy till the year 1160 he celebrated, stopping then abruptly, perhaps because while he was writing, about 1166, Bergamo, having changed sides, deserted Frederick and joined the Lombard league. A tolerably good versifier and a vivid colourist, if he does not add much to our knowledge of those times, at least he modifies for us some of the details, while others he either confirms or denies. Hitherto only a short sample of this

---

[1] *Ottonis Frisingensis Opera* (I. *Chronicon*. II. *Gesta Friderici Imperatoris*), in Mon. Germ. Hist. Script. vol. xx., reprinted in R. Wilmans' edition *in usum scholarum*, Hanover, 1867. Another work of Otho's on the history of Austria is lost. The continuation of the *Gesta* by Ragevinus (erroneously called Radevicus in the older editions) was further continued by an anonymous writer, while Otho de Sancto Blasio carried the bishop of Freising's *Chronicon* down to the year 1209. Touching Otho of Freising much has been written, and we may mention among others the researches of Giesebrecht and Wattenbach, and the fine prefaces of Wilmans to the edition above mentioned.—*Guntheri Ligurini De Rebus gestis Friderici I. Ænobarbi*, ed. pr. Basileæ, 1569.—*Gotifredi Viterbiensis Opera*, in Mon. Germ. Hist. Script., vol. xxii.

poem has been published, which contains a narrative of the coronation of Barbarossa, and the encounter between the Romans and the imperial troops— a far more probable version than that given by Otho of Freising,—and closes with a touching digression regarding the doctrines and punishment of the reformer Arnold of Brescia, whom he exhibits to us calmly intrepid in the presence of the rack and the halter, an unshaken martyr to his faith :—

"But when he saw that the punishment was prepared, and that his neck was to be bound by hurrying Fate in the halter, being asked if he would renounce his false doctrines, and confess his sins after the manner of the wise, he, wonderful to relate, fearless and confident in himself, answers that his own doctrine appears to him the sound one, nor would he hesitate to undergo death for what he had said, in which there was nothing either absurd or dangerous. And he asks a short delay for time to pray in, for he says he would wish to confess his sins to Christ. Then on his bended knees, with eyes and hands raised to heaven, he groaned, sighing from the depths of his breast, and silently communed in spirit with Almighty God, commending to Him his soul; and after a short delay he gives over his body to death, prepared to suffer with constancy. Those who were looking on at the punishment shed tears, even the executioners yielded to a movement of pity, while he hung suspended from the noose which held him."

The fact of this book being not exactly a history but an historical poem, the difficulties of the versification, and the classical reminiscences especially in the descriptions of battles, sometimes rather takes from the historical exactitude of what it tells ; yet the love of, and insight into the truth which it shows are precious qualities, as is also its secret of rendering in a single line the important details of a given fact, or the hidden causes of many. Thus when he speaks of the fascination exercised by Arnold's eloquence in many towns of Italy, and adds that it was potent also over the—

"Romanam facilem nova credere plebem,"

he depicts vividly in these words that people so restless through the whole Middle Age, always too keenly conscious of its past overwhelming greatness, always discontented with its present municipal life, which never rose above mediocrity.[1]

With the peace between the Communes and Frederick, signed at Constance in 1183, ceases the first period of municipal history, and another opens

---

[1] Ernesto Monaci, *Il Barbarossa e Arnaldo da Brescia a Roma*, in the *Archivio della Società Romana di Storia Patria*, vol. i., and W. v. Giesebrecht, *Sopra il poema recentemente scoperto intorno al l'imperatore Federico I.*, lettera al professore Monaci, ibid. vol. ii. The manuscript which contains the poem is of the thirteenth century and bears the title, *Gesta per Imperatorem Federicum Barbam rubeam in partibus Lumbardie et Italie.*

out still more fruitful in activity and in internal changes, an age of fierce and continual civil wars, an age of commerce, of arts, of literature. Historical research is a gainer; and while the increase of learning and the widespread desire for information add to the number of those compilations, which embrace the whole of history from the beginning of the world to the times of the compiler, each city also, great or small, has its chroniclers, and among them some who, extending their labours beyond the walls of their own town, become in reality historians of the whole or of a great part of Italy. Also the life-giving breath of true art penetrates into these pages of history, and writers begin to appear full of thought and graceful in style, whether they make use of the ancient tongue, or of the new living language which is forming slowly and becoming classic. We shall treat very briefly the authors of general compilations, and only just allude to some of the minor chroniclers, in order to be able to dwell a little longer on the more important ones. Among the former our attention is drawn to Sicardus, chosen bishop of Cremona in 1185, a zealous and warmhearted man, who exerted himself much at Frederick I.'s court in favour of his country, exhorted the inhabitants of Cremona to send assistance to the Crusaders in the East, and betook himself thither in person in 1203, pushing on as far as Armenia in company with an apostolic legate. He was the author of various books, among the rest a chronicle, abounding in fables in the early period, but extremely careful and exact in the part relating to the occurrences of his own day. Other writers of the same kind are John Colonna, archbishop of Messina, who in 1257 was in England as the legate of Alexander IV., and wrote a *Mare Historiarum* which is still unedited; Ricobaldus Ferrariensis, who at the end of the thirteenth century wrote a universal history, called *Pomarium*; James of Acqui, John deacon of Verona, and Landulph Colonna a Roman; all writers whose works, like that of Sicardus, are worthless in the early part, but from which we can extract useful facts relating to the age in which they were written. Plenty of information also is to be derived from the friar Franciscus Pipinus, a Bolognese Dominican, who translated from the French into Latin a history of the wars in the Holy Land, and the travels of Marco Polo. After having been himself in the East, he described also his own journeys, closing so many labours with a general chronicle from the origin of the Frankish kings till 1314, the last part full of facts which took place in different parts of Italy, and which are related by him with care and accuracy.

Franciscus Pipinus in his chronicle represents a literary tendency of the Dominican order, which, all intent on preaching and controversy, required to have extensive compilations that should afford facilities for a certain amount of learning. These compilations, embracing a wide series of events taken from the Scriptures, from histories, from traditions, form real encyclopedias, presenting a mixture of truth and mere legend. Different, on the other hand, was the tendency of the Franciscans, who went about among the people, and shared their feelings, their fancy, and their instincts. The *Fioretti* of St. Francis are admirable in their simple and popular freshness, while in the poems of Jacopone of Todi there are to be found both ardour inflamed by zeal, and a spirit of biting sarcasm, the first revealed in his *Stabat Mater*, the second in the terrible satires against Boniface VIII. The Franciscan order was democratic, and even when, feared and caressed, it penetrated like a wave of popular feeling into palaces and courts, it never abandoned its first tendencies, but entered with the easy contempt of a democracy conscious of its own strength. It was natural that the Guelph movement of the thirteenth century should find its painter in a Franciscan,—for Fra Salimbene of Parma, more than the historian, is the painter of his times. He was born at Parma in 1221. At the age of fifteen he left his father's house to become a Franciscan friar, and firmly withstood the entreaties, bribes, even the maledictions of his father, who implored him to return to the home where he was loved. From convent to convent he wandered through all central and northern Italy, stopping for a longer or shorter time in the principal places; he travelled through France for about two years, and on his return to Italy resided for a time at Ferrara, then resumed his wanderings from place to place, coming and going at random according to chance circumstances, the will of his superiors, and a certain restless craving in himself for change and novelty. He saw and knew a great number and variety of people of different nationalities, conditions and characters; popes, kings, bishops, barons; peasants and prophets; saints, buffoons and rogues. He negotiated several matters for his order, and co-operated in 1256, by naming an arbitrator, in settling certain differences between the communes of Bologna and Reggio. Soon after we find him near Piacenza, at the bedside of a plague-stricken patient; in 1260 he is at Modena, organizing one of those strange processions of flagellants, which just in those years excited the disordered religious passions of the people. Going to the Romagna, where he occupied himself with literature, and at Ravenna examined the Pontifical Book of Agnellus, he was spectator of many remarkable occurrences, and was thus "always with one foot in the cloister and one in the world, always in the midst of a confused movement of ideas and feelings, of repentance and crimes, of freedom and tyranny."[1]

---

[1] Marco Tabarrini, *La Cronaca di Fra Salimbene da Parma*. In all that we say of Salimbene we follow principally the essay on that subject by the Senator Tabarrini, one of the most finished works which we have from the pen of this eminent writer. It has been

He lived certainly until 1288, and probably till after 1290, thus traversing in his life the longer and more characteristic portion of the thirteenth century. After having composed various theological and historical works, most of which are lost, he finally collected for the use of a niece of his, nun in a convent at Parma, all that he had learnt from books or seen in the world, and mixing all this together formed from it a huge chronicle, which has come down to us safely.

In this chronicle, as in a faithful mirror, Salimbene reproduces the age in which he lived. Unlike most of the other principal Italian chroniclers, this friar was rather spectator than actor in the history of his day, but an acute and discerning spectator, with a turn for observation, and sufficiently free from the prejudices of his time and party to judge independently, sufficiently influenced by them to reflect them unconsciously in his pages. As a Franciscan of the thirteenth century he was drawn into an ascetic mysticism foreign to his nature, which was frank even to rudeness, and full of a rough common sense. In writing he tells what he knows about every one, whether they wore

republished among his *Studi di Critica Storica*, Firenze, 1876. As to the *Chronicon Fr. Salimbene Parmensis*, it was published for the first time in 1857, at Parma, from a modern and incomplete copy of the Vatican manuscript, which is unique. Several times a wish has been expressed for a new edition, and after having had reason to compare many passages with the Vatican text, we also add our voice to those of others.

helmet, cowl, or mitre, and in the same way judges freely of things, writing in a careless but picturesque style, and in a rude Latin so full of Italian forms as hardly to retain anything of the original language. He is not an historian but a story-teller who describes things one by one as he happened to see them, familiarly, without order, almost without design, among continual digressions, and every now and then introducing into his narrative subtle observations and criticisms, which show a mind prompt to grasp the truth of things. The struggle between Frederick II. and the Guelph communes of Lombardy is related fragmentarily, in a thousand episodes in which a number of those secondary, and more than secondary, figures appear and act, who, though playing so large a part in history, seldom receive other than passing notice from professional historians. And not only the lesser men are portrayed by him with a few bold strokes, but also the great ones, including the Emperor Frederick II., who "was without faith ; a cunning man ; sly, sensual, malicious, prone to anger ; yet a man of parts when he chose to show good nature and courtesy ; fond of amusement, cheerful, industrious ; he could read, write and sing, and compose songs and poems ; . . . he knew and could speak many languages ; and to sum up briefly, had he been a good Catholic he would have had few equals among the emperors ; he was a handsome man, well made but of middle stature. For I saw him,

and sometimes I loved him." And after having
spoken of some cruelties committed by Frederick
from a curiosity for scientific inquiry, he adds that
he was an Epicurean, and "whatever he could find
in the Holy Scriptures either by himself or his
philosophers, about there being no other life after
death, he found it all;"[1] and it was his intention
that "the pope as well as the cardinals and the
rest of the prelates should be poor and go on foot;
and he did not mean this to be done for holy zeal,
but because he was very mean and greedy, and
wished to have the riches and treasures of the
Church for himself and his children, and this he
said to some of his secretaries." And in another
place he says that Frederick, "together with his
princes, strove to undo the liberty of the Church, and
destroy the unity of the faithful." This accusation,
which must have been very general in those days,
agrees also with the view taken by those modern
writers, who attribute to Frederick and Petrus de
Vinea the design of breaking with the papacy and
founding a new Church, and would explain the
favour accorded by the popes to Charles of Anjou
against the house of Hohenstaufen. And this

---

[1] Suo cimitero da questa parte hanno
Con Epicuro tutti i suoi seguaci
Che l'anima col corpo morta fanno.
  *   *   *   *
Qua entro è lo secondo Federico.
     DANTE, *Inferno*, x.

fortunate prince, with his hypocritical affectation of piety, who, through self-interest and without any attachment to the cause, became the head and ruin of the Guelph party in Italy, is also described in his real colours in several places throughout the chronicle of Salimbene, who first saw him in a French monastery with his brother St. Louis. But what is especially attractive and valuable in this chronicle is the bold, and at the same time minute, picture of the state of Italy, which stands out clearly in every page and in every episode. The general agitation regarding theological dogmas is admirably depicted, as also the firm determination of Rome in the presence of this new speculative movement, which inclined, either like Frederick to a sort of Epicurean negation, or like the Joachimites to a visionary mysticism. Salimbene himself was for a time a follower of the Abbot Joachim, but did not remain long under that influence, owing to his practical character, which had little in common with the fantastic dreams of the Calabrian visionary. Hence he turns naturally in his chronicle to many incidents descriptive of the life and the various classes of the clergy, their virtues and vices, and their relations with the populace, of whose religious extravagances he approves partly and partly disapproves. In the same way he depicts the political life of his times, the wide expanding of republican freedom, and the misery to which Frederick II.'s wars reduced Lombardy, which he describes as

" reduced to a desert, without any one cultivating it or travelling through it. . . . Nor could men plough or sow or reap or plant vineyards, or live in villages. . . . But near the towns men worked with a guard of soldiers, . . . and this had to be done on account of the highwaymen and robbers, who had greatly increased. And they carried off men and held them captive, till they might redeem themselves with money. And at that time a man would see another man passing him on the road as gladly as he would have seen the devil:" a sad state of things, still further aggravated by the continual local disputes, described everywhere by Salimbene, between the popular Guelph party and the old Ghibelline nobility irritated by the democracy, which forced it to bend before the law. But it is impossible to follow this chronicle in all its endless meanderings, wholly consisting as it does of digressions, episodes, and incidents great and small. It would be the same as trying to give in a few pages a complete picture of the men and manners of Italy in that era of changes, when municipal life was stretching out hardy shoots on all sides, and the blood was coursing hotly through the veins of a reinvigorated people.

Salimbene's chronicle reaches to the year 1288, and there is good reason for attributing to him another chronicle which comes down to 1290, and which was published anonymously by Muratori, under the name of *Memoriale Potestatum Regien-*

sium. It concerns itself chiefly with the affairs of the city of Reggio, and also enlarges on the history of Lombardy and Emilia. And beginning now to speak of other local chronicles, we may say that hardly any city in those provinces is to be found, between the thirteenth century and the first years of the fifteenth, which does not possess its one or more chronicles, generally full of valuable information. Bologna, Ferrara, Modena, Parma, Piacenza, are among those whose chronicles deserve most attention, especially Piacenza, whose history has lately been enriched by the discovery of two other chronicles, most valuable for the times of Frederick II., published first by Huillard Bréholles, and then again in an improved edition by the Historical Society of Parma and Piacenza. At Milan, Stefanardus of Vimercate, a Dominican, a theologian, and a learned author of books on canonical law, wrote in an elegant poetical form on the events which occurred in that town between 1262 and 1295, while Otho Visconti was archbishop. Another Dominican friar, Galvanus Flamma, a Milanese, born at the end of the thirteenth century, wrote various works important for Milanese history and for that of the Viscontis, of which the best known, called *Manipulus Florum*, was published by Muratori in his great collection. Also Milanese and a friend of Flamma's was the notary John of Cermenate, who had some share in his country's vicissitudes, and narrates with great precision and vigorous purity of style those which occurred between 1307 and 1313. With less elegance as a writer, but in equally good faith, Petrus Azarius of Novara composed the history of the Visconti family from 1250 to 1362. An anonymous writer wrote the life of Fra Dolcino, a heretic of Novara, and Bonincontrus Morigia the history of Monza, up to 1349,—an eye-witness and actor in the scenes which he describes. Of the less numerous chronicles of Piedmont, it will be enough to name that of Asti, written by a certain Ogerius, a member of the same family of Alfieri to which later the great tragic writer belonged another chronicle, also of Asti, by William Ventura, and the *Chronicon Imaginis Mundi* by James Acqui. On the other hand the province of the Marca Trivigiana, and especially the towns of Verona, Vicenza and Padua were abundantly supplied with writers of merit. In the first of these cities the Guelph chronicler Parisius de Cereta deserves mention for the simplicity and impartiality with which he wrote of what occurred in the early part of the thirteenth century, with special reference to Ezzelin da Romano and Mastinus della Scala. But the greatest historians of all that region are those of Vicenza and Padua. Often actively mixed up in the events of his narrative, Gerardus Maurisius of Vicenza gives us the exploits of the Da Romano family between 1182 and 1287, from an ardently Ghibelline point of view; dwelling especially on the early days of

Ezzelin, and bestowing praises on him which would astonish us, did we not remember that in those days Ezzelin had not yet revealed the monstrous cruelty of his character. Besides, the original work of Maurisius was remodelled into its present form by his contemporary Thaddeus, a notary, who put it into Leonine verse, and very probably exaggerated the laudatory passages. It was also of Vicenza and the places with which she was on terms of hostility or friendship in the fourteenth century, that Antonius Godi and Nicholas Smerego wrote, the work of the latter being continued by an anonymous monk of Santa Giustina of Padua. Superior as historians, however, to all these are Ferretus of Vicenza, and Rolandinus and Albertinus Mussatus of Padua.

Ferretus Ferreti, born towards 1295 of a good and wealthy family of Vicenza, was attracted to literature through his quick and imaginative turn of mind, his lively and satirical disposition. His guide in poetry was Benvenuto dei Campesani, famous for a poem in abuse of Padua and in praise of Henry VII. and Cangrande della Scala. Following the salutary impulse of his age, Ferretus studied the classics with great ardour, and strove to imitate them. Although regarded by Muratori as one of the best Latin writers of the time, he nevertheless did not succeed in avoiding that stiffness and affectation from which only the most finished writers of Latin escaped in the two following centuries of renaissance. He wrote a history of what occurred in Italy between 1250 and 1318, especially in connection with those events which happened near him, showing great skill in grouping and selecting facts, with a view to placing them vividly before the reader's imagination. But this very skill, which arose from a rich vein of fancy, led him, rather than to minute researches, to look for the dazzling side of human actions, in order to produce striking effects in the picture he was painting. "Rerum gestarum splendida facta percurrimus," he exclaims: and indeed, as Professor Zanella observes in his fine essay on Ferretus, "he could not desire a better field for his talents; for that period which he undertook to describe, from 1250 to 1318, is among the most brilliant and most fertile in events that are to be found in Italian history. No one can deny that Charles of Anjou, Peter of Aragon, Boniface VIII., the Tuscan factions, Corso Donati, Clement V., Henry VII., Cangrande, Matteo Visconti, Uguccione della Faggiuola are not vividly depicted by Ferretus, who likewise takes pleasure in describing in florid language localities, battles, sieges, entries, coronations, deaths of popes and emperors. But as to his profession of always telling the truth and never letting himself be induced, either by love or hatred, to utter falsehood, I think that he often forgot his promise. It is to be noted that among many rumours circulated regarding any fact, he never fails to select that which redounds to the dishonour of some one in power—a satirical propensity not easily to be reconciled with a real love of truth." Ferretus also tried historical subjects in verse, and his poem on the origin of the Scaliger family, dedicated to Cangrande, abounds in information relating to the principal towns of Venetia, and especially, besides Vicenza and Padua, to Verona, which, on account of the wide influence of the Scaligers who resided there, comes to be treated of by all the chroniclers of that part of Italy. And as he had sung the Scaligers, so also Ferretus dedicated a poem to the death of the great exile, who at their court had found his first refuge and entertainment, and who was probably known to him personally; but unfortunately this ancient tribute to the tomb of Dante is lost.

Rolandinus of Padua wrote the history from 1200 to 1260 of his native town. He had studied at the University of Bologna, and received there, in 1221, the title of Master and Doctor in Grammar and Rhetoric. On his return home, his father, who was a notary in Padua, gave up to him some notes which he had been preparing on the more remarkable events of his day, and exhorted him to write the history of their town. Rolandinus did not forget his father's advice, and, enlarging on the original idea, composed by the aid of his academical studies a work in twelve books, which displayed such clearness, and such careful knowledge and classification of facts, as to gain immediately for its author a great reputation as historian. In 1262, two years after he had completed it, his history received the honour of being publicly read in the University of Padua, in the presence of professors and students, who conferred on it their formal approbation. Time has confirmed this judgment.[1]

After Rolandinus came another even greater historian, indeed one of the most distinguished men of letters of whom Italy could then boast. Albertinus Mussatus, the friend and contemporary of Ferretus of Vicenza, was born in 1261, in Padua, of poor parentage. Being left an orphan at an early age, he supported himself and his younger brothers by copying books for the students of the university, until having gradually learnt much from the very fact of copying, he began to plead in the courts. His powerful talents and generous greatness of character gained him general favour, and raised him rapidly to honours and riches, so that in 1296 he was knighted and called to the Council of Padua, which then administered the free Republic.

---

[1] *Ferreti Vicentini Historia Rerum in Italia gestarum ab an.* 1250 *usque ad* 1318, and *De Scaligerorum origine poema*, in Muratori, Rer. Ital. Script., vol. ix. *Rolandini Patavini De factis in Marchia Tarvisina, lib. xii.*, ibid., vol. viii., and in Mon. Germ. Hist. Script., vol. xix. The other writings mentioned above are also to be found in Muratori's collection. The Piedmontese chronicles have been republished a few years ago at Turin in the *Historiae Patriae Monumenta.*

There he increased so quickly in reputation, that in 1302 he was sent as ambassador to Pope Boniface VIII., and from that time till the end of his life, whether as statesman, soldier, historian or poet, he remained a man of mark, and esteemed even by his enemies, throughout all his country's vicissitudes, and the storms of fortune which sometimes threatened him with ruin.

When, in the midst of Italy's troubles between the Guelph and Ghibelline factions, Henry VII. of Luxembourg, called upon by the latter party, came to take possession of the imperial crown, a great ferment resulted in the northern and central provinces of the peninsula. Not that the new emperor had a position of any real strength, but the different parties, receiving a fresh impulse from his coming, and shaken by a thousand vague hopes and fears, burned with a hotter and more impetuous flame. The Guelph cities of Lombardy, jealous of their liberties, and remembering the resistance made in the past to emperors of a very different stamp, either received this last one coldly, or resolutely opposed his entrance. On the other hand, he was favoured in the Ghibelline cities, but in neither one nor other, full as they were of independent life, had he any authority worth mentioning, and in his efforts as peacemaker he was quite unsuccessful. Far more powerful than reverence or hatred for the Empire were the local irritations, which divided each city into two parties, of which the prevailing one strove to maintain its position, while the other was constantly agitated by the hope of its turn coming, and its being then able to steer the helm of government in a different course. Hence a continual rise and fall of the two factions, and the Guelph cities changing to Ghibelline, and the Ghibelline to Guelph, and within the walls citizens fighting against citizens, and the victors destroying the houses of the vanquished, while these latter carry into exile a rancorous desire for revenge, and the ever-present hope of returning to wreak it. Such was also the troubled life of Padua. She was Guelph in her sympathies, both from the prevalence of that faction within the walls, and for fear lest Vicenza, her dependant, should shake off her yoke and go over to Cangrande della Scala, the master of Verona and head of the Ghibellines. On the first arrival, however, of Henry VII. in Italy, Padua prudently, though with some reluctance, sent an embassy to greet him at Milan (A.D. 1311). One of the ambassadors was Albertinus Mussatus, now eminent among the literary men of his day, and already known as one of the first revivors of Latin poetry in Italy. Henry VII. received him with such special favour, as to inspire him with an affection which never cooled, even when his duty as a citizen obliged him to stifle his personal feelings, and to take up arms against the imperial cause. After some time Mussatus was again sent on an embassy to Henry VII., to ask for guarantees for the liberties of Padua, which were granted, though not unconditionally. On the return, however, of the ambassadors, they found their fellow-citizens violently agitated by a report that Henry had appointed Cane della Scala Imperial Vicar of Padua, a title hateful to the Guelphs, and almost always synonymous with master and tyrant. In consequence they would not accept Henry's conditions, which made him angry; and, the moment appearing favourable, Vicenza rebelled and threw herself into the arms of the Scaliger. This was the beginning of a long and obstinate war between the two cities (A.D. 1311). Mussatus, who had done all in his power to avert it, had several times to return to Henry VII., in his efforts to conclude a peace, and have the former concessions confirmed. But he found it an ungrateful task to negotiate between the angry sovereign, and the excited spirits of his fellow-citizens, who lent an ear to peaceful counsels only when the danger was at its height. The ambassador felt the effect of this constantly changing tide in the reception he met with on his return, sometimes enthusiastic as for the saviour of the city, sometimes gloomy and threatening as were he bringing treason and dishonour. Things continued very serious: in September, 1311, Henry selected, according to certain conditions which had been agreed to, among four persons proposed by the Paduan council itself, one Gerardus da Enzola as imperial vicar for Padua. This hated name of Vicar increased the discontent among the people, and it grew more and more difficult for pacific proposals to prevail in the council. In 1312, returning from Genoa with the last conditions obtained from the emperor, Mussatus found the city in great uproar. The Scaliger had been named imperial vicar for Vicenza, and would certainly be named so for Padua before long; perhaps already the decree appointing him was signed, and its publication only delayed till the opportune moment presented itself. Such the rumours which excited this proud and warlike city, and the indignation of the entire people found its echo in the hearts of the councillors convened in the great Sala della Ragione. A thrill ran through the whole assembly when Roland of Piazzola, who had been one of Mussatus' companions in the embassy, rising with great vehemence, and going back over the calamities inflicted by former vicars, prophesied that the Scaliger would prove another Ezzelin. "I saw," he exclaimed with fire, and referring to his recent journey to the emperor, "I saw cities but lately flourishing now in ruins, and their citizens fugitives, the country districts deserted and covered with unaccustomed weeds, the aspect of the nobles grown sordid from hunger, while the poor people are exhausted by famine. Oh, shame! Lombardy, this fertile land, now uncultivated, may be compared to a forest wilderness. And who are the inhabitants of its noble cities? The inhabitants are its old tyrants dressed up in the name of imperial vicars; by these the remnants of Lombardy are consumed. . . . I saw Genoa beautiful, I saw her disfigured in three days; beautiful, from the joy of her citizens welcoming this image of felicity, I saw her disfigured from the change in the aspect of her community who had to alter the customs of their country into an absolute rule. Thus it would be if our president were removed, O citizens, and a stranger substituted, and your votes were annulled and interfered with by laws, and this senate dissolved, your tribunes, whom you call *Gastaldiones*, being basely and shamefully deposed. . . . Was he ashamed to make this Cane, a wicked man, the Vicar of Vicenza almost at the very gate of our most prosperous city, having broken the alliance of Vicenza and Padua, at peace with each other? Not for this was he ashamed, but rather followed the advice of his partisans that this Cane might drag you into servitude, and stir up civil war in this State through its neighbours. Oh, may the cruel and horrible slaughter of your fathers come into your memory at this thought, namely by that son of Satan, Ezzelin da Romano, whom Frederick, the impious predecessor of this Henry of Luxembourg, under the false name of imperial vicar, appointed only as a minister of destruction!" Then turning to the imperial vicar, he continued: "And thou, Gerardus, if thou wouldst indeed agree to this, renounce being vicar, resume the sweet and holy office and name of our Podestà, rule this city in freedom for half a year, and swear to continue thus with all thy strength! But if not, take thy salary and go; we have at hand an excellent man, Rudolph of St. Miniato, whom I propose to fill and attend to this free and blessed office of Podestà."[1] There was a general shout of applause. Vainly Mussatus strove to introduce calm into their counsels; in vain he explained the uncertain state of things in Italy, showed how the Ghibelline party, still vigorous, might become a dangerous assistance to the emperor whom they were defying; vainly he prayed, he implored for milder measures. All his eloquence was powerless against the popular wrath, and the war party conquered.

A few days later the war began; a war every now and then interrupted and again resumed, and carried on for many years; varied in fortunes, but always alike in the hatred with which those passionate spirits threw themselves into the fratricidal struggle. Albertinus Mussatus, who had shown himself so mild a counsellor, proved a lion in the fight; always in the most perilous enterprises, always the first to confront danger, the last to retire from it. It appeared as if he had forgotten that Henry to whom he was once so attached, and

---

[1] *Albertini Mussati Historia Augusta,* in Muratori, col. 417.

whose exploits he had celebrated, when, like Dante, he fondly hoped that they were destined to be beneficial to Italy. Padua, his beloved country, was engaged in war, and he was fighting her enemies. In the November of 1313 there was a momentary lull in this fierce contest. Mussatus and another native of Padua went to discuss terms of peace, which the Scaliger had proposed, but the discussion proved fruitless, and war became again imminent. In the mean time Henry VII. was dead (August 24, 1313), and with him faded away many hopes of the more ardent Ghibellines, many illusions of those who had looked to him as to an angel with a message of peace. The Guelph party became puffed up with pride, and at Padua, under the pretext of reforms, it seized upon all authority, treated with outrage not only the Ghibellines, but all the more moderate citizens, and quickly degenerated into tyrannical anarchy (A.D. 1314). There resulted a violent uprising of the people, of which, without a show of reason, Mussatus became the victim, and his house was attacked by an infuriated mob, breathing death and destruction. In sight of this danger Mussatus did not lose his presence of mind. He refused to conceal himself when advised to do so, and would allow no defence to be made, for fear of shedding the citizens' blood. Mounting a horse, he rode courageously out of the besieged gateway, and dashing at full speed through the crowd, escaped unharmed from the city, and retired to a place of safety. It inflicted a sharp pang on his generous heart, and he felt all the more bitterly injustice and exile, from the sense of how faithfully he had always served his beloved and ungrateful country. In an oration which he made in his defence, and then inserted in his history, he exclaimed in grief and indignation, "Need I be ashamed or blush to express my own praises, if I have deserved well in anything, being surrounded by such ingratitude? Need I be ashamed even to be arrogant? No. For when a past danger renders it necessary to speak, in order to repulse further injuries, a violent apprehension overcomes the calmness of the most courageous man. The other day, after the slaughter by those wicked ones and the horrible massacre, the tumultuous mob rushed to the house of Albertinus Mussatus, which was besieged by the raging multitudes demanding my goods, my children, and my blood. If one might say with the world's Redeemer, 'O my people, what have I done to thee? I have led thee,' saith He, 'forty years in the wilderness,'—I say, I, Mussatus, have led thee, O Paduan People, nearly for as many months through great dangers, in my footsteps, under my guidance, from which thou thyself confessest to have stepped aside through thy own fault." And after enumerating a long series of services rendered by him to his country, and the mild counsels he gave them in good fortune, he continues, alluding to their timidity in dangers: "But repentance comes too late after the hail. And what remedies can be invented for all misfortunes? O Tribunes of the people, remember. I speak the truth. Lo, I speak to you who were aware of, and the causes of all that I foresaw. You held that Cæsar was to be pacified if possible: you, O Magnates of the city, took counsel how to do it. And how should it be done? By what contrivance? By what means? How? That need, that fatigue called upon Albertinus Mussatus. It was asserted that *he could save the Republic, could restore her from ruin*. In case there was still anything to be done in the matter, you ran to him, prostrate as he was and deprived of all hope of public action, you took counsel with him, you implored him alone. When Vitalianus de Basiliis, then in command of the people, with his hands joined, falling on his knees and weeping, implored me, together with all you Tribunes, to go to the King. . . . I confess that I regard myself with wonder and pity. I must hand down for posterity the reasons in writing. When at the head of this Republic, did I ever fail? I leave out the daily, nightly, yearly labours. Let me not, as a reward for my work, have to allege the bitter vigils, cares and anxieties. There is no want of witnesses; let them testify that I may be believed. Did I exhaust the treasury? How? When? Have I enriched myself at the expense of private persons? Who are they? Let one who has been hurt or despoiled by me say so. Take this, O Tribunes, as a sufficient proof of our rectitude: on the kalends of last December (not to go back to an infinite series), the lots selected me for the office of Elder. This honour is almost equal to that of consul among the Romans. I then called to judgment, to make restitution, that Peter of Alticlino against whom there was a popular accusation, a most powerful and formidable man, and several others of the military and civil orders: I desired them to be bound, convicted them and obliged them, with great firmness and severity, to return to the treasury the moneys they had stolen. Thus was I led to act by my habits, my daring, my love of the Commonwealth, by the atrocity of their thefts, and by justice." And after these fiery words, he adds others, telling of his deeds in time of war; also explains why he had desired the imposition of a tax, which appeared to him useful and fair, but which had led to his being hated by the people, and driven into exile; and concludes with proud indignation: "But it is natural that the unclean herd should hate the sheep with golden fleece. Be it far from you, O Tribunes, to imitate the ferocity of wild beasts thirsting for innocent blood. If I can save my health, fortunes and faculties, I dedicate them with whatever remains that I may be able to do, to the Fathers, the Magnates, and the wiser part of the People."

Pages of a true eloquence, which excited the

admiration of contemporaries, as they still do that of posterity, to whom they recall the Roman Republic, and those virile utterances which burst forth in Greece and Rome, when political passions boiled over, and the democracy exercised its agitating influence! At length, when the period of uproar had ceased and quiet was restored to the city, the council met, and having abolished the extravagant reforms, and re-established the old order of things, unanimously decreed the recall of Mussatus, and public honours to be paid to him in compensation for the insult he had suffered. This was a great satisfaction to the faithful citizen, but before he could return, the Paduan forces advanced unexpectedly against Vicenza, and he joined the army. In the engagements which followed he fought with his habitual valour, until in a chance encounter he fell from a bridge into a ditch, where, surrounded by Cangrande's men, and having received eleven wounds, he was taken prisoner and conducted to Vicenza. There he remained in honourable captivity, was visited by Cane accompanied by his court, and held discourse with him, both grave and jocular,—an example not rare in that day, that as soon as the bloody swords were sheathed, wrath could give place to admiration, and a powerful baron was disposed to honour the virtues and talents of a simple citizen. In the November of 1314, on the conclusion of a peace, Mussatus was liberated, and returned to his native town to receive the distinctions decreed to him, and that crown of poetic laurel, for which Dante vainly sighed all his life, in the hope that his sacred poem might overcome the cruelty which kept him far from his country. With natural satisfaction Mussatus describes in his history, at length, and with characteristic touches, the festival held in his honour, which proved a great solemnity owing to the presence at it of the Senate, the university, and the whole town, which had grown proud of this son, whose literary fame was now universally recognized throughout Italy.

And indeed the works of Albertinus Mussatus deserved this recognition.[1] An excellent writer of Latin for his day, he was one and perhaps the best of those like Giovanni del Virgilio, Dante and

---

[1] *Albertini Mussati Opera*, Venetiis, 1636. *De Gestis Heinrici VII. Cæsaris*, *Historia Augusta*. *De Gestis Italicorum post mortem Heinrici VII. Eccerinis Tragœdia*, in Muratori, Rer. Ital. Script., vol. x. Besides the preface of Muratori and what Tiraboschi has said, various writings have appeared lately on this author, among which a very good one by Professor Giacomo Zanella, *Di Albertino Mussato e delle guerre tra Padovani e Vicentini*, in which he examines with great subtlety not only his historical works but also other literary compositions of his, among them one entitled "The Dream," in which he finds some affinity with the Divine Comedy. See also the writings on Mussatus of Wychgram, Cappelletti and Zardo, none, however, worthy of the subject. Indeed hitherto Mussatus has been his own best historian. The two Cortusi and the two Gatara, the former uncle and nephew, the latter father and son, wrote about Padua after Mussatus, but are very inferior to him. We must content ourselves with mentioning them in this note. Their works were published by Muratori, op. cit. vols. x. and xvii.

others of their contemporaries, who prepared the way for the renaissance which was realized by Petrarch; and while he studied the ancients and often attempted to imitate their expressions, he is nevertheless a very original writer in the ideas and the conception of his works. As a poet he wrote letters, eclogues, elegies, all of some merit, but especially showed a powerful creative faculty in his tragedy of Ezzelin. Freeing himself from all preconceived theories, without abandoning the classical foot-prints of Seneca, he was the first among Italians to choose a modern subject, nay, one still living in the memory and in the fears of the people, —a subject gloomily tragic, which he handled with dramatic force, and especially in the choruses with wonderful lyric impetus. The historical subject which he choose, and which added so much to the popularity of his work, indicates his turn for history. Mussatus, enamoured as he was of the writers and times of Rome, and gifted with vigorous powers of thought and imagination, felt himself naturally and irresistibly impelled to relate the story through which he had lived, to tell of the things seen and felt amidst scenes of such violent action, of such grandeur of vices and virtues. And if we have related this writer's life at great length, it is because his life has appeared to us to be the compendium of his age, as he has described it, and as it really was. He wrote the *Historia Augusta*, a narrative of the deeds in Italy of Henry

VII. of Luxembourg (A.D. 1308-1313), a prince of good intentions but of little power, eagerly invoked by the Ghibellines, esteemed even by the Guelphs, but never really feared or obeyed. He crossed the Alps to restore the mere ghost of an Empire, which had lost all reality, in the midst of so many republics, and of the popes, hostile and powerful still, owing to the assistance of the Guelph and Anjou factions. Mussatus wrote with great impartiality, but with the warmth of one who has taken part in public life, and placed in it all his hopes of doing good. His frequent journeys, generally as ambassador, in many parts of Italy—in the last years he went on an embassy also to Germany—gave him opportunities for seeing the condition of the different localities which were the scenes of his history, as also for knowing the principal personages, and gaining or verifying much of his information. Neither wholly Guelph nor wholly Ghibelline, he seems to vacillate between the two, and such vacillation is not uncommon among the most elevated spirits of that day. He would have hoped from the Empire that strong unity of government which could alone silence party discords, while on the other hand he inclined towards the Guelphs from a love of Republican traditions and of liberty which could not choose but be suspicious of the imperial eagle, and of the petty tyrants who, with the name of Vicars, grew up and prospered under the shadow of its wings. A friend and admirer of Henry's, to whom he dedicated his history, but at the same time an independent and severe historian, he warns the emperor that he would not find in those pages either flattery or only the record of his praiseworthy actions, but also the faults from which as a man he could not be free. The death of Henry interrupted the work, but later Mussatus continued it in a second history, that described the *Gesta* of the Italians after Henry VII.'s death, and was divided into twelve books, of which three are in verse and describe the siege of Padua by Cangrande in 1320. This unfinished work, interrupted by many gaps, is far less perfect in style than the *Historia Augusta*, but is not second to it in historical importance, and shows even greater freedom of judgment. He undertook it at the suggestion of Pagano della Torre, then bishop of Padua, and continued it for many years through all his laborious occupations,[1] to finish it at last in exile at Chioggia, where he also made the sketch of a writing on Ludovic the Bavarian, of which, however, there is only a fragment. For, about the year 1330, Albertinus Mussatus closed his valiant and honoured life in exile. After many other

---

[1] Scis quippe tu nostrorum actuum in Rempublicam, fide testis Episcope, quantis domi militiæque solertiis implicer, ut nec nox agendorum variis meditationibus suppetat, nec agendis lux diurna sufficiat. . . . Sed quamquam sic agitantibus vexatus anfractibus, quia in parte laborum ipse fuerim, scribendi laborem recusasse nolim, præsertim tanto permotus auctore.

services rendered to his country and many changes of fortune, he was again driven forth, and this time he was not recalled. He was left to die away from home, in a misery and old age rendered more oppressive through a friend's treason, a son's ingratitude, and the sight of Padua's liberties crushed in the hands of tyrants. A melancholy end, which moves to compassion, and yet is not without consolation, nor without that moral beauty which shines forth from a pure and consistent life, equally firm in good and evil fortunes; one of those lives which, while they present the inexplicable problem of earthly destinies, bear certain witness to the Eternal Justice.

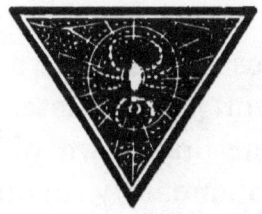

CHAPTER VII.

THE CHRONICLERS OF THE MARITIME REPUBLICS: VENETIAN CHRONICLES—MARTIN DA CANALE —ANDREA DANDOLO—THE GENOESE ANNALISTS FROM CAFFARO TO JAMES D'ORIA— PISA : PETRUS PISANUS—BERNARD MARANGO —THE CHRONICLERS OF THE REST OF TUSCANY AND PRINCIPALLY THE FLORENTINES—DINO COMPAGNI—THE VILLANI.

WHEN we turn to the chroniclers of the maritime cities, the first to attract our attention are those of Venice. After the chronicles of Altina and Grado had, in the earliest times, thrown some light on the dimness of her origin, and later John the deacon had written in the first dawn of her municipal life, she was always abundantly supplied with historians worthy of her magnificent fortunes.[1] After those

---

[1] The sources of Venetian history are naturally the object of continual researches and discussions for the learned. Besides what Muratori, Foscarini, Tiraboschi, and Pertz have left us on the subject, we should mention specially, as having been of great use to us, the works of Simonsfeld on the *Chronicon Altinate* and on Andrea

first chroniclers followed an anonymous one, who composed the Venetian annals from the middle of the eleventh to the end of the twelfth century, and among other information regarding her political history, left many important particulars touching local events in connection with the city. A fragment of a chronicle, written certainly after the death of the Doge Sebastian Ziani (A.D. 1229), and already published as part of the *Chronicon Altinate*, is also useful for the history of the relations of Venice with other States, and more especially with the East, where she, now mistress of the Adriatic, was extending on all sides her power and influence. And from the thirteenth century onwards her historical literature increases in vigour, and finds inspiration in the poetry of the spot and in the greatness of that political insight which, besides managing its home interests with such wisdom, directs also distant enterprises in every known quarter of the globe. Prompted by this poetry and this greatness, the chronicler Martin da Canale wrote the story of Venice down to near the end of the thirteenth century, in the form rather of a romance than a history. He makes use, however, of his predecessors, of tradition, and, for the times in which he lived, of his own observation or of oral information derived from trustworthy eye-witnesses,

---

Dandolo, published in the *Archivio Veneto*, and an excellent study by Professor G. B. Monticolo, entitled *La Cronaca del diacono Giovanni e la Storia Politica di Venezia sino al* 1009. Pistoia, 1882.

so that in what concerns the thirteenth century he is, on the whole, a truthful writer, and often, even in particulars, as well-informed and accurate as he is vivacious. Hardly anything is known of him personally, not even whether he was really a Venetian; but in any case he lived for long in Venice, and shows the greatest affection and admiration for her. Like the *Tresors* of Brunetto Latini, and like Marco Polo's book, his also is written in French, because, as he says, "*lengue franceise cort parmi le monde et est la plus delitable a lire et a oir que nule autre.*" On the origin of Venice he gives the Trojan legends and those about Attila, but is very brief till he comes near the times of Henry Dandolo. With this famous doge, Martin's narrative expands, and becomes still fuller when he reaches the Doge Jacopo Tiepolo (A.D. 1229-1249), and till 1275—the last date in his chronicle,—when, his details, especially of Venetian manners, are a treasure-house for the modern historian. They include particulars concerning the personages of his day, the church and square of St. Mark, the celebrated tournaments which took place in this latter, the dresses and splendour of the doges, their appearances in public, and the processions of the corporations of arts in the solemn festival of the Maries; all these form so many pictures of a singular age, painted on a fairy-like background. Martin da Canale is a writer with whom it is necessary to use some circumspection, he having, as we said, almost as much of the romance writer as of the historian; yet such is the ingenuous vivacity of his fancy, that as a colourist none of his contemporaries can rival him in his description of Venice. We shall extract from this charming book the following episode, which describes the taking of Zara by the Doge Dandolo, when on his way to the East with the Crusaders for the conquest of Constantinople:—

"So what shall I now tell you? The Count of St. Pol, and the Count of Flanders, the Count of Savoy, and the Marquis of Montferat, in the year 1202 of the incarnation of our Lord Jesus Christ, sent their messengers to the noble Doge of Venice, Messire Henry Dandolo, and prayed him to give them ships to cross the sea. And when my lord the doge heard the prayers which the messengers of these barons of France made for their lords, he rejoiced, and said to the messengers, 'Go and tell your lords, that at whatever hour they will come to Venice, they shall find ships ready to cross the sea; and that the doge will in his own body cross with them in the service of the holy church.' Then returned the messengers to their lords, and told them all this as the lord doge had commanded. And when the barons of France heard it they were very glad, both of the ships which the lord doge had promised them and also that he would in his own body cross the sea with them; for they said that better company they could not have in the whole world. Messire Henry Dandolo, the noble doge of Venice, sent for the carpenters and ordered transports and ships and galleys in great number to be speedily prepared; and had silver coins quickly made to pay the masters and the workmen, because the small ones were not so convenient for them. And it is from the time of my Lord Henry Dandolo that in Venice they began to strike large silver coins, which are called ducats, and are current throughout the world for their excellence. The Venetians made great haste to prepare the ships, and as soon as the French were ready, they set out on their way, and rode till they came to Venice, where they were very well received, and the Venetians made great joy and feasting for them; and my lord the apostle had sent them his legate, who should absolve them from their sins. To this legate my lord the doge paid great honour, and took the holy cross from his hand; and many noble Venetians took it, and the people with them. With great joy and great feasting, Messire Henry Dandolo entered a ship to cross the sea with the barons of France, in the service of the holy Church; and the barons each placed himself in his ship, and the knights entered transports and other ships in which their horses were placed. And when they were out at sea the sailors tightened the sails to the wind, and let the ships run at full speed before the wind. And my lord the doge had left in Venice his son, called Messire Rainieri Dandolo, in his place. He governed the Venetians in Venice very wisely. My lord the doge went on across the sea, till he came to Zara, with all his company. The men of Zara were at that time so proud that they had refused the lordship of my lord the doge, and had robbed travellers on the sea, and had raised walls round their town. And the weather had changed and the sea was angry: it behoved them to take to the land to save the ships, and they went to Malconsiglio, an island just in front of Zara. And when they were in safety inside the harbour, my lord doge said to the barons, 'My lords, you see that town. Know that it is mine: but those in it are so proud, that they refuse my rule. I wish you would wait for me here, for I would show them what those deserve who refuse the rule of their lord.' When the barons heard this, they said to my lord the doge, 'Sire, we are ready to come with you, and with us our knights.' 'In God's name (this said my lord the doge), none of you shall put foot there, for I want you to see what I can do, and the Venetians with me.' They made no more delay, when they were ready with their arms and ladders, except that Messire Henry Dandolo, the high doge of Venice, placed himself first, and the Venetians behind him; and they went to attack Zara, and the battle was begun. And it happened that, in spite of all the defence the people of Zara could make, the Venetians descended on the dry land. Then the battle was fought with spears and swords, and those on the walls threw javelins and sharp stones and pointed stakes, and defended the city with all their might. But their defence availed nothing, for now the Venetians put their ladders to the walls, and mounted on them, and beat the men of Zara down, and took the town quickly, and drove out the men of Zara, and placed my lord Henry Dandolo in possession of Zara."[1]

In the same way that Martin da Canale had taken largely from the historians who preceded him, so another chronicler of the name of Mark made great use of him in his turn, in compiling a Latin chronicle, of which only some fragments have been published. Of much greater weight again are his successors, Marin Sanudo Torsello and the friar Paulinus, two of the principal sources whence the great mediæval chronicler of Venice, Andrea Dandolo, drew his historical information.

Descended from an illustrious family of warriors, statesmen, and prelates, Andrea Dandolo was born in the first years of the fourteenth century. While still very young he filled high offices—in 1331 as procurator of St. Mark, as podestà of Trieste in 1333, and three years later as general purveyor in the campaign against Mastino Della Scala. In 1343,

---

[1] *La Cronique des Veniciens de Maistre Martin Da Canal*, edited by Polidori, with an Italian translation opposite by Galvani, in the *Archivio Storico Italiano*, First Series, vol. viii. The same volume contains also the *Chronicon Altinate*, published by A. Rossi, and the fragments of Mark's chronicle published by Angelo Zon.

when only thirty-six years old—or, as some think thirty-three—Andrea was raised to the ducal throne, an unusual example of such early advancement. His contemporaries all unite in pronouncing him just, liberal, and beneficent. Deeply versed in jurisprudence and history, he used his knowledge for the good of the State and of letters, which gained him the friendship of many distinguished scholars, and especially that of Petrarch. His disposition and tastes inclined him to peace, but the troubled times in which he held the reins of government rendered wars inevitable, and a great part of his thoughts had to be devoted to warlike matters. In the first years of his reign his activity was called forth by many and varied cares, among others the continual commercial and warlike relations between Asia Minor and Venice, to whose ships the ports of Egypt and Syria were then beginning to open; the commercial difficulties with the Tartars, which had arisen and been again smoothed away; the rebellion of Zara in Dalmatia quelled, notwithstanding the hostile efforts of the king of Hungary, and that of Justinopolis in Istria also put down; and finally a terrible pestilence in Venice itself. These cares only increased with the progress of time, from the growing rivalry between the Venetians and Genoese, the latter also wishing to engage in commerce with the Tartars of the sea of Azof. The rivalry soon became war, and such war as might be expected between the two greatest maritime powers of the day in Europe—a war, long and adventurous, of varied victories and defeats, difficult to conduct on account of the numerous alliances it was necessary to court and to maintain in readiness against the alliances of the enemy. And here one remembers with pleasure how the voice of Petrarch was raised, midst that clashing of arms, a counsellor of peace to the doge. But he was powerless against the force of circumstances which rendered it necessary to prosecute the war. In it the Venetians had met with a serious defeat, and while preparations were being made to defend the city against a possible attack, Andrea Dandolo died the 7th of September, 1354, either from a broken heart at the misfortunes of his country or from the fatigues undergone during those preparations, having lived less than fifty years, and reigned twelve.

The many cares of State and the warlike nature of the times did not prevent him from pursuing his studies as lawyer and historian. He added a book to the statutes of Venice, superintending the work as it was being gradually prepared, and perfecting it. He ordered and assured the arrangement of the Venetian archives by the compilation of two valuable books, entitled the *Liber Albus* and *Liber Blancus*, the first containing the treaties made by Venice with oriental countries, the second those concluded with the different states of Italy. Before he rose to the ducal dignity he had undertaken some historical labours, which he afterwards incorporated in his great book, the Chronicle, or as others call it, the Annals of Venice, written while he was doge. It is an excellent work, for which he made use of every kind of materials, and it embraces the whole history of Venice to the end of the thirteenth century collected with great diligence and learning. His free access to the archives gave him all facility for consulting documents, and of this he availed himself, inserting many extracts, and even whole documents, in his book. He also read many authors not belonging to Venice from whom he could draw useful facts, and of the Venetian writers who preceded him hardly one escaped his attention, while he may well have known some who have not reached us. And he used this mass of information with much critical judgment, so that it is not too much to say that, had all the rest been lost, the chronicle of Andrea Dandolo would have preserved the pith of the earlier works, and the history of Venice would have come down to us the same. As a writer he is not very attractive. Always simple and clear, but without imagination, he takes little pains to arrange his facts or to present them artistically. Nor is this worthy chronicler a perfect historian. As Muratori says, he is not sufficiently on his guard against mere fables when relating remote events, and he is also apt to be confused in his chronology, and to fall into the errors of his predecessors. But these are slight imperfections in comparison with his great merits, and what he tells us of the origin and growth of Venice is of immense value, for we certainly have no writer of greater authority on this subject.[1] He does not speak in his chronicle of his own times, but of those still near his own he treats with calm and honest impartiality of judgment. On the life and political institutions of Venice he has the clearest possible understanding, and as he narrates the facts he also gradually describes the historical development of that admirable constitution ; and this quality alone is of such importance that it would in itself be enough to make him one of the greatest historians in the whole of the Italian Middle Age. An introductory letter was prefixed to the work by Benintendi de Ravegnanis, the chancellor of the republic, a famous man of letters, who was also a friend of Petrarch's, and author of a Venetian history which was not finished, and only extends over the first centuries of the city's existence. Another chancellor, Raphael—or Rafainus—de Caresinis, continued the work of Dandolo, and carried on the annals to the year 1383, with great accuracy but less impartiality than the doge, though the book has much interest as that of a contemporary and of a citizen devoted to his country's service.[2]

---

[1] "Certe graviorem de iis rebus scriptorem nullum proferam." (Muratori in his preface to Dandolo's chronicle.)

[2] *Andreae Danduli Chronicon Venetum a Pontificatu S. Marci ad an. usque* 1339: *succedit Raph. Caresini continuatio usque ad an.* 1388

Nor did Genoa the Superb fail to emulate her rival in wisely providing for the city a series of historical writers, who successively described her vicissitudes during about two centuries, from the year 1100 to 1293. It was an illustrious Genoese citizen called Caffaro who imagined and founded this series. Born about 1080, he served as soldier and general in many expeditions and took great part as consul in the affairs of the republic, and also as ambassador to Pope Calixtus II., and to Frederick Barbarossa. When about twenty years of age, at the time of the expedition to Cesarea in 1100, he began to think of describing the achievements of his fellow-countrymen, and from that time he constantly wrote down all that either he saw himself or knew of from the ocular testimony of other consuls or similar personages, and in 1152 presented his book in full council to the consuls of the republic. They decreed that the work should be copied with great care and elegance, and then preserved in the public archives. Notwithstanding his now advanced age, Caffaro, flattered by this proof of appreciation, returned to his labours with redoubled zeal, and carried on his annals till 1163, the eighty-third year of his age, when the civil discords which were then agitating Genoa prevented his

---

nunc primum evulgata, in Muratori, Rer. Ital. Script. vol. xii. Here also we may mention the chronicle written in Italian by Daniele Chinazza of the war of Chioggia between Venetians and Genoese (A.D. 1378 and following years). Ibid. vol. xv.

continuing his book for the remaining three years of his life. On his death in 1166, he left besides the annals a *Liber de Expeditione Almariae et Tortuosae*, an expedition in which he took part (1147–1148), and another, *De Liberatione Civitatum Orientis*, which describes the Genoese exploits in Syria and Palestine. In these works, as in the annals, Caffaro shows himself exactly what he is—a well-informed writer, generally an eye-witness of what he relates, a courageous, religious, guileless man, much attached to his country, and a careful examiner of all that regards the public and private life of the citizens. He was also thoroughly experienced in business matters, and on intimate terms with the leading men of his day, especially with the Emperor Frederick and the Popes; tenacious of justice in all that related to the empire as well as to the Church; and after a life spent nobly in peace and war, he had the happiness in his old age to see his son Otho consul of the republic. Such is the full and well-merited eulogy with which Pertz concludes his account of Caffaro.

By order of the republic, the chancellor Obertus continued the history from 1164 to 1173. Obertus was also mixed up in the politics of his country, and had opportunities for seeing and knowing whatever of importance for Genoa was going on, whether within the city or at a distance, so that we find his times vividly portrayed in his work. The negotiations for peace with the emperor of Con-

stantinople, the armaments prepared at Porto Venere against Pisa, the explanations given by him to Frederick Barbarossa of the disagreements between the Pisans and Genoese touching Corsica, the assistance rendered to Milan in the building of Alessandria—these are some among the many episodes in which he had a share. After him Genoa was without an historian for fifteen years, until, in 1189, Ottobonus, a municipal notary, resumed the work; and after briefly supplying the interrupted thread for those fifteen years, continued the annals with greater fullness down to 1196. He also was present at many undertakings, and could bear personal testimony to his narrative. He writes in that simple and fluent style which is the natural outcome of a mind accustomed to attend to business, and to look at things from the real and practical side. In 1194, he assisted at the siege of Gaeta with the Genoese fleet sent to Henry VI.'s aid, and when the town was taken, it was he who received from its inhabitants the oath of allegiance exacted by Genoa. In 1196, he was near Bonifazio at the conflict between the Genoese and Pisan fleets, and from the minute details which he gives, we may infer that he was present at other actions described in the course of his work. He has also left us valuable information on the internal political changes which occurred in Genoa in 1194, when the consuls of the commune were replaced by a podestà elected annually and not belonging to the city, as
IT. X

was then the general custom of the Italian republics. Ogerius Panis succeeded to Obertus in the office of chronicler (A.D. 1197–1219), a man employed by the republic in various negotiations with the king of Arragon, Ildefonse, with the city of Marseilles, and with Frederick II. After Ogerius there came Marchisius (A.D. 1220–1224) and Bartholomeus (A.D. 1225–1248), both good writers and also employed largely in State business. They both, especially the second, had to relate a very important period in history, and to show Genoa in her relations with the neighbouring and distant States of the Mediterranean, and the varied part she took in the struggle, of which Italy was the scene, between Frederick II. and the Church.

After an anonymous continuation, lasting from 1249 to 1264, the charge of the Genoese annals was entrusted no longer to one but to several writers at the same time, who, extending their labours somewhat beyond the limits of Genoese territory, continued them from 1264 to 1279 with great zeal, and, in the midst of the strong party-feeling which disquieted Genoa, were admirably impartial in their narrative and in their judgments. Among the last called to this office was James D'Oria, who, having worked at them with others from 1269, was commissioned in 1280 to continue them alone, which he did until 1294. Born in 1234, and grandson of the famous Admiral Obertus D'Oria, he served his country through many vicissitudes with pen and sword. In 1284, in a great battle against Pisa, he was with many of his relations on board a galley belonging to the D'Oria family, but when returning victorious he was exposed to a violent storm near Porto Venere, and barely escaped with his life. On his return home he attended to the rearrangement of the city archives, had many documents registered, and turned them to account in his history. Intimately acquainted with the ancient writers, he searched in them for all the information he could find, in order to compose a brief sketch of the history of Genoa prior to the times of Caffaro. Of all that related to his own day he gave copious details, especially of the relations between Genoa and Charles of Anjou, and of the expedition to Corsica conducted by Percival D'Oria. As a writer he was very discerning, and superior to all his predecessors for the acuteness of his observation, the width of his views, and for a precision of mind which led him to omit no particular which could be of interest to posterity. It is to these qualities of D'Oria's that the history of Genoa owes the preservation of a quantity of facts concerning her constitution, her army, fleet, and coinage. On the 16th of July, worn out by bad health rather than by age, he handed in his work to the magnates of the city, who received it with the praises due to such conscientious labours. With him closes this series of annals, the only one written by commission for an Italian republic and the most complete during the whole age of the Communes. As the history of a mercantile and warlike people, it reflects their characteristics in every page, in spite of the variety of the writers and the times. These writers have much in common. A Latin full of Italian forms and phrases, hardly any rhetorical ornament, but complete simplicity of language and precision of style, great abundance of facts, names, and dates, profound patriotism and remarkable impartiality of judgment—these we find in all, from Caffaro to D'Oria, the first and the last of the series, and the two greatest for their enlightenment and the sagacity shown in their researches. The Genoese annals serve to prove more and more clearly that contemporary history, in order to give a vivid picture of events, must be presented to us by an eye-witness, and by one whose share in the action adds warmth to his description.[1]

Pisa was less rich in annals, yet some we find there also. When in 1088 she was the ally of Genoa and Amalfi in a brilliant enterprise against

---

[1] *Cafari et continuatorum Annales Ianuenses*, ed. Pertz in Mon. Germ. Hist. Script. vol. xviii. To the annals is prefixed an excellent preface by Pertz, to which we have adhered very closely in what we have said of the annalists. In connection with Genoa it is also useful to mention the *Chronicon Genuense ab origine urbis usque ad an.* 1297, by Jacobus de Varagine, the well-known author of the *Legenda Aurea*. Muratori published it in the ninth volume of his collection, making a compendium of the ancient and legendary portion, but preserving intact the list of bishops and the part of the chronicle which is nearest to the author's own times.

the Saracens in Africa, which was like a prelude to the Crusades, one of her citizens commemorated the exploit in a rude rhyme full of patriotic fire. Also the taking of Majorca (A.D. 1115) was celebrated in a Latin poem in seven books, remarkable for the many facts it contains and the classical turn of the verse; and the same feat of arms was described by the cardinal Petrus Pisanus. We have already spoken at length of this latter among the compilers of the Pontifical Book, and mentioned how he accompanied his fellow-countrymen in the expedition to the Balearic Isles, and on his return home wrote an account of it.[1] And indeed while writing it he enlarged on the first plan of his work, and going back to the earliest Crusade and to the taking of Jerusalem, composed the *Gesta triumphalia per Pisanos facta*, in which he celebrates with much warmth and vividness the deeds of his countrymen. But the principal chronicler of Pisa was Bernard Marango, who lived in the twelfth century, filled many public offices at home, and was sent abroad as ambassador in various places, among others to Rome in 1164 to sign a peace agreed upon between his fellow-citizens and the Roman people. After some short chronological notes his annals begin in the year 1004, briefly at first, then from 1136 to 1175 become fuller and contain a wider range of facts. In 1175 his work

---

[1] See above, chap. v. p. 198.

ceased, but was carried on to 1269 by Michael de Vico, a canon of Pisa in the fourteenth century. Marango is an uncouth writer but clear, and his Latin also is full of Italian words and forms. He is in substance a well-informed annalist and truthful, and much that he tells us we should not have known but for him, as he had access to sources of knowledge now lost to us. He has a special importance for the history of Pisa's relations with the Empire and the Popes, with Genoa and with the rest of Tuscany, which was in those days brought into a more prominent position in consequence of the growing political importance of Florence, and for that wonderful uprising of arts and letters which left so deep an impress on the history of civilization.[1]

And it was indeed about that time that chronicles began to appear in every city of Tuscany, invaluable commentators of Italy's history from the twelfth to the fifteenth century. Among the best are the chronicles of Lucca, Siena and Pistoia, of which we may mention in connection with Lucca the annals (A.D. 1061–1394) by that same Ptolomaeus Lucensis whom we have already met with

---

[1] *Laurentii Vernensis De bello Maioricano libri VII.*, Rer. Italic. Script. vol. vi. *Gesta triumphalia per Pisanos facta*, ibid. *Bernardi Marangonis Annales Pisani*, 1004–1175, Mon. Germ. Hist. Script. vol. xix., and with the continuation by Michael de Vico in Muratori, op. cit. vol. vi. The other writings mentioned immediately after these are also to be found in Muratori, op. cit. vols. xi., xv., xviii.

as author of a Church history, the life of Castruccio by Nicholas Tegrimus (A.D. 1301–1328), and the chronicle of John Ser Cambio (A.D. 1400–1409). For Siena, without touching on later ones, should be named the chronicle of Andrea Dei (A.D. 1186–1352), and the annals of Neri Donati (A.D. 1352–1381); while for Pistoia we have the *Annali Pistolesi* (A.D. 1300–1348), written in Italian, and in Italian also were many of the chronicles mentioned as well as others omitted. This fact adds not a little to their value, since it assisted the development of the language, and also because the authors, writing in their own tongue, no longer had the flow of their thoughts interrupted, but could express them with the vivacity and clearness with which they presented themselves.

Above the rest of Tuscany towers Florence after the twelfth century. From beginnings humble and little known she rose rapidly to the first place, and became celebrated for her wealth, her arts and literature. Her people full of talent and activity, had a greater similarity than any other in modern history to the ancient Athenians, with their lively, keen, riotous and quarrelsome disposition. The Florentines ended by developing instinctively a wonderful democracy that possessed all the merits of that form of government combined with its defects. The personal sentiment, so strong in all Italians, was especially strong in the Florentines, and brought about astonishing results both for good and evil. On one hand rivalries for office and private enmities excited ferocious struggles between two parties, called at first Guelph and Ghibelline, and later, when the democratic Guelph party prevailed, renewed under the appellation of White and Black (*parte bianca* and *parte nera*), —struggles which aroused to mutual intolerance family against family, the nobility against the people. On the other hand, and notwithstanding this disturbing state of things, there was great prosperity in commerce, industry and finance, and the guilds of the artizans grew so strong as to become the real basis of the State, and obliged the nobles, if they wished to share in public affairs, to enroll themselves among them, and of this we have an example in Dante. The Tuscan tongue was now formed, and letters and arts made such progress as had never been dreamed of before in modern times, and has never been surpassed since. It is a great truth that only people of strong feelings in everything can in everything be great; and there was no kind of beauty of which those proud and passionate spirits were not enamoured, nor loftiness of thought nor grace of feeling to which they did not attain, in spite of the fratricidal wars, the assassinations and exiles which formed part of their daily experience. In the mean time a fraternal and almost mystic affection united the great artists who came to clothe with beauty the realms of thought, and especially all turned with instinctive sympathy to Dante, then young and dreaming of love and poetry. While he was composing the *Vita Nuova*, Casella was putting to music his song, *Amor che nella mente mi ragiona*,[1] and Giotto portrayed him beautiful in grace and tenderness, and Guido Cavalcanti and Cino of Pistoia wrote verses for him to which he replied. They were in that springtime of the mind which brings with it buds and flowers; but soon the angry tide of civic discord swept Dante along with it, and flung him upon the desolate shore of exile, where his powerful spirit reached maturity through pain. Wandering from city to city the immortal fugitive gained keen insight into men and things, learned, one by one, the long list of Italy's virtues, crimes, and misfortunes, and in composing the sacred poem—

"To which both heaven and earth have set their hand,"

he engraved on it the history of Italy, and indeed laid in it the foundation of all medieval history. It does not come within the scope of this book to inquire into the historical value of Dante's poem, but it is well to have dwelt on it for a moment that the divine figure of the poet might shed its radiance across these pages.[2]

---

[1] "Amor che nella mente mi ragiona,"
Cominciò egli allor si dolcemente
Che la dolcezza ancor dentro mi suona.
                    DANTE, *Purgatorio, II.*

[2] We do not feel called upon to speak of Petrarch, for his action

The origin of Florence is shrouded in darkness. It appears to have been first of all founded two centuries before Christ, and then again by Augustus, but its history up to the eleventh century has hardly any basis except the well-known fabulous legends of Troy, of Catiline, and of Totilas, popular in the Middle Ages among the Florentines.[1] Around these legends the imagination of the chroniclers delighted to hover, and hitherto hardly anything but matter of pure conjecture has been gathered from the most ancient records, a brief description of which will suffice. The *Gesta Florentinorum* of Sanzanome, starting from these vague origins, begin to be more definite about 1125, at the time of the union of Fiesole with Florence, and show us this latter in 1231 already well advanced on its course of material and intellectual prosperity. The *Chronica de origine civitatis* seems to be a compilation, made by various hands and at various times, in which all the different legends regarding the city's origin have been gradually collected. The

---

as an historian was confined to the study of classic times, a study which owes so much of its revival to him. The only one of his works which seems to us to have any interest for contemporary history are his letters. The same may be said of Boccaccio, whose life of Dante and commentary on the *Divine Comedy* we do not mention, since they would carry us to Dante's other commentators, and beyond our limits.

[1] L'altra traendo alla rocca la chioma
Favoleggiava con la sua famiglia
De' Troiani e di Fiesole e di Roma.
DANTE, *Paradiso, XV.*

Annales Florentini primi (A.D. 1110-1173) and the *Annales Florentini secundi* (A.D. 1107-1247), together with a list of the consuls and Podestàs of Florence from 1197 to 1267, and another chronicle formerly attributed, but it appears without good reason, to Brunetto Latini, complete the series of ancient Florentine records. To these must, however, be added a certain quantity of facts which under various forms were to be found in various manuscripts, were used by the old Florentine and Tuscan writers, and quoted from by them under the general name of *Gesta Florentinorum*. This source of information, as Professor Paoli remarks, was the result of "a labour of continual compilation and recompilation which was multiplex, anonymous and universal; not a really literary work, but the basis of a splendid historical literature, such as was that of Florence in the fourteenth century."

Until now this literature was considered to have originated somewhat earlier, and to have begun with the chronicle which bears the names of Ricordano and Giacotto Malespini, who lived in the second half of the thirteenth century, and of whom but little is known and that with uncertainty. This was considered the most ancient chronicle written in the vulgar tongue, after the *Diurnali* of Mathew Spinelli were declared apocryphal. But now some of the learned have attacked it, and with such strong arguments that it hardly seems any longer possible to assert its authenticity, notwithstanding some grave objections set forth by those who sustain it. In any case it is now admitted by all, that even if the chronicle is in substance authentic, it has certainly come down to us completely altered. So far there are not sufficient grounds for arriving at a definite conclusion, and we cannot get beyond hypotheses, among which that of Professor Paoli seems to us probable, namely that this chronicle is a remodelling of more ancient records unknown to us, and made use of by various chroniclers, either without mentioning them at all, or doing so but vaguely. This chronicle of the Malespini as it has reached us, is, however, a most attractive book, beginning with the early legends and continuing down to the twelfth and thirteenth centuries, during which it relates in detail the history of Florence. It contains old forms of style and linguistic archaisms, which give picturesqueness of colouring to its mass of information, and to the many facts and episodes almost all of which we find narrated in the same words in the great chronicle of Villani. This latter, whom we are now approaching, has till now been accused of having copied and moulded into his own the work of the so-called Malespini, whereas now it would appear that they had copied from him. But before anything can be affirmed one way or other, we must wait for the results of fresh researches into the manuscripts, and of more profound critical studies; yet in any case, even if this chronicle is finally decided to be apocryphal, it has some merits which will prevent its ever being entirely effaced from Italian literature.

Of late years the chronicle of Dino Compagni, one of the fairest jewels in the Italian language, has been the subject of long and passionate controversy.[1] The author of the chronicle was born about 1260, of an old burgher family, and while still young found himself, like Dante, taking part in public life at a time when Florence was entering on a disturbed period of civil discord, and her popular constitution was growing more and more democratic in its form. The city was divided by the enmity of several powerful families, the people engaged in a successful struggle with the nobility,

---

[1] Here also the controversies were concerned with the authenticity of the chronicle, which by some critics, principally Italian and German, was violently attacked, and as violently defended by others. The importance of the book, and the learning of the contending parties, made the question a serious one, and it was treated with a great display of erudition, but not always nor by all with moderation and good faith. The voluminous but very thorough work of Professor Isidoro Del Lungo (*Dino Compagni e la sua Cronica*, Florence, Le Monnier, 1879-1880) is full of learning and discernment, and has in our opinion disposed satisfactorily of the question, besides rendering a twofold service to literature in proving the authenticity of the chronicle and, at the same time, providing us with an excellent edition of it. We must, however, leave on one side all this question of Dino Compagni, as it is called; only we wished to allude to the matter, and to mention Professor Del Lungo's work, which has been our guide in the following pages, and to which all who study this chronicle will henceforth be greatly indebted.

and in its animosity disposed to repress their arrogance with the arrogance of the law. After the defeat of the Ghibellines of Arezzo in the battle of Campaldino (A.D. 1289), which brought with it that of all the Tuscan Ghibellines, the prevailing Guelph party began to turn against itself, and broke up, as we have said, into two factions, the *Bianchi* and *Neri*, the first taking part with the family of the Cerchi, the second with that of the Donati. To these latter the pope, Boniface VIII., inclined favourably, being suspicious of the Bianchi because they did not seem to him sufficiently distinct from the Ghibellines. On this account the pope sent his legates to Florence to support the Neri, and later brought upon her the interference of Charles of Valois, a princely adventurer, poor, and greedy of riches and honour, whose stay in Italy was a perpetual disgrace, and brought with it nothing but discord. A few years before, the Florentines, under the leadership of a public-spirited tribune, Giano della Bella, had established, by means of the *Ordinamenti di Giustizia*, one of the proudest democratic constitutions which can be imagined. Then Giano went into exile, persecuted by the envy of many men in power, and by another and very different tribune, the butcher Pecora, who had pushed himself into notice by flattering the evil passions of the populace, and taking advantage of them. In the mean time, Corso Donati, the Catiline of Florence, was plotting against the *Ordina-*

menti di Giustizia, and having placed himself at the head of the Neri, he tried to shake off the yoke imposed by the popular party on the nobility. Through the coming of Charles of Valois, Corso Donati and the Neri had grown more powerful, and used their power to oppress the other party, so that the residence in Florence of the Frenchman, who came with the title of *Paciere*, or Peacemaker, only served to let loose party passions, and to stain the city and suburbs with murders, robberies, and violence of every kind. Then the Valois left Florence to her desolation; Boniface VIII. before long died, after undergoing the disgrace of Anagni; Corso Donati was killed, but the discords and struggles did not cease. In the mean time many of the Bianchi, who had been exiled from their country, and Dante among them, in consequence of the state of matters and the common enemies were beginning to draw nearer to the Ghibellines, and they did so the more when in Tuscany also was hailed that ray of hope, which for a moment illumined Italy, weary with her long sufferings. It seemed as if Henry of Luxembourg, when he came to be crowned emperor, was bringing in his hand the olive branch instead of a sceptre. It was the fond dream of tired and peace-desiring men, and we have seen how at Padua the Guelph Mussatus sang the praises of Henry, and celebrated his exploits. Yet for all this the discords were not lulled, and when Henry directed his steps towards

Tuscany, the Ghibellines there exulted, and among the Bianchi of the Guelph party the hope of a return to power revived. But the Florentine Neri did not yield. Joining with the Anjous of Naples, they showed themselves openly hostile to Henry, who was prevented by death from continuing the struggle. With him the *parte bianca* lost all influence, and every hope of ever regaining it.

Dino Compagni had been present in Florence at all these occurrences and shared in them, having been several times between 1282 and 1301 prior of the city, and in 1293 Gonfalonier of Justice. Spotless in his integrity, kindly in his feelings, simple, sincere, and straightforward, he made every effort in those turbulent days to recall his countrymen to thoughts of peace, and for this holy object expended, but in vain, all the resources of his fervid eloquence and of his honest will. His temperate disposition led him to join the Bianchi, and when his party fell and he was obliged to withdraw from public life, he, while mourning over his country's misfortunes, pursued in retirement his trade of silk merchant, and sought consolation in literature, which he had already attempted, and to which he contributed certain lyrics, and, as it seems, a poem entitled *La Intelligenza*. With his mind full of the impressions made by what he had seen, and of the affectionate regret with which the state of his country inspired him, he felt himself induced to write an account of the matters at which he had been present. "The memory," he says, "of ancient histories has long urged my mind to write the dangerous and unprosperous vicissitudes through which this noble city, the daughter of Rome, has passed during many years, and especially in the time of the jubilee in the year 1300. And I, making excuses to myself, as being incompetent, thinking that some one else might write, omitted to write for many years, while the danger and important aspect of things has so increased that silence can no longer be kept. I proposed to write for the benefit of those who will inherit years of prosperity; that they may recognize the blessing of God, who in all times rules and governs. When I began, I proposed to tell the truth of things certain which I had seen and heard, providing they were matters worthy of note, of which surely none saw the beginnings as I did; and those which I had not actually seen, I proposed to write of according to hearsay, and because many, according to their corrupt wills exceed in what they say, I proposed to write according to the most general report."

Having thus described the plan of his work and the reasons which made him undertake it, and given a rapid account of the city of Florence and the origin of her civil discords, he enters on his history, which from 1280 to 1312 embraces all the events alluded to by us. In this history he lives, breathes and moves, and in such a way that we know of no modern historian who equals him in his gift of lighting the same flame in his readers' breasts as that which burned in his own. Among the ancients he has by preference been compared to Thucydides and Sallust, and perhaps he is most like the former in a natural simplicity which is lacking to the latter, to whom, however, Dino sometimes approaches in the nervous picturesqueness of his style. In Dino's chronicle we have the whole man reproduced, with all his love and devotion for his country and all his generous indignation. Patriotism is indeed the moving passion of his soul, whether he exults over virtuous actions, or judges with severity and brands as infamous those unworthy citizens, who were ruining their country for private or party interests. Against these he is especially implacable, as in the following passage: "Arise, O wicked citizens, and take the sword and fire in your hands, and spread your iniquitous deeds. Show your impious will, and evil intentions; delay no more; go and reduce to ruin the beauties of your city. Shed the blood of your brethren, strip yourselves of faith and charity, and deny each other help and service. Sow your lies which will fill your children's granaries. Do as Sylla did to the city of Rome, when all the evil which he did in ten years, Marius in a few days avenged. Do you think that the justice of God has failed? Even that of the world repays one for one. See how your ancestors received the reward of their discords: barter the honours they acquired. Lose no time, ye miserable: for more is consumed in one day of war than is gained in many years of peace; and small is the spark which brings destruction on a great kingdom."

The frank and amiable disposition of Dino was little suited to the turbulent age in which he lived. In the midst of such excitement of feeling if he, as statesman, remained always in the right and kept his actions in harmony with the purity of his intentions, he did not however always find in his ingenuous candour the best remedies for preventing or repressing the civic dissensions. And this he feels himself, and when he reflects on the past and judges it in his narrative, he of his own accord recognizes and confesses his own errors and those of his colleagues; as he is fair in dispensing praise and blame to all, so he does not hesitate to accuse himself. He is not occupied with his own person, but with the facts which influenced his action, and this makes it interesting to follow him when he speaks of himself, and reveals in his simple narrative the generosity of his character and the calm impartiality of his judgment. There is no episode more touching than the one in which he tells what he did, when he was prior and Charles of Valois was about to enter Florence. Fearing civil discords in presence of a stranger, he follows the dictates of his heart, and thinking that it must speak with equal strength in every one where the honour of their country is concerned, he invokes it in his compatriots with a sublime and trusting ingenuousness. Here is the passage:—

"Things being in these terms, there came to me, Dino, a holy and honest idea, for I thought: 'This lord will come, and will find all the citizens divided, and great scandal will follow from it.' So I concluded, for the office that I held and for the goodwill that I found in my companions, to call together many good citizens in the church of St. John; and so I did. And there were all the authorities; and when it seemed to me time, I said: 'Dear and worthy citizens, who have all of you in common received baptism from this font, this reason impels and binds you to love each other as dear brethren; and also because you possess the most noble city in the world. Among you some discontent has arisen, from ambition of offices, which as you know my companions and I have promised you with an oath to extend to all. This lord is coming and we must honour him. Put away your discontent and make peace among yourselves, that he may not find you divided. Put aside all the offences and ill will there has been among you in times gone by; let them be forgiven and forgotten for love of your town. And over this sacred font, whence you received holy baptism, swear among yourselves a good and perfect peace, so that the lord who is coming find all the citizens united.' To these words all agreed, and did so, touching the book with their hands, and swore to maintain good peace, and to preserve the honours and jurisdiction of the city. And this being done we departed from that place. But the wicked citizens, who had feigned tears of tenderness, and kissed the book, and shown the most zealous mind, were the principals in the city's destruction. Whose names I will not tell for shame's sake. But I cannot pass over the name of the foremost, since he was the cause of the others following, and he was Rosso dello Strozza; violent in looks and deeds, leader of the others; who soon after paid the forfeit of that oath. Those who were evil disposed said this loving peace was held forth as a deception. If there was any fraud in the words, I must suffer the penalty, though one should not receive an evil reward for a good intention. I have shed many tears for that oath, thinking how many souls have been lost for their wickedness."

"Words of true piety," exclaims Father Tosti, quoting them in one of his books,[1] "and would that they were impressed on every Italian mind!" But these pious words, which after six centuries fired the holy patriotism of the monk of Monte Cassino, were not sufficient in those troubled times, and perhaps it might have been better to "sharpen the

---

[1] Tosti, *Storia di Bonifazio VIII. e dei suoi tempi.*

swords," as on another occasion Dino regrets not having done. His great object was to see harmony ruling among the different parties, and he hoped to reach it by gentle persuasions, as he shows us in another episode no less worthy of record, nor less vivid a picture of the times, and of the efforts which really were being made to bring back peace to the harassed city. "The Signiors were greatly urged by the more important citizens to make new Signiors. Although it was against the law of justice because it was not the time for electing them, yet we agreed to call them, more out of compassion for the city than for any other reason. And I was in the chapel of St. Bernard in the name of the whole office,[1] and had there many of the more powerful of the people, for without them nothing could be done. There were Cione Magalotti, Segna Angiolini, Noffo Guidi for the party of the Neri; and Messers Lapo Falconieri, Cecc Canigiani and Corazza Ubaldini for the Bianchi. And I addressed them humbly and with much affection, saying, 'I wish to make the office in common, since from the rivalry about the offices there comes such discord.' We agreed, and elected six citizens in common, three of the Neri, and three of the Bianchi. The seventh whom we could not divide we chose of so little weight that no one

---

[1] The Signory, composed of six, afterwards eight priors and the Gonfalonier.

could suspect him. Which names I placed in writing on the altar. And Noffo Guidi spoke and said: 'I shall say something for which you will hold me a cruel citizen.' And I bid him be silent; and yet he spoke and with such arrogance as to ask me to be pleased to make their part in the office greater than the other; which was as much as saying 'Undo the other part,' and would have put me in the place of Judas. And I told him that before I would do such treason, I would give my children to be eaten by the dogs. And so we separated from the meeting."

Thus unconsciously reproducing himself, this man, after his fall from public life and power, passed his days modestly, as we have said, between his commerce and his pen, and so quietly that we hardly hear any more of him till the year 1323 when he died. Admirable as historian, just and kind-hearted as a man, he was a worthy contemporary and fellow-citizen of Dante, to whom he has more resemblance than any other writer of his age, from the ardour of his feelings, from the mixture of love and indignation in his character, from his singular gift of looking at things from above, of judging men and portraying them in a phrase. Many writers have spoken of him, but none perhaps with so much acumen as the great modern historian of Florence, Gino Capponi, who says of him, "Dino Compagni, an honest man, somewhat narrow in his political views, but a warm defender of what was good and right . . . the cheerful companion of the first founders of a popular government, devoted to whoever had satisfied the wrath felt against the nobles, and then but little contented with the new men, and the commonalty which had risen to the seat of government; a Guelph, but from his love of order ready to receive an emperor; at last afraid of this same emperor, against whom it seemed to him that a mad and useless war was being waged; thoroughly honest in each of these ideas, but in all finding himself at length mistaken; full of fancy and passion, and always a rigid moralist. . . . His history is entirely composed of a series of impressions, the clearness, vivacity and force of which prove their sincerity; the writer in describing himself depicts his time; and it is exactly in this that the merit of Dino Compagni consists, for in it he has few equals. . . . The Florentine Dino Compagni in that chronicle of his rises far above the prose writers of the thirteenth century. Alighieri tyrannizes with his haughty intellect over language which is raised as a fair captive to the favour of her lord; Dino, whose eloquence is so bright and efficacious, does not however succeed in hiding some effort in his composition; sincerely impassioned, yet ambitious of giving to his narrative an historical form, in which he may have taken Sallust as a model. In subtle facility of style, Compagni leaves far behind him Villani, who is infinitely superior to him in width of subject and in knowledge of facts."[1]

Contemporary with Dino but by some years younger was the great chronicler Giovanni Villani, who applying himself to commerce, in accordance with the traditions of his family, was busied in it both at home and abroad. In the first years of the fourteenth century he travelled to Rome, in France and in the low countries, where he saw and observed many men and things. On his return to his country, he began to occupy himself with public affairs about the time that Dino was quitting them, and when a period of comparative calm was succeeding to the turmoils and agitations described by this latter. In the year 1316 and 1317 he belonged to the office of the priors, and took part in the crafty tactics of the Florentines when they concluded a peace with Pisa and Lucca. In 1317 he was also officer of the money, and while administering the mint, collected its records with diligence and composed, chiefly by himself, a register of the coins struck in Florence up to his time. Prior again in 1321, he superintended the rebuilding of the city walls with a great zeal which was ill repaid, for later his work was subjected to suspicions, which however he was able to refute triumphantly. Later he was in the Florentine

---

[1] Gino Capponi, *Storia della Repubblica di Firenze.* Barbèra, Firenze, 1876.

army, when it attacked Castruccio Castracani and was defeated by him at Altopascio. In a distressing famine which desolated many provinces of Italy in 1328, he exhibited his usual activity in diminishing its evil effects within Florence, and left us a record of the prudential measures then taken, in a chapter of his chronicle which bears witness to that economical wisdom in which the Florentines of the Middle Ages were in advance of their time, and often in practice came near the theories of modern economists. Two years later he superintended the making of the bronze gates of St. John, "very beautiful and of wonderful work and costliness, and they were formed in wax, and afterwards the figures were cleaned and gilt by a master Andrea Pisano, and they were founded in a furnace by Venetian masters." In 1341 he was as hostage of war at Ferrara, and there he remained for some months together with the other hostages, and was treated with great honour and courtesy. Among the subsequent vicissitudes of Florence which he saw on his return and described vividly, was the brief usurpation and then the expulsion of the duke of Athens. Involved without fault of his in a great bankruptcy of the company of the Bonaccorsi, he was retained in prison for some time. He died in 1348, a victim to the plague rendered famous by Boccaccio's description.

In the year 1300, on the occasion of the solemn jubilee announced by Pope Boniface VIII., Rome was visited by a vast concourse of the faithful who had betaken themselves there in pilgrimage from every part of the Christian world to pay homage to the tombs of the apostles. Thither among other pilgrims went Villani, and while wandering through that city of wonders he fell under the spell, and in presence of the majestic solitude of its ruins, found his mind returning to the past, and his heart being inflamed by those memories. So that while Dante, who was also that year treading the Roman streets, felt the great idea of his poem stirring vaguely in his mind, the keen and observing spirit of the Florentine merchant seemed suddenly to divine its own historical gifts.[1] "In the year of Christ 1300, according to the birth of Christ, it being said by many that formerly, every hundred years of Christ's nativity, the pope who then was made a great indulgence, Pope Boniface VIII., who was then the Apostolic, made this aforesaid year in honour of Christ's nativity a special and great indulgence after this manner; that whatever Roman, within that year and for thirty days following, should visit the churches of the blessed Apostles St. Peter and St. Paul, and for fifteen days the whole of the remaining people who were not Romans, to all he gave a full and entire pardon of their sins from

---

[1] "Like our own Gibbon musing upon the steps of Ara Cœli, within sight of the Capitol, aud within hearing of the monks at prayer, he felt the *genius loci* stir him with a mixture of astonishment and pathos."—J. A. SYMONDS, *Renaissance in Italy*.

blame or punishment if they had confessed aright or would confess. And for the consolation of the Christian pilgrims, every Friday and solemn festival there was shown in St. Peter's the sudarium of Christ. On which account a great portion of the Christians then living made this aforesaid pilgrimage, women as well as men, from different and distant countries, from afar off as from the neighbourhood. And it was the most astonishing thing that ever was seen, how continually throughout the whole year they had in Rome beside the Roman people two hundred thousand pilgrims, without those who were on the road going and coming, and all were furnished and satisfied with food in just measure, men and horses, with great patience, and without noise or contentions; and I can bear witness to it for I was present and saw it. And from the offerings made by the pilgrims the Church gained great treasure, and the Romans, from supplying them, all grew rich. And I finding myself in that blessed pilgrimage in the holy city of Rome, seeing her great and ancient remains, and reading the histories and great deeds of the Romans as written by Virgil, Sallust, Lucan, Livy, Valerius, Paulus Orosius and other masters of history who wrote the exploits and deeds, both great and small, of the Romans and also of strangers in the whole world, to give recollection and example to those who are to come. So I took style and form from them, though as a disciple

I was not worthy to do so great a work. But considering that our city of Florence, the daughter and offspring of Rome, is on the increase and destined to do great things, as Rome is in her decline, it appeared to me fitting to set down in this volume and new chronicle all the facts and beginnings of the city of Florence, in as far as it has been possible to me to collect and discover them, and to follow the doings of the Florentines at length, and briefly the other remarkable matters of the world, so that it may be pleasing to God, in the hope of whose grace I made this undertaking rather than by my poor knowledge; and so in the year 1300, on my return from Rome, I began to compile this book, in honour of God and of the blessed John, and in praise of our city of Florence."

The work begun by Villani in 1300 goes back to biblical times and comes down to 1346. Nor is the idea of his work vast only for his researches into the dimness of the distant past, and for his collecting the few facts known and the many legends among which the first origin of Florence lies concealed. The wide universality of his narrative, especially in the times near him, while it attests to the author's travels and to the comprehensiveness of his mind, makes one also feel that the book has been inspired within the walls of the universal city. Indeed, as Dino Compagni's chronicle is confined within definite limits of time and place, this of Villani's is a general chronicle extending over the whole of Europe; Dino Compagni feels and lives in the facts of his history, Villani looks at them and relates them calmly and fairly, with a serenity which makes him appear an outsider, even when he is mixed up in them and is himself their originator. While very important for Italian history in the fourteenth century, it is quite the corner-stone of the early medieval history of Florence, whose traditions he goes over and groups, and after collecting all the knowledge he can reach, relates with more or less order everything connected with past and present times. Of these latter he has a very exact knowledge. Sharer as he was in public affairs, and in the intellectual and economical life of his city, at a time when in both she had no rival in Europe, he depicts what he saw with the vividness natural to a clear mind accustomed to business and to the observation of mankind. He was Guelph, but without strong feeling, and his serenity is diffused throughout his book, which is much more taken up with an inquiry into what is useful and true than with party considerations. He is really a chronicler, not an historian, and has but little method in his narrative, often reporting the things which occurred long ago and far off just as he heard them and without criticism. Every now and then he falls into some inaccuracy, but such defects as he has are largely compensated for by his valuable qualities. He was for half a century eye-witness of his history, and provides abundant information on the constitution of Florence, her customs, industries, commerce and arts; and among the chroniclers throughout Europe, he is perhaps unequalled for the value of the statistical data preserved by him. Giovanni Villani as a writer is less profound than he is clear and acute, and though his prose has not the force and colouring of Compagni, it has the advantage of greater simplicity, so that taking his work as a whole we find him to be without doubt the greatest chronicler who has written in Italian. It is astonishing that there is not yet in Italy a really good edition of his book, and that among the many learned students of history whom Florence can boast of, not one has yet been found disposed to prepare it.

The thread of the narrative, interrupted by Giovanni Villani's death, was taken up again by his brother Matteo, who carried the chronicle on to 1363, when he also being struck down by the plague left to his son Filippo the care of continuing the work down to 1364. Of the first we know very little: the life of the second, who was chancellor of the commune of Perugia, is better known. He was a man of learning and letters, chosen in 1401 and 1404 to expound publicly the *Divine Comedy* in the Florentine *Studio*, and author of a celebrated collection of Lives of illustrious Florentines. Though a more accomplished man of letters than either his father or uncle, he is inferior to them both as a chronicler; and even his father, while following laudably in Giovanni's steps, was very far from equalling him.

In Florence, as in other parts of Italy, there is no absence of chroniclers in the age succeeding that of the Villanis, and some of them excellent. Among others Marchionne Stefani, Piero Minerbetti, the two Boninsegni, Giovanni Morelli have all merit as chroniclers, and generally have one advantage over those of the rest of Italy in a more facile and graceful use of their native language. The best of them all perhaps was Gino Capponi, who wrote an account of the tumult of the Ciompi (A.D. 1378), and also either by him or his son Neri is a commentary on the conquest of Pisa (A.D. 1402–1406). But with the Villanis the series of medieval chroniclers may be said to close. After them comes history, superficial still, and in its form but a servile imitation of the classic models during the humanistic movement of the fifteenth century, but in the following century displaying thought, acumen and vigour in many writings, and above all in the unsurpassed pages of Macchiavelli and Guicciardini. These two writers, while differing in their manner of thinking and feeling, both tended nevertheless towards the new life which they presaged in the midst of their country's decay, and by their meditations on the causes of that decay, they opened out new horizons to human thought. But it was from the past that their minds drank in their strength, and from these humble and vigorous chronicles that their histories drew a vital part of their substance. Great is the service rendered by these chronicles, nor can we leave them without a sense of gratitude and reverence. By them the times of antiquity are united to ours, and by their aid we are enabled to follow for almost ten centuries the throes suffered by humanity in one of its greatest efforts on the path of progress.

INDEX.

A

Agathias, 37
Agnellus of Ravenna, 96-103
Alfanus, 163
Alferius, Ogerius, 271
Alighieri, Dante, 313
Amatus of Salerno, 164, 182
Anastasius Bibliothecarius, 93
Andrew of Bergamo, 118
Annales Casinenses, 229
—— *Cavenses*, 182
—— *Ceccanenses*, 230
—— *Romani*, 195, 196
Annali Pistolesi, 311
Anonymus Barensis, 181
Arnulph, 245, 246
Auxilius, 104
Azarius, Petrus, 271

B

Bardo, 220
Bartholomew, annalist of Genoa, 306
Bartholomew of Neocastro, 239, 240
Benedict of Soracte, 142-144
Benno, 207
Benzo, 207
Bernardus Guidonis, 242
Boetius, 5, 13

Boncompagnus Magister Florentinus, 248
Bonizo, 209-220
Boso, 202-206
Bruno of Segni, 171, 186, 187

C

Caffaro, 303, 304
Canale, Martin da, 293-298
Caresinis, Rafainus de, 302
Cassiodorus, 4-19
Catalogues, 115
Chronicon Casauriense, 230
—— *Normannicum breve*, 182
—— *Novaliciense*, 183-185
—— *Salernitanum*, 182
—— *S. Bartholomæi de Carpincto*, 230
Colonna, John, 262
—— Landulph, 262
Compagni, Dino, 317-328
Constructio Farfensis, 106-108

D

Damiani, Peter, 208, 209
Dandolo, Andrea, 298-302
Dei, Andrea, 311
Desiderius, abbot of Montecassino, 16

Destructio Farfensis, 109
Dolcino, Fra, life of, 271
Domnizo, 220-222
Donati, Neri, 311
D'Oria, James, 306-308

E

Ennodius, Magnus Felix, 38, 39
Erchempert, 116-118

F

Falcandus, Hugo, 231-235
Farfa, the monastery of, 106-111, 149; its chronicle, 158; its register, 150-152
Ferretus of Vicenza, 272-274
Flamma, Galvanus, 270
Frederick Barbarossa, poem on, 258-260

G

Gesta Episcoporum Neapolitanorum, 95, 96
Godfrey of Viterbo, 257
Godi, Antonius, 272
Gregory of Catino, 149-159
—— the Great, 42-64, 224
—— VII., 222-225
Guaiferius, 164
Guntherus Ligurinus, 256

J

James of Acqui, 262
Johannes Diaconus, principal author of the *Gesta Episcoporum Neapolitanorum,* 95
—— of Venice, 144, 145, 292
—— of Verona, 262
—— Vulturnensis, 159, 160
John of Cermenate, 270
Jordanes, 19-21

L

Landulph, the elder, 246
——, the younger, 246, 247

Leo Ostiensis, 164-173
Liber Pontificalis, the, 93-95, 186, 187, 195-206, 241, 242
Libuinus, 187
Liutprand, 123-142
Lupus Protospatarius, 181

M

Malaspina, Saba, 237-239
Malaterra, Godfrey, 182
Malespini, Giacotto, 315-317
——, Ricordano, 315-317
Marango, Bernard, 309
Marcellinus Comes, 37
Marchisius, 306
Marius Aventicensis, 38
Maurisius, Gerardus, 271
Montecassino, the monastery of, 105, 111, 160; the minor writings of, 163; the chronicle of St. Benedict, 111-115
Morena, Acerbus, 249
——, Otho, 249
Morigia Bonincontrus, 271
Moyses, Magister, 247
Mussatus, Albertinus, 275-291

N

Nicholas of Curbio, 242
Nicholas of Iamsilla, 236, 237

O

Obertus, 304
Oderisius, abbot of Montecassino. 163, 165, 173
Origo Langobardorum, 64
Orthodoxa Defensio Imperialis, 206
Otho of Freising, 250-256
Ottobonus, 305

P

Pandulph, 201, 202
Panegyricus Berengarii, 119, 120
Panis, Ogerius, 306

Parisius de Cereta, 271
Paul of Bernried, 188-194
Paulinus, 298
Paulus Diaconus, 65-90
Peter of Eboli, 235
Petrus Crassus, 206
Petrus Diaconus, 174-180
Petrus Pisanus, 196-201, 309
Pipinus, Franciscus, 262
Placidus Nonantolanus, 208
Procopius, 25-37
Ptolomæus Lucensis, 242, 310

R

Ragevinus, 256
Raoul, Sire, 247, 248
Richard of St. Germano, 236
Ricobaldus Ferrariensis, 262
Rienzo, Cola di, life of, 243-245
Rolandinus of Padua, 274, 275
Romuald of Salerno, 230
Rothari, King, edict of, 64

S

Salimbene, Fra, 263-269
Sanudo Torsello, Marin, 298
Sanzanome, 314

Secundus, bishop of Trent, 65, 89
Ser Cambio, John, 311
Sicardus of Cremona, 261
Smerego, Nicholas, 272
Speciale, Nicholas, 239, 240
Stefanardus of Vimercate, 270
Stefanus, Magister, 65
Subiaco, the monastery of, 105, 150; its register, 150

T

Tegrimus, Nicholas, 311

V

Ventura, William, 271
Vico, Michael de, 310
Villani, Filippo, 335, 336
———, Giovanni, 329-335
———, Matteo, 335
Vinea, Petrus de, 238
Vulgarius, Eugenius, 104, 105

W

Wibert of Toul, 188
Wido, 206
William of Apulia, 182

PRINTED BY WILLIAM CLOWES AND SONS, LIMITED, LONDON AND BECCLES.

Society for Promoting Christian Knowledge.

Publications on
THE CHRISTIAN EVIDENCES.

BOOKS. Price.

Steps to Faith.
Addresses on some points in the Controversy with Unbelief. By the Rev. Brownlow Maitland, M.A., Author of "Scepticism and Faith," &c. Post 8vo. ......*Cloth boards* — *s. d.* 1 6

Theism or Agnosticism.
An Essay on the grounds of Belief in God. By the Rev. Brownlow Maitland, M.A., Author of "The Argument from Prophecy," &c. Post 8vo. ....*Cloth boards* 1 6

Argument from Prophecy (The).
By the Rev. Brownlow Maitland, M.A., Author of "Scepticism and Faith," &c. Post 8vo. ....*Cloth boards* 1 6

Scepticism and Faith.
By the Rev. Brownlow Maitland. Post 8vo. *Cloth boards* 1 4

Modern Unbelief: its Principles and Characteristics. By the Right Rev. the Lord Bishop of Gloucester and Bristol. Post 8vo. ....*Cloth boards* 1 6

Some Modern Religious Difficulties.
Six Sermons preached, by the request of the Christian Evidence Society, at St. James's, Piccadilly, on Sunday Afternoons after Easter, 1876; with a Preface by his Grace the Archbishop of Canterbury. Post 8vo.......*Cloth boards* 1 6

Some Witnesses for the Faith.
Six Sermons preached, by the request of the Christian Evidence Society, at St. Stephen's Church, South Kensington, on Sunday Afternoons after Easter, 1877. Post 8vo.
Cloth boards 1 4

When was the Pentateuch Written?
By George Warington, B.A., Author of "Can we Believe in Miracles?" &c. Post 8vo. ....*Cloth boards* 1 6
9-1-82.] [Sm. Post 8vo.

	Price.
	s. d.

Theism and Christianity.
Six Sermons preached, by the request of the Christian Evidence Society, at St. James's, Piccadilly, on Sunday Afternoons after Easter, 1878. Post 8vo.......*Cloth boards* 1 6

The Analogy of Religion.
Dialogues founded upon Butler's "Analogy of Religion." By the Rev. H. R. Huckin, D.D., Head Master of Repton School. Post 8vo... *Cloth boards* 3 0

"Miracles."
By the Rev. E. A. Litton, M.A., Examining Chaplain of the Bishop of Durham. Crown 8vo. .... *Cloth boards* 1 6

Moral Difficulties connected with the Bible.
Being the Boyle Lectures for 1871. By the Ven. Archdeacon Hessey, D.C.L. Preacher to the Hon. Society of Gray's Inn, &c. FIRST SERIES. Post 8vo. ...*Cloth boards* 1 6

Moral Difficulties connected with the Bible.
Being the Boyle Lectures for 1872. By the Ven. Archdeacon Hessey, D.C.L. SECOND SERIES. Post 8vo.
Cloth boards 2 6

Prayer and recent Difficulties about it.
The Boyle Lectures for 1873, being the THIRD SERIES of "Moral Difficulties connected with the Bible." By the Ven. Archdeacon Hessey, D.C.L. Post 8vo.
Cloth boards 2 6
The above Three Series in a volume ....*Cloth boards* 6 0

Historical Illustrations of the Old Testament.
By the Rev. G. Rawlinson, M.A., Camden Professor of Ancient History, Oxford. Post 8vo ....*Cloth boards* 1 6

Can we Believe in Miracles?
By G. Warington, B.A., of Caius College, Cambridge. Post 8vo... *Cloth boards* 1 6

The Moral Teaching of the New Testament
VIEWED AS EVIDENTIAL TO ITS HISTORICAL TRUTH. By the Rev. C. A. Row, M.A. Post 8vo...................*Cloth boards* 1 6

Scripture Doctrine of Creation.
By the Rev. T. R. Birks, M.A., Professor of Moral Philosophy at Cambridge. Post 8vo.............................*Cloth boards* 1 6

Publications on the Christian Evidences. 3

	Price.
	s. d.

The Witness of the Heart to Christ.
Being the Hulsean Lectures for 1878. By the Rev. W. Boyd Carpenter, M.A. Post 8vo. ....*Cloth boards* 1 6

Thoughts on the First Principles of the Positive
PHILOSOPHY, CONSIDERED IN RELATION TO THE HUMAN MIND. By the late Benjamin Shaw, M.A., late Fellow of Trinity College, Camb. Post 8vo. ....*Limp cloth* 0 8

Thoughts on the Bible.
By the late Rev. W. Gresley, M.A., Prebendary of Lichfield. Post 8vo. ....*Cloth boards* 1 6

The Reasonableness of Prayer.
By the Rev. P. Onslow, M.A. Post 8vo. ....*Paper cover* 0 8

Paley's Evidences of Christianity.
A New Edition, with Notes, Appendix, and Preface. By the Rev. E. A. Litton, M.A. Post 8vo..........*Cloth boards* 4 0

Paley's Natural Theology.
Revised to harmonize with Modern Science. By Mr. F. le Gros Clark, F.R.S., President of the Royal College of Surgeons of England, &c. Post 8vo. ....*Cloth boards* 4 0

Paley's Horæ Paulinæ.
A new Edition, with Notes, Appendix, and Preface. By J. S. Howson, D.D., Dean of Chester. Post 8vo. *Cloth boards* 3 0

The Story of Creation as told by Theology
AND SCIENCE. By the Rev. T. S. Ackland, M.A. Post 8vo.
Cloth boards 1 6

Man's Accountableness for his Religious Belief.
A Lecture delivered at the Hall of Science, on Tuesday, April 2nd, 1872. By the Rev. Daniel Moore, M.A., Holy Trinity, Paddington. Post 8vo ....*Paper cover* 0 3

The Theory of Prayer; with Special Reference
TO MODERN THOUGHT. By the Rev. W. H. Karslake, M.A., Assistant Preacher at Lincoln's Inn, Vicar of Westcott, Dorking. Post 8vo. ....*Limp cloth* 1 0

Publications on the Christian Evidences.

	Price.
	s. d.

The Credibility of Mysteries.
A Lecture delivered at St. George's Hall, Langham Place. By the Rev. Daniel Moore, M.A. Post 8vo......*Paper cover*   0   3

Analogy of Religion, Natural and Revealed,
TO THE CONSTITUTION AND COURSE OF NATURE: to which are added, Two Brief Dissertations. By Bishop Butler. NEW EDITION. Post 8vo...............................*Cloth boards*   2   6

Christian Evidences:
intended chiefly for the young. By the Most Reverend Richard Whately, D.D. 12mo...................... *Paper cover*   0   4

The Efficacy of Prayer.
By the Rev. W. H. Karslake, M.A., Assistant Preacher at Lincoln's Inn, &c. &c. Post 8vo. .... *Limp cloth*   0   6

Science and the Bible: a Lecture by the Right
Rev. Bishop Perry, D.D. 18mo. *Paper cover* 4d., or *Limp cloth*   0   6

A Lecture on the Bible. By the Very Rev.
E. M. Goulburn, D.D., Dean of Norwich. 18mo. *Paper cover*   0   2

The Bible: Its Evidences, Characteristics, and
Effects. A Lecture by the Right Rev. Bishop Perry, D.D. 18mo..*Paper cover*   0   4

The Origin of the World according to
REVELATION AND SCIENCE. A Lecture by Harvey Goodwin, M.A., Bishop of Carlisle. Post 8vo....*Cloth boards*   0   4

*** For List of *TRACTS* on the *Christian Evidences*, see the Society's Catalogue B.

DEPOSITORIES:
NORTHUMBERLAND AVENUE, CHARING CROSS, W.C.;
43, QUEEN VICTORIA STREET, E.C.; 48, PICCADILLY, W.,
AND 135, NORTH STREET, BRIGHTON.

www.ingramcontent.com/pod-product-compliance
Lightning Source LLC
Chambersburg PA
CBHW030258240426
43673CB00040B/998